WORKBOOK

AQA KS3 ENGLISH LANGUAGE YEAR 7

PREPARING FOR PAPER 1 AND PAPER 2

Helen Backhouse

CONSULTANT: DAVID STONE

OXFORD

UNIVERSITY PRESS

Contents

Introduction to this workbook

How this workbook will help you

The main aim of this workbook is to prepare you for the AQA Year 7 English Language tests. The workbook is designed to give you confidence and to help you understand what you need to do to answer each question in the test papers.

How the AQA Year 7 English Language tests are structured

There are two test papers, Paper 1 and Paper 2, both of which contain a Reading and a Writing section. Each Paper includes five questions: four reading tasks and one writing task. Paper 1 includes a Reading section with a fiction text to assess your reading skills and a Writing section to test your creative writing skills. Paper 2 includes a Reading section with two non-fiction texts to assess your reading skills and a Writing section to assess your skills in presenting a point of view.

How this workbook is structured

This workbook is divided into two parts: Paper 1 and Paper 2. For each Paper, there is a unit on each of the five questions that you will face in the test. Each of these units will give you a clear idea of the format of the question, what to include in your answer and how to organize your response. A range of activities is included, as well as a sample test paper question at the end of each unit.

Exploring new texts

This workbook introduces you to a range of fiction and non-fiction texts from different historical periods (from the 19th, 20th and 21st centuries), which will prepare you for the type of texts you can expect to find in the AQA Year 7 English Language tests. Some of the texts are linked by theme to help you practise comparing texts.

Which features are included?

To help you develop your reading and writing skills, there are some additional features in this workbook. Key terms, Top tips and a Glossary will support your understanding of important terms and ideas, as well as helping with more difficult words in the source texts. There is also a focus on improving your technical accuracy (also known as SPAG – Spelling, Punctuation and Grammar).

How to check your progress

Each Reading and Writing Section of the workbook ends with a Progress Check for you to assess how well you are learning and to target the skills you need to improve.

Key terms

Top tip

SPAG

A note on spelling

Certain words, for example 'synthesize' and 'organize', have been spelt with 'ize' throughout this book. It is equally acceptable to spell these words and others with 'ise'.

Question 1

Understanding texts

Objective

- Identify information and ideas

Key terms

explicit stating something clearly and openly

implicit suggesting something without stating it openly

The first question on Paper 1 is about information and ideas. Fiction texts are full of them. Some are clear and **explicit**. Others are less clear or hidden, so you have to read between the lines and work out the meaning for yourself. These are **implicit**.

Read the text below and then complete Activity 1.

The Dragon's Dream by Kate Thompson

Once upon a time and far, far away, there was a young king who lived in a castle high up in the mountains. The king was very wealthy, and the great hall in his castle was piled high with treasure, but still he was not happy. Noblemen came
5 and went, and there were always servants scurrying through the castle, but even so, this king was lonely. He was lonely because in all the length and breadth of his land he could find no one who would marry him.

Now, the reason that no one would marry him was that his
10 castle was so cold. All through the winter it was covered in snow, and even during the summer, when the people in the valleys were enjoying the sunshine, icy winds blew through the castle in the mountains.

Activity 1

Even very simple texts like fairy tales have both explicit and implicit meanings. Read the statements below about the extract from *The Dragon's Dream* and circle whether they are explicit or implicit in the text.

1. The king lives in a castle in the mountains. EXPLICIT / IMPLICIT

2. The king thinks love is worth more than riches. EXPLICIT / IMPLICIT

3. The king has been searching for a wife for a long while. EXPLICIT / IMPLICIT

4. The king has servants and noblemen at the castle. EXPLICIT / IMPLICIT

For Question 1 of Paper 1, you need to focus on information and ideas that are clear and explicit. This question asks you to list four things you have learned about a particular aspect of the text, for example, a character or a place. Before you write each of the four things down, you need to ask yourself the following questions:

1. Is it *in the text*?
2. Is it *true*?
3. Is it *accurate*?
4. Is it *about the subject of the question*?

Activity 2

A student was asked to write four things they had learned about the king from the text on page 4. The four answers below are all wrong. Read them and work out what is wrong with each one. Write your reason on the line next to each statement. The first one has been done for you.

1. The king had lots of gold. _Not accurate. Text says 'treasure', not gold, which might be jewels._

2. The king was greedy. _____

3. The king had no brothers. _____

4. There were lots of servants. _____

So to answer Question 1, you need to identify information and ideas from the text that are true, accurate and about the subject of the question.

Top tip

Put the subject of the question as the first words of your answer, for example, 'The castle…', to help you focus.

Activity 3

Using all that you have learned about identifying explicit information from pages 4–5, complete the following task:

List four things about the castle from the text on page 4.

1. _____

2. _____

3. _____

4. _____

Question 2

Language features

Objectives

- Identify language features
- Use subject terms correctly

The second question on Paper 1 is about how the writer uses language. You are asked to write about the words, **phrases** and language features the writer has used, and what effect they have on you, the reader. This means you have to read the text very carefully and notice how the writer has chosen words and phrases to create effects.

Key term

phrase a group of words without a main verb

Activity 1

Match the language feature on the left with the definition on the right by drawing a line between them. One has been done for you.

Alliteration	A word used to describe a noun (a person, place or thing)
Simile	When the word sounds like the noise it describes
Onomatopoeia	When something is described as being something else
Metaphor	When words starting with similar sounds are put together
Adjective	When something is described as being *like* or *as* another thing

Activity 2

Imagine you are writing a description of a city. Look at the language features below and write two or three examples of each that you could use in your description.

1. Adjective _____

2. Alliteration _____

3. Onomatopoeia _____

4. Simile _____

_____

5. Metaphor _____

_____

It is useful to identify language features in a text, but it is much more important to write about what *effect* the language has on the reader. Writers choose their words very carefully to make the reader respond in specific ways. The writer might want the reader to feel fear or excitement, for example, so they choose their words to match their **purpose**.

Read the text below about an Indian boy, Jaspal, who lives in London.

> **Key term**
>
> **purpose**
> the reason for writing a text, e.g. to entertain, to describe or to persuade

---

The Eye of the Horse by Jamila Gavin

Jaspal leaned over the old metal bridge and looked down onto the railway tracks below. The shining metal slithered away like parallel serpents, till they reached a point in the distance where they merged as if one – but he knew that this was only an optical illusion.

5   The sight of the tracks always gave him an intense feeling of excitement. Sometimes, when the sun was shining in a particular way, he could block from his view the grubby backs of those London houses and flats, with their grimy windows and straggles of grey washing hung out to dry. He could fix his eye on the patch of blue sky between the tenements[1], and imagine he was back in India. For a while, he could

10   try and forget the pain which sat in his stomach like a hard lump.

Trains reminded him of his village back home in Deri. Beyond the mango and guava groves[2] and between the fields of wheat, mustard seed and sugar cane, the railway track ran the length of the Punjab[3] skyline.

He and his best friend, Nazakhat, had loved trains. On many an afternoon after

15   school, they would take the long way home so that they might get over to the track and walk on the rails. There was no chance of being run down by a train, as you could see as far as the horizon in each direction. Anyway, long before the train was in sight, you could feel the hum of its power beneath your feet. It was often the smoke they saw first, streaming a long trail in the sky, and then they would hear the piercing

20   shriek of its whistle, which carried all the way to the village.

Glossary

1   tenements – a block of flats with rented rooms

2   mango and guava groves – small woods where mangos and guavas (a tropical fruit) are grown

3   Punjab – a region in India

Activity 3

Using a coloured pen, highlight or circle five words or phrases that you find most interesting in the text above. If you recognize any language features, write down what the language feature is alongside the text above.

Language effects

Objective

- Comment on the effects of language

Question 2 is about how writers use language to create effects. Most language features appeal to the reader's senses – what they see, hear, smell, touch or taste. **Similes** and **metaphors** are examples of language features that create images. The writer uses these features to surprise the reader, to make them see things differently and to spark their imagination.

Activity 1

In the first paragraph of the text on page 7, the writer describes the railway tracks: 'The shining metal slithered away like parallel serpents.' Think about the words the writer uses. Shut your eyes and repeat the words in your head. Let your imagination explore the connections and sensations in your mind. What can you see, hear or feel when you think about these words?

Open your eyes and write down your thoughts and feelings below.

1. 'Shining metal' reminds me of _

_ _

2. 'Slithered' suggests a feeling of _

_ _

3. 'Serpents' creates an image of _

_ _

Key terms

metaphor when one thing is described as being another to create an image, e.g. 'the sea was an ogre, wild and enraged'

simile when one thing is compared to another, using 'as' or 'like', e.g. 'the fish darted from under the rock *like* silver bullets'

The sentence describing the railway tracks is also a simile: 'The shining metal slithered away *like* parallel serpents.' It is effective because there are lots of things that train tracks and serpents have in common, so it is possible for the reader to imagine one looking like the other.

Read what one student wrote about how the writer uses language below.

The writer compares the train tracks to 'parallel serpents', which highlights how the tracks are like long, thin, twin snakes moving in lines away from Jaspal. The simile suggests that the train tracks are swerving and shimmering as if they are alive and dangerous. It creates a sense of the boy's excitement about the railway, as well as his fear. The writer uses alliteration in the words 'slithering' and 'serpents', which makes the reader imagine the hissing sound and smooth, gliding motion of the snakes.

Top tip

The highlighted words and phrases are very useful when you are writing about the effects of language.

Another group of language features appeal to the reader's sense of hearing. Examples of these language features are **alliteration** and **onomatopoeia**. A writer uses these features to suggest sounds that add to the mood or atmosphere of the description.

Activity 2

A student was asked to read the following extract from the text on page 7:

> '… he could block from his view the grubby backs of those London houses and flats, with their grimy windows and straggles of grey washing hung out to dry.'

The student was then given the following question:

> How does the writer use language here to show how Jaspal feels about London?

Read the student's answer below and fill in the gaps in the response.

> The writer uses words like 'grubby,' '_ _ _ _ _ _ _ _ _ _ _ _ _ _ _ _' and 'grey' to describe London. This use
>
> of _ creates a sense of how dirty and _
>
> London looks. The sound of the words is harsh and suggests a _ mood.
>
> It makes the reader think that the city is a _ place for Jaspal to live.
>
> The 'straggles of grey washing' makes me think of _
>
> _
>
> I think Jaspal feels that London is _
>
> _

Activity 3

Using all that you have learned about how the writer uses language from pages 6–9, read the extract below and answer the question that follows.

> '… long before the train was in sight, you could feel the hum of its power beneath your feet. It was often the smoke they saw first, streaming a long trail in the sky, and then they would hear the piercing shriek of its whistle…'

> How does the writer use language to bring to life the sounds of the railway?

Write your answer on separate paper.

Question 3

Structure

Objective

- Identify structural features

The third question in Paper 1 is about **structure**. You are asked to write about how the writer organizes their ideas and how they present the story to the reader.

Think of it like a film. In a film, do you see the action from a distance or up close, from one character's **point of view** or from different points of view? How does the film introduce the characters and establish the **setting** and the mood? This is very similar to how a writer structures a story.

The structure of a written text is about the **sequence** of ideas: how the writer moves from one character to another, from one place or time to the next, or from writing description to **dialogue** or action.

> ### Key terms
>
> **dialogue** conversation between two or more characters
>
> **flashback** a section in a text that is set before the events of the main story
>
> **future tense** a verb that describes something that will happen in the future, e.g. 'they will laugh'
>
> **narrator** the person who tells the story
>
> **past tense** a verb that describes something that happened in the past, e.g. 'they laughed'
>
> **point of view** the way a character regards events or people
>
> **present tense** a verb that describes something that is happening now, e.g. 'they laugh' or 'they are laughing'
>
> **sequence** the order in which things happen
>
> **setting** where the events take place
>
> **structure** the organization of a text

Read the text on page 11. It is taken from the opening of a story about Jack, who has found a letter from his dad who left home five years ago and hasn't been seen since. Then answer the questions in Activity 1.

Activity 1

1. Which characters are we introduced to? _____

   _____

2. Who is the **narrator** and how can you tell? _____

   _____

3. Is the story written in the **past**, **present** or **future tense**? _____

   _____

4. How does the writer signal the start of the **flashback**? _____

   _____

Hit the Road, Jack by Mimi Thebo

I had the letter in my hand. I flipped it over and I saw Dad's name signed on the other side. And then I got so excited that I couldn't read it for a moment. The
5 blue ink just seemed to swim about on the cream coloured paper.

And I remembered…

Dad is telling me to read something. It's the same handwriting, but it's black
10 ink on white paper. It seems to swim around in front of my eyes. I can feel his hand on my shoulder, holding on to it hard, as if he's never going to let me go. Around the page is the top of the
15 kitchen table and I'm looking down at it. I remember that. And I remember that the back of my head is hurting.

I'm having trouble reading it – I don't know why. Maybe it's because my head
20 hurts. And I can hear Dad encouraging me, saying, 'Go on… read it, read it…'

Then it stopped.

I was back in the toilet with the letter in my hand. I couldn't hear Dad's voice any
25 more. I could only hear Mum crying in her bedroom and my own breath in the small space, sounding quick and excited.

I turned the page over in my hand again. There was no date or address or
30 anything like that. But the paper didn't feel old to me. It had that crisp feeling.

Dear Laura,

I'm working hard, but I miss you so much. I just don't like
35 being apart.

It gets really cold here, and the food is terrible. But the worst part is being all alone.

I know what we planned and I
40 know it would be better for us if I stayed here and kept on at it, but I just don't think I can.

I'll try and speak to you this weekend. Maybe I can make
45 you understand and you'll let me come home.

You are my only darling Laura,

John

It was so sad it made me feel sick. My
50 dad was out there somewhere, working hard. He only wanted to come home. But instead, my mother was going to marry Richard.

Activity 2

Use the statements below to complete the flowchart and show the sequence of what happens in the text above. Write the letter for each statement in the boxes in the correct order.

A Jack reads the letter.   **B** Jack looks at the letter.   **C** John's letter to Laura

D Jack hears his mum crying.   **E** Jack reflects on his parents' relationship.

F Jack remembers something happening in the kitchen.

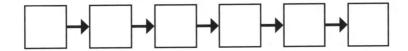

Structure and effects

Objective

● Comment on the effects of structural features

For Question 3, you have to write about not only *how* the writer structures the text but also what the *effects* of the **structural features** are. Ask yourself: 'What effect does the way the writer has organized the story have on me?'

For example, the writer of *Hit the Road, Jack* (page 11) uses a structural feature called flashback in lines 7–22. The effect of the flashback is to give us clues about what happened in the past and help us understand more about the characters. It provides a snapshot of a moment from the family's history, portraying Jack as a younger boy, anxious and in pain as he struggles, and his dad encourages him, to read. The flashback in this text is deliberately short and has few details, which makes us curious about what happened. We are intrigued and want to find out more about the relationship between Jack and his dad.

Activity 1

Below is a list of some structural features used in the text on page 11. Complete the table by adding line numbers to show where each of the structural features is used in the text. One has been done for you.

Structural feature	Line numbers	Effect of structural feature
Shift in **narrative voice**	32–48	Shows us different characters' thoughts and feelings
Switch to present tense		Gives readers a more dramatic sense of events happening right now
Switch to focus on details		Little things make the story more realistic and believable
Flashback in time		Gives clues about the past to help us understand characters now
Shift from narrative to letter		Gives a different **perspective** from another character's point of view

Key terms

narrative a written story or account

narrative voice the person telling the story from their point of view

perspective a particular view of something

structural feature a feature that helps to structure a text

When you write about effects, it is important that you relate every point you make to the text you have read. Read the two student examples below. Student A and Student B have written about the effect of switching to present tense as a structural feature in the text on page 11.

Specific detail about the text

Student A

The writer switches to present tense to give readers a sense of the events happening right now and makes the reader feel as if they are there in the story with the characters, feeling the same emotions.

Student B

The writer, Mimi Thebo, switches to present tense during the flashback to the kitchen scene to give readers a vivid sense of the family drama unfolding around us, almost as if we were Jack in the centre of what's happening. It transports us back in time and makes us feel more connected to Jack, to feel his anxiety and confusion about the events taking place.

Activity 2

Student A could be writing about any book, whereas Student B writes about the same structural feature as Student A but relates everything to the specific text. Use a highlighter or coloured pen to show where Student B refers to details from the text on page 11, *Hit the Road, Jack*, in their answer above. The first one has been done for you.

Activity 3

Choose one structural feature from the table in Activity 1 that hasn't been covered by Student B. Follow Student B's example and write about the effect of using this structural feature in *Hit the Road, Jack*.

Activity 4

Re-read the text on page 7, *The Eye of the Horse* by Jamila Gavin. Using all that you have learned about structure and effects from pages 10–13, answer the following question:

> How does the writer use structure to show the differences between Britain and India?

Write your answer on separate paper.

Question 4

Evaluation

Objectives

- Interpret the task
- Identify the methods the writer uses
- Explore the effects of the methods

Question 4 is an **evaluation** question. That simply means you are being asked to comment on how successful you think the writer has been in writing the text. You will need to ask yourself:

1. Which aspect of the writer's work is the focus of the question?

2. Which methods does the writer use to achieve that purpose?

3. What effect does each of the methods have?

Key term

evaluation a judgement about the value of something

The question

So you need to start with the question itself. This usually includes an opinion from someone who has read the text and focuses on one particular aspect. The key words are highlighted in the question below.

> A student said, 'I love the way Jamila Gavin brings to life the experience of the railway for us.' How far do you agree?

Top tip

Your first task is to work out from the question what the focus of the answer should be.

Activity 1

Read the sample quotations below about the text on page 11. Underline the key words to identify which aspect of the writer's purpose is the focus of the quotation.

1. 'In *Hit the Road, Jack* the characters are introduced in a very intriguing way.'

2. 'I think Mimi Thebo is really good at creating a mood of tension in this opening section.'

The writer's methods

When you are clear about the focus of the question, you need to consider how the writer has used particular methods to achieve that purpose, so Question 4 is asking you to bring together what you have understood in the text about both language and structure.

Read the extract on page 15 about a girl called Ella who is babysitting her younger brother Sam. Her older brother Fin has gone out and left her alone in the house at night.

Storm Catchers by Tim Bowler

There's nothing wrong, she told herself, and started to walk down the stairs. It's just a storm coming. But it was no use. Polvellan was a house that had always frightened her even though she'd lived here all her life. It wasn't just that it was such an old building. There was something else, something she didn't understand; she felt
5   uneasy here even when the others were around.

Tap! The sound snapped in the night again. She opened her mouth to call out and ask if anyone were there, then closed it again. If somebody were in the house, the last thing she should do was give herself away. She thought of Sam and wondered if she should go back and guard him.

10 No, check the downstairs rooms first. Make yourself do it. Then go back to Sam. [...]

Tap! She gave a start and looked to the left. The noise had come from the sitting room. There was no doubt about it. She stared at the door; it was ajar and the lights inside the room were switched off. She reached for the telephone. Ring Billy. Get him to send Fin home.

15 But she drew her hand back. She had to master this. She had to check the noise out for herself. It was bound to be something simple. She walked to the sitting room door and gave it a push. It brushed over the carpet a few inches and stopped. She stared through the gap, then took a deep breath, pushed the door a little further, and craned her head round.

20 The old room looked dusky but reassuringly familiar. Behind the drawn curtains she could hear the rain lashing against the window; but at least there was no one here. She pushed the door fully open and switched on the light. The features of the room sprang into focus: the piano, the fireplace, the armchairs, the sofa, the music stand with her flute beside it. She walked into the room.

25 Tap! She jumped. It was the window. Someone must be out there, hidden by the curtains. She hurried to the phone, picked it up and started to dial 999; then put it down. This was stupid. The tap wasn't regular. It might not be a person at all; it might be something trivial. What would Dad say if she called the police out for nothing? She strode to the window, pulled back the curtain, and burst out laughing.

30 It was nothing after all. A chain from one of the hanging baskets had broken loose and gusts were throwing it up at the window so that every so often the metal ring at the end struck the glass. Tap! There it was again. She chuckled and reached out to close the curtain; then froze in horror.

Reflected in the glass was a figure standing behind her in the doorway.

A typical evaluation question about the text above might be:

A student wrote: 'This story is really creepy. The writer is brilliant at building up suspense.' How far do you agree with this view?

The key words of the statement on page 15 are highlighted, so you can see that the focus for this question is how the writer uses methods to create **suspense** and a creepy atmosphere.

The writer of *Storm Catchers* uses six main methods to create suspense in the text:

Language

- Description of sounds – using words such as 'snapped' and 'tap' for effect
- Sentence length – changing the length of sentences to create effects
- Choice of **verbs** – appropriate and interesting verbs to tell the reader how the action happens

Structure

- Shift in narrative voice – changing the voice from the narrator to Ella
- Focus on setting – describing the scene to create an effect
- **Rising action/falling action** – changing the pace and drama of the action

Key terms

falling action the pace of events slows down and becomes calmer and more reassuring

rising action the pace of events speeds up and becomes more dramatic and exciting

suspense a feeling of uncertainty about what might happen

verb 'doing' or action words, e.g. 'ran', 'laugh', 'screamed'

Read the first section of the text again, below. The text is highlighted to show where each of the six methods has been used.

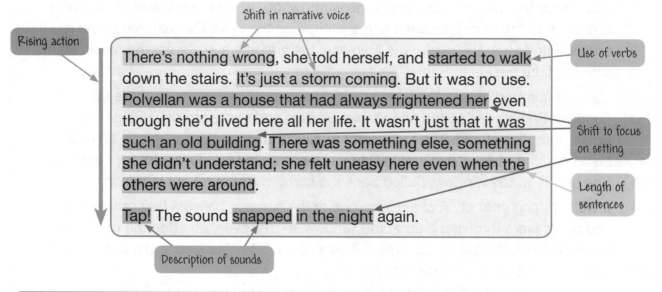

There's nothing wrong, she told herself, and started to walk down the stairs. It's just a storm coming. But it was no use. Polvellan was a house that had always frightened her even though she'd lived here all her life. It wasn't just that it was such an old building. There was something else, something she didn't understand; she felt uneasy here even when the others were around.

Tap! The sound snapped in the night again.

Activity 2

Turn back to the whole text on page 15 and highlight where the same six methods listed above are used in the rest of the text.

You should choose two or three of the methods listed above to write about in your answer to an evaluation question. Choose at least one structural and one language feature.

The effects of the writer's methods

Your next task is to consider the effects of your chosen methods. Below is a spider diagram showing the six methods listed on page 16 and some of the effects they have in creating suspense and a creepy atmosphere in the text on page 15.

Language features and effects have been coloured blue, while structural features and effects have been coloured green.

Key term

climax the most exciting point in a story

Activity 3

Read the diagram below carefully to see what effects the methods have on the reader. Remember, some of these are the effects these features would have in *any* text. When you write about them, you need to relate everything to the text you are studying.

Structure

Language

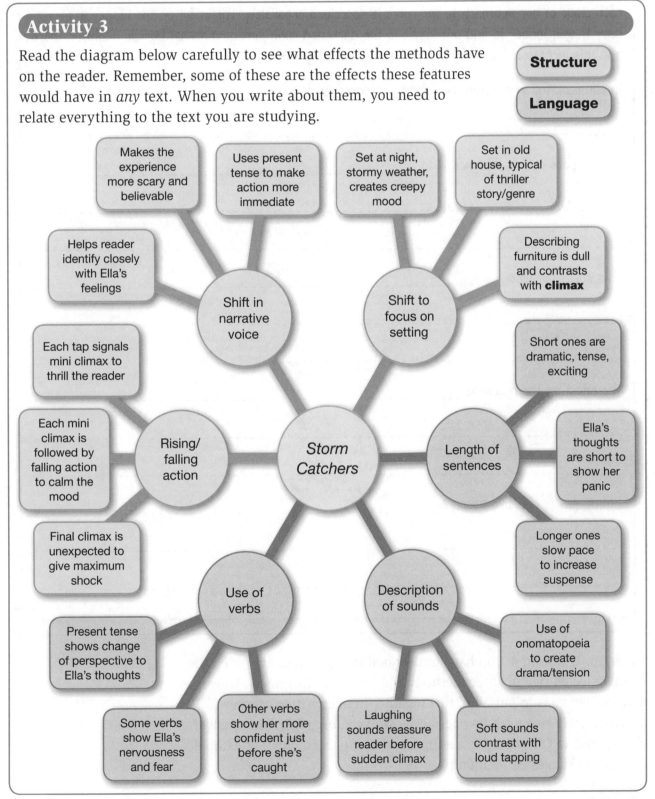

Activity 4

Read what one student wrote about the length of sentences in the text on page 15 and complete their answer.

To create a feeling of suspense the writer uses some long sentences, such as 'She stared through the gap, then took a deep breath, pushed the door a little further, and craned her head round.' The purpose of this sentence is to slow down Ella's search for the intruder. This works because each stage of her approach to the room is described separately. The effect on the reader is they have to wait longer to find out what's in the darkened room, imagining what horror might be there and this increases the reader's nervousness and suspense.

In contrast, the writer also uses short sentences, such as _____

_____.

The purpose of this sentence is to _____

_____

_____.

This works because _____

_____

_____.

The effect on the reader is _____

_____

_____

I think this is effective because _____

_____

_____

So far, for Question 4, you have understood the question, identified the focus, selected two or three methods and explored the effects. Now the final challenge is to put all of this together in one written answer of approximately two to three pages. The way you organize your answer in response to Question 4 is a simple series of paragraphs. For example, look at the suggested plan on page 19.

Paragraph 1: Introduction – a single sentence to sum up what happens in the text and the writer's purpose

Paragraph 2: First method, Quotation and Effects

Paragraph 3: Second method, Quotation and Effects

Paragraph 4: Third method, Quotation and Effects

Paragraph 5: Conclusion – your opinion on the overall success of the text

Top tip

It is important to use quotations and evidence from the text to support your answer to Question 4 in the test.

Activity 5

Using all that you have learned about evaluation from pages 14–19, answer the following question about *Storm Catchers* on page 15:

> A student wrote: 'This story is really creepy. The writer is brilliant at building up suspense.' How far do you agree with this view?

Write your evaluation on separate paper.

Progress check

It's time to check your progress. For each Question, start at the bottom of the chart and decide if you think you have achieved that level. If you have, put a tick in the box and then read the text above. Have you achieved that level too? Do the same for all the Questions in the Reading section.

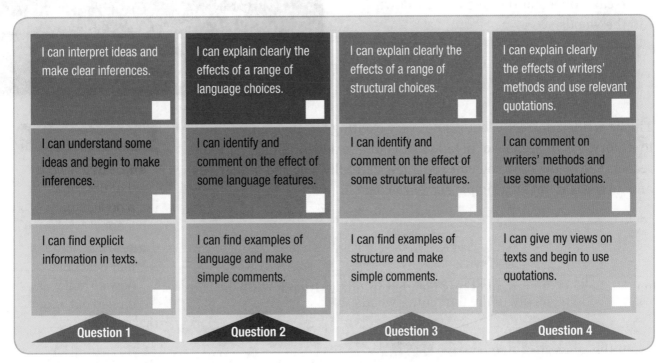

I can interpret ideas and make clear inferences. ☐	I can explain clearly the effects of a range of language choices. ☐	I can explain clearly the effects of a range of structural choices. ☐	I can explain clearly the effects of writers' methods and use relevant quotations. ☐
I can understand some ideas and begin to make inferences. ☐	I can identify and comment on the effect of some language features. ☐	I can identify and comment on the effect of some structural features. ☐	I can comment on writers' methods and use some quotations. ☐
I can find explicit information in texts. ☐	I can find examples of language and make simple comments. ☐	I can find examples of structure and make simple comments. ☐	I can give my views on texts and begin to use quotations. ☐
Question 1	Question 2	Question 3	Question 4

Question 5

Narrative writing

Objectives
- Explore narrative perspective
- Develop a character

Top tip

You will not have time to write a whole story in the test, so focus on writing an exciting opening section.

For the first question of the Paper 1 Writing section (Question 5) you are given two tasks and you must choose one. Both are creative writing questions, asking you to write either a description or a narrative (a story), so you need to prepare for both. One of the questions will have a picture as a starting point for your ideas.

An example of a narrative writing question might be:

> Write the opening section of a story about someone who is scared.

or

> Write a story suggested by the picture.

The picture might be of a place or a person. It might suggest a mood or a feeling. It is up to you to decide how the story develops, but your story must be linked to the picture in some way.

Let's start with an opening sentence:

> The car stopped at the gate leading down to the woods.

This is written correctly, but it's not very exciting for an opening line to a story. There are lots of details that could be added to interest the reader. See below how you can add a few carefully-selected **adjectives** and **adverbs** to make a simple sentence come to life:

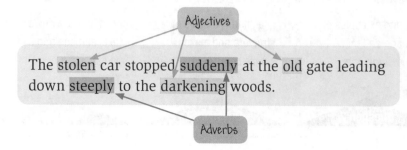

Adjectives

The stolen car stopped suddenly at the old gate leading down steeply to the darkening woods.

Adverbs

Key terms

adjective a word that describes a noun, e.g. 'happy'

adverb a word that describes how an action is carried out, e.g. 'happily'

Activity 1

Use the same starting sentence, 'The car stopped at the gate leading down to the woods', but add your own adjectives and adverbs to bring the opening line of the story to life. Think carefully about the mood you want to create before choosing your adjectives and adverbs.

When you write a story, you need to decide who the narrator is. A **first-person narrative** is when one of the characters tells the story from their own point of view. A **third-person narrative** is when the story is narrated by someone who is not a character.

For example, the second sentence in this story about the stolen car could introduce the narrator as either a first-person or third-person narrator:

> *I moved my head away from the window and crouched even lower in the boot of the car, terrified I would be discovered.*

or

> *The girl moved her head away from the window and crouched even lower in the boot of the car, terrified she would be discovered.*

Key terms

first-person narrative
a story told from the point of view of a character involved in the action, using 'I'

third-person narrative
a story told by someone not involved in the action, using 'he', 'she' or 'they'

Activity 2

Now write a second sentence for your story using either a first- or third-person narrator.

Characters are very important when writing stories. The details you include about your characters make them come to life. Look at the spider diagram below which shows details about the character of the girl in the boot of the stolen car.

Top tip

In a short story, it is a good idea not to include too many characters – perhaps two or three at most.

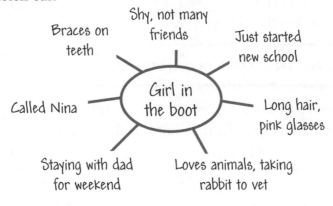

It would be very dull for the reader if you gave all the details about your characters at the start. It is better if you can drop details about your characters into the story as it develops. For example, below are the next two sentences in the same story, giving more details about the girl and her rabbit:

> *Nina shook the hair from her face and pushed her pink glasses more firmly onto her nose. She stroked her rabbit's soft long ears as he sat very still beside her.*

Activity 3

Use the blank spider diagram below to build up details about a character in your story.

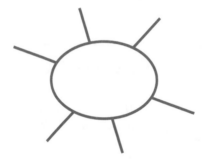

Another way to bring characters to life is to include dialogue. See below how, as the story continues, giving characters a voice makes them more realistic.

> *'How's your poor leg, Jerry?' Nina whispered to the rabbit. 'I'm glad you're here. I'm so scared!'*

Activity 4

Using descriptive details and dialogue, as well as the plans you have made in this section, complete the following task:

> Write a story suggested by the picture on page 20.

You have about 45 minutes to answer Question 5 in the test, so it is a good idea to practise writing within a time limit. Write your story on separate paper.

Descriptive writing

Objectives

- Vary vocabulary and imagery
- Use structural features
- Develop sentence forms

Question 5 on Paper 1 might ask you to write a description rather than a story, such as 'Write a description of a place you know well.' The purpose of descriptive writing is very similar to writing a story or narrative, but is more focused on bringing to life the sights, sounds, sensations and mood of a particular place, person or event. The descriptive task may have a picture to give you some ideas.

Descriptive writing is a great opportunity for you to show off your vocabulary. It is also an opportunity to use **imagery** and other language features. Look at the diagram below to see how it has been used to develop vocabulary and images linked to the picture above:

Key term

imagery
descriptive language that creates an image in the reader's mind

Patchwork of blue and green · Glinting · Twinkling like stars · A green parasol · Dappled shade · Sun shining through leaves · The sun is like a spotlight · Shafts of light

Activity 1

Create your own bank of vocabulary and imagery based on one of the options below. Add your ideas to the spider diagram.

Tree in autumn

A fallen log

A squirrel

Frost on a leaf

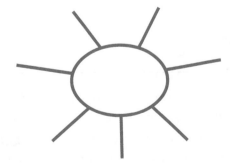

Descriptive writing does not usually include much action. This means you need to use a different sort of structure to move from one paragraph to the next than you would if you were writing a story.

For example, in a description, you might start a new paragraph because the weather changes or because you suddenly see a squirrel or because you climb a tree to describe the view from the top. These are called shifts, when your focus moves from one place, person or mood to another.

See below how the focus shifts from looking down to looking up:

> As I stood by the tree, a shaft of golden light fell to the ground, amongst the fallen leaves spread out like an orange carpet at my feet.
>
> I looked up and saw the sky was a huge patchwork of blue and green, like a tent over my head.

Activity 2

Write a plan to structure your description. Make notes on what your focus will be in each paragraph.

Paragraph 1 _____

_____

Paragraph 2 _____

_____

Paragraph 3 _____

_____

Paragraph 4 _____

_____

Paragraph 5 _____

_____

Another way for you to develop your descriptive writing skills is to use different sentence forms. Sentences can be short or long, simple or complex; they can be **exclamations** or **questions**. They can start with adjectives, adverbs or verbs. It makes your writing more interesting to use a wide variety of sentence forms.

Key terms

exclamation a word, phrase or sentence that expresses strong emotion, often ending with an exclamation mark (!)

question a sentence that asks for information and ends in a question mark (?)

Activity 3

Read each of the following examples and then write your own sentences using a similar form. For example, the first sentence begins with an adjective.

1. 'Dappled shade gave the wood a chilly feel.' _Damp leaves squelched underfoot._ ___

2. 'Softly, the leaves floated to the ground.' ___

3. 'A leaf fell.' ___

4. 'Climbing higher, I could see the sky above.' ___

5. 'How do leaves know when to fall?' ___

6. 'What a sinister silence there was!' ___

Activity 4

Using all you have learned about descriptive writing from pages 23–25, complete the following task:

> Write a description of a place you know well.

Write your description on separate paper.

Top tip

Many of the skills you develop in this section are useful for writing both stories and descriptions.

Progress check

It's time to check your progress. For each Question, start at the bottom of the chart and decide if you think you have achieved that level. If you have, put a tick in the box and then read the text above. Have you achieved that level too?

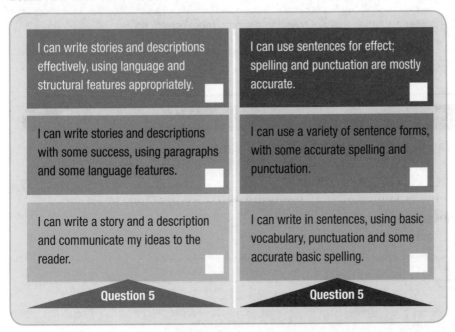

I can write stories and descriptions effectively, using language and structural features appropriately. ☐	I can use sentences for effect; spelling and punctuation are mostly accurate. ☐
I can write stories and descriptions with some success, using paragraphs and some language features. ☐	I can use a variety of sentence forms, with some accurate spelling and punctuation. ☐
I can write a story and a description and communicate my ideas to the reader. ☐	I can write in sentences, using basic vocabulary, punctuation and some accurate basic spelling. ☐
Question 5	Question 5

25

Question 1

Understanding texts

Objective

- Interpret information and ideas

Key term

non-fiction
writing that is factual, rather than fictional or made up

The first question on Paper 2 is about information and ideas. You will be asked to read a **non-fiction** text and then say which of the given statements are true. The statements include both explicit and implicit ideas.

Read the text below and then complete Activity 1.

No Strings International is a charity that uses puppets to teach life-saving messages to children and their families who live in the developing world[1].

5 Many children in other parts of the world cannot read and write or even go to school, so using puppets is a really good way of teaching them in a fun and interesting way.

10 No Strings is running an important project in Afghanistan. Afghanistan has a long history of war, and as a result there are nearly eight million landmines in the country. A landmine is a small 15 unexploded bomb buried under the ground. If a person steps on one it can be very dangerous as it can seriously injure or even kill them. No Strings has created an educational puppet film,

20 *ChucheQhalin*, which teaches children where landmines are most likely to be lurking, and how to avoid them. It uses characters based on traditional Afghan stories, and is told in their own 25 languages. The main characters are Chuchi, a little boy made of carpet, and his camel, Jaladul, who have lots of adventures together. Thousands of children have already seen the film 30 thanks to their Afghan partner OMAR. They have their own TV station, and they also take it into schools on a mobile media motorbike. This eRanger motorbike is very special as it turns 35 into a cinema so can show the film to children who live in the most far-away places.

Glossary 1 developing world – poorer countries that are trying to become more advanced

Activity 1

1. Why are puppets a good way to teach children in Afghanistan?

----

2. Why is the No Strings project important?

To answer the questions in Activity 1, you had to interpret the meaning of the text on page 26. Most of the information and ideas in non-fiction texts are clear or explicit, but there are also ideas that are suggested or implicit.

For example, read the final sentence of the text again: 'This eRanger motorbike is very special as it turns into a cinema so can show the film to children who live in the most far-away places.' The sentence has lots of implicit ideas. The following are ideas that you could interpret from the final sentence of the text and are all true:

- Some Afghan children live a long way from a city or town.

- Travelling in Afghanistan is not very easy.

- A motorbike which turns into a cinema is a clever invention.

- The charity cares about teaching all children.

- Many people in Afghanistan don't have access to TV or the Internet.

Activity 2

Is the following statement about the text on page 26 true or false? Explain your answer.

Eight million children have been injured by landmines in Afghanistan.

TRUE / FALSE

Top tip

Read every word of the statement slowly and carefully to check each part is correct.

Activity 3

Read the following statements about the text on page 26 and decide which four are true and which four are false.

1. The two main characters in the film are a boy and a camel. TRUE / FALSE

2. The charity No Strings only works with children in Afghanistan. TRUE / FALSE

3. There are no schools in Afghanistan. TRUE / FALSE

4. The purpose of the film is to teach children how to avoid landmines. TRUE / FALSE

5. The puppet film is called *ChucheQhalin*. TRUE / FALSE

6. No Strings is running a project to clear landmines in Afghanistan. TRUE / FALSE

7. Chuchi and Jaladul are characters based on traditional stories. TRUE / FALSE

8. Afghan children go to school on motorbikes. TRUE / FALSE

Question 2

Summarize and synthesize

Objective
- Select and use quotations

In Paper 2 there are two texts, Source A and Source B. Both are non-fiction texts and will be about the same subject or theme. One will be a modern text from the 20th or 21st century (1900–present day) and the other will be from the 19th century (1800–1899). Question 2 will ask you to write a summary of the differences or similarities between the texts.

Quotations are very important when you are summarizing texts because they are the evidence you need to show what you have understood from the text. In Question 2 you need to find and use quotations from both texts.

Read the following news article.

Source A

Travel chaos in England as snow and gales shut roads, harbours and airports

Flights delayed and cross-channel ferries suspended while snow sees drivers stranded in Sheffield

5   Heavy snow and gale-force winds have caused major disruption to travellers across the UK, with flights delayed, cross-channel ferries suspended and motorists stranded.

The north of England was worst hit by the cold snap, with blizzards closing Leeds Bradford International airport in Yorkshire and Liverpool's John Lennon airport for
10   several hours while flights at Manchester airport were also delayed on Saturday.

The freezing weather also brought treacherous conditions to roads, with many motorists in Sheffield forced to abandon their cars overnight after snow left roads impassable.

A band of wet, cold and blustery weather crossed England from Merseyside and
15   north Wales through the Midlands and Yorkshire. The north and the Midlands were worst hit by the snow, with 11cm (4.3in) falling in Leek, Staffordshire. Nottinghamshire and Bingley, near Bradford, saw flurries of up to 7cm (2.8in).

Motorists have been advised to check ahead before travelling, and in some parts to avoid journeys unless they are essential. [...]

20   Thousands in the Midlands were left without electricity as heavy snow brought down power lines. The Met Office warned that more snow may fall on Saturday, but added that the major threat would be from ice, which would affect almost all of the country.

When you choose a quotation you should use the smallest number of words possible. For example, if you wanted to choose a quotation from the text to show that the weather was windy as well as snowy, you might look at line 5 and choose the words 'Heavy snow and gale-force winds' or perhaps line 14 and choose the words 'wet, cold and blustery weather'.

Top tip

Don't forget to use quotation marks to show the words you have selected from the text.

Activity 1

Complete the table below by finding a quotation from Source A to support the following statements.

Statement	Supporting quotations
It is windy as well as snowy.	
Different types of transport are affected.	
People's lives are disrupted by the snow.	

When you use a quotation to support a statement, try to include it as part of the sentence you are writing. For example:

In Source A, the writer informs the reader that the disruption is not just caused by snow but also by 'gale-force winds'.

Activity 2

Write one sentence about the different types of transport affected and a second sentence about how people's lives are disrupted by the snow according to Source A. Use quotations from your completed table in Activity 1 to support what you have understood.

1. _____

_____

2. _____

_____

Making connections

Objective

- Make connections across texts

Paper 2 has two non-fiction texts to read on the same subject or theme. Question 2 asks you to write a summary of the differences or similarities between the texts.

The first text in this section, Source A, is a news article from 2014 about the effect of snow (page 28). The second text, Source B, is also about snow.

Source B

Diary entry from 1867

Wednesday, 2 January. Since midnight, snow had silently fallen, to the depth of 6 to 8 inches; by breakfast time it was all over except a slight flaky dropping, &[1] the day was calm & very cold. Nothing could be more beautiful; no change more complete & charming. The trees around the fountain near Garden Court were loaded with snow:
5   an exquisite tracery[2] of white branches, relieved against the dark red house fronts. But in the streets the transformation was greatest. All traffic, except afoot, was stopped; no cabs, no omnibuses, no waggons. The snow lay in heaps in the road; men were scraping & shovelling the footways; & people in thick coats & wrappers stepped noiselessly along. The Strand[3] was as quiet and empty as a village street at nightfall;
10   even the foot passengers were far fewer than usual. Here in the heart of London, & at midday, there was absolute cleanliness & brightness, absolute silence: instead of the roar & rush of wheels, the selfish hurry, the dirt & the cloudy fog, we had the loveliness & utter purity of new-fallen snow. It fell without force or sound; & all things huge & hasty & noisy were paralysed[4] in a moment. I walked along enjoying the wondrous lovely scene.

Glossary   **1** & – and   **2** exquisite tracery – beautiful, delicate pattern
           3 The Strand – a busy central London street   **4** paralysed – unable to move

Activity 1

Answer the following questions using quotations from Source B (above) to support what you have understood.

1. How does London look different because of the snow? _____

_____

2. What effect does the snow have on the sounds of London? _____

_____

3. How does the writer feel about the snow? _____

_____

There are lots of similarities between Source A and Source B: both are about wintry weather and in both texts daily life has been affected by the snow. There are also lots of differences.

Activity 2

Read each of the statements below and decide if it is true about Source A (page 28) or Source B (page 30) or both.

Statement	Source A, B or both?
The effect of the snow is negative.	
The writer informs us about one city.	
The writer is annoyed by the snow.	
The snow is dangerous.	
The writer is enchanted by the snow.	
Traffic is affected by the snow.	

Key term

connective a word used to connect words, phrases, clauses and sentences, e.g. 'and', 'but', 'however'

To answer Question 2 in the test, you have to make connections between the texts. For example, one student noticed a connection in the way Source A and Source B show how snow affects the traffic:

Similarity

Quotation: Source A

Quotation: Source B

Difference

Both texts show how traffic has been affected by the snow. In the news article, the writer states that motorists were 'forced to abandon their cars overnight' because the roads were 'impassable'. In the diary entry, the writer also describes how all the traffic was stopped: 'no cabs, no omnibuses, no waggons'. However, the news article suggests that the roads are 'treacherous' because the snow is so dangerous, whereas the writer of the diary thinks that it is 'wondrous' without 'the roar & rush of wheels' because it is so peaceful.

Making connections between texts is easier if you have spotted the similarities and differences between them. It is also easier to write about the connections if you use **connective** words like:

Similarly   Although   Equally

Whereas   In contrast   However

Activity 3

Using all you have learned about choosing quotations and making connections from pages 28–31, complete the following task:

> Write a summary of the differences and similarities between the effects of the snow in Source A (page 28) and Source B (page 30). You should include:
>
> • the type of weather   • the effect of the weather   • how people respond.

Write your summary on separate paper.

Question 3

Language and effects

Objectives

- Analyse words and phrases
- Develop comments on effect

Key term

autobiography a personal account of someone's life, written by that person

Question 3 on Paper 2 is about how the writer uses language to create effects. In the test, the text will be one of the same texts that you wrote about in Question 2. The text which follows here is an extract from an **autobiography** written by chef and cookery writer, Nigel Slater.

Toast by Nigel Slater

Apple Crumble

Snow has fallen upon deep snow. The sky, lavender, grey and deep scarlet-rose, is heavy with more. Cars, barely one every half-hour, make their way slowly home, their tyres crunching on the freezing snow. The white boulder I rolled yesterday and left
5 on the grass verge shines amber under the street lamp. My mittens are stiff. My face numb. Everything glistens.

There are shouts from the boys up the road firing snowballs at one another. I am playing alone, about a hundred yards away from them. My mother is watching me through the dining-room window. She looks worried. I am the proprietor[1] of an
10 imaginary cheese shop, carving slices of Cheddar from the huge rock of snow lit by the street lamp. As I ask my next customer what they want, I catch my mother's eye. I smile and wave at her and she looks down, embarrassed. The front door opens and she calls to me.

'It's time to come in now.'

15 'Oh, can't I stay out just a bit longer? There's a queue.' [...]

She comes out and looks anxiously up the road at the boys having fun, yelling and running and sliding in the snow. Five of them, four from my own class. She looks disappointed. A cold little smile. She puts her arm round me, wincing at the frozen hairs on my cold duffel coat.

20 'Come on in, I've made a crumble.'

Glossary 1 proprietor – owner

All words have **connotations** – these are the associations we have with words, what they make us think or feel. For example, the word 'green' has connotations of freshness, nature and new life, but it can also have connotations of sickness, poison or mould.

Key term

connotations the underlying ideas and feelings suggested by a word

The connotations of words and phrases are important because they give the text a depth and richness. For example, by using the word 'glistens' the writer is able to make you imagine the idea of brightness, shininess and a sense of magic. When you write about language, you need to consider these connotations in your answer and explain the effect the words and phrases have on you.

Read what one student wrote about the word 'glistens'.

Abstract noun

Adverb

Adjective

> The writer uses the word 'glistens' to describe the snowy scene. It suggests how the snow-covered street is shiny, with pinpricks of brightness. It reminds me of diamonds glinting tantalizingly on the ground. The word 'glistens' is almost magical and creates a sense of wonder and enchantment or a fairy-tale world.

The student has used adjectives, adverbs and **abstract nouns** to describe the effect of the word 'glistens'.

Activity 1 (SPAG)

Complete the table below to show adjectives, adverbs and abstract nouns.

Adjectives	Adverbs	Abstract nouns
magical	magically	
		gentleness
	brightly	
	beautifully	beauty
		peace

Activity 2 (SPAG)

Choose one word or short phrase that you find interesting from the text on page 32 and write about the connotations, using at least one adverb, one adjective and one abstract noun.

Top tip

Use your imagination when you write about language to explore what effect the words and phrases have on you, like the student does here, imagining the snow to be like 'diamonds'.

Key term

abstract noun
a word used to identify emotions, ideas and qualities, rather than physical things, e.g. 'bravery', 'happiness'

In the text on page 32, the writer uses a wide range of language features. To answer Question 3 on Paper 2 about how the writer uses language, you are expected to identify the language features used in the text, as well as to describe the effect created by using them. For example, this is what Student A wrote about one language feature:

Student A

The writer uses onomatopoeia in the text when he writes 'their tyres crunching on the freezing snow'. Onomatopoeia is when the word sounds like the noise it is describing. He does this to show the noise the tyres make.

Student A is correct in identifying the language feature used – it is onomatopoeia – and is correct in explaining what effect the feature can have. But Student A has not written about what effect the onomatopoeia has in this particular text. This is what Student B wrote about the same language feature:

Student B

The writer uses onomatopoeia to describe the soft crushing sound the cars make as their tyres are 'crunching on the freezing snow'. The word 'crunching' sounds slow and heavy, which suggests how the cars are barely moving in the deep snow. It has the sharp sound of 'cr' to sound like new snow being crushed and the gentler 'ch' sound to suggest the noise is muffled by the snow.

You can see that Student B has thought much more carefully about the sound of the word 'crunch' and described the effect it has on the reader.

Activity 3

Choose one example of a language feature from the text on page 32 and write about the effect it has on the reader.

Language can have a wide variety of effects on the reader. Some words create a visual effect, such as a description of a 'colourful sunset', and some words create sound effects, such as car tyres 'crushing' snow. Some words, like 'lavender', can create a sensation, such as softness or warmth, and some words, like 'frozen', can create an emotion or feeling, such as fear or sadness. All these effects combine to create a mood or atmosphere in the text.

Top tip

Try using abstract nouns to describe the atmosphere, for example, 'a mood of enchantment' or 'a mood of sadness and anxiety'. This will help to make your writing more sophisticated.

Activity 4

1. Circle the adjectives to show which words you think best describe the mood of the text on page 32. You can choose more than one word.

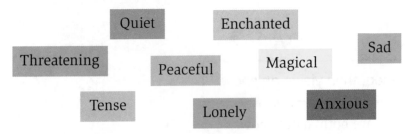

Quiet   Enchanted   Sad   Threatening   Peaceful   Magical   Tense   Lonely   Anxious

2. Explain your choices, using quotations from the text.

Activity 5

Using all you have learned about language from pages 32–35, answer the following question:

> How does Nigel Slater use language to create a wintry mood in the text on page 32?

Choose three or four interesting examples of language that the writer uses to describe the wintry day and describe their effects on the reader. Write your answer on separate paper.

Question 4

Comparison – points of view

Objective
- Identify point of view

The two non-fiction texts in Paper 2 have the same subject or theme. However, the writers will present different points of view on the subject. Your task in Question 4 is to compare the different points of view and also to compare how the writers use different methods to present their points of view.

A typical question might be:

> Compare how the writers present their views on snow.

Read the two texts opposite, which are both about snow.

Activity 1

Read the statements below and decide if you think they are more likely to be the view of the writer of Source A or Source B.

1. The snow has turned the whole city into a magical wonderland. **SOURCE A / SOURCE B**

2. The snow is a serious inconvenience and there is more to come. **SOURCE A / SOURCE B**

3. The snow is dangerous and affects motorists and homeowners alike. **SOURCE A / SOURCE B**

4. The snow has stopped the traffic, which makes the roads very peaceful and quiet. **SOURCE A / SOURCE B**

To compare the different points of view, it is helpful to use words such as 'whereas', 'although', 'however' or 'in contrast'. You can use these connectives to compare the texts. To show you have understood the points of view, you need to include quotations to support your statements. For example:

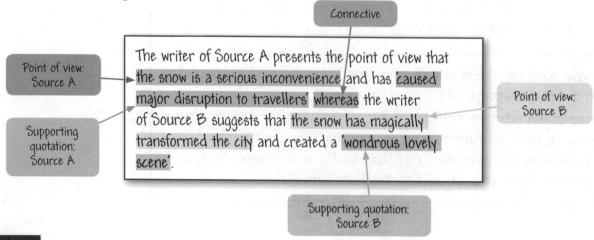

Connective

Point of view: Source A

The writer of Source A presents the point of view that the snow is a serious inconvenience and has 'caused major disruption to travellers' whereas the writer of Source B suggests that the snow has magically transformed the city and created a 'wondrous lovely scene'.

Point of view: Source B

Supporting quotation: Source A

Supporting quotation: Source B

Source A

Travel chaos in England as snow and gales shut roads, harbours and airports

Flights delayed and cross-channel ferries suspended while snow sees drivers stranded in Sheffield

Heavy snow and gale-force winds have caused
5 major disruption to travellers across the UK, with flights delayed, cross-channel ferries suspended and motorists stranded.

The north of England was worst hit by the cold snap, with blizzards closing Leeds Bradford
10 International airport in Yorkshire and Liverpool's John Lennon airport for several hours while flights at Manchester airport were also delayed on Saturday.

The freezing weather also brought treacherous
15 conditions to roads, with many motorists in Sheffield forced to abandon their cars overnight after snow left roads impassable.

A band of wet, cold and blustery weather crossed England from Merseyside and north
20 Wales through the Midlands and Yorkshire. The north and the Midlands were worst hit by the snow, with 11cm (4.3in) falling in Leek, Staffordshire. Nottinghamshire and Bingley, near Bradford, saw flurries of up to 7cm (2.8in).

25 Motorists have been advised to check ahead before travelling, and in some parts to avoid journeys unless they are essential. [...]

Thousands in the Midlands were left without electricity as heavy snow brought down power
30 lines. The Met Office warned that more snow may fall on Saturday, but added that the major threat would be from ice, which would affect almost all of the country.

Source B

Diary entry from 1867

Wednesday, 2 January. Since midnight, snow had silently fallen, to the depth of 6 to 8 inches; by breakfast time it was all over except a slight flaky dropping, &[1] the day
5 was calm & very cold. Nothing could be more beautiful; no change more complete & charming. The trees around the fountain near Garden Court were loaded with snow: an exquisite tracery[2] of white branches, relieved
10 against the dark red house fronts. But in the streets the transformation was greatest. All traffic, except afoot, was stopped; no cabs, no omnibuses, no waggons. The snow lay in heaps in the road; men were scraping &
15 shovelling the footways; & people in thick coats & wrappers stepped noiselessly along. The Strand[3] was as quiet and empty as a village street at nightfall; even the foot passengers were far fewer than usual. Here
20 in the heart of London, & at midday, there was absolute cleanliness & brightness, absolute silence: instead of the roar & rush of wheels, the selfish hurry, the dirt & the cloudy fog, we had the loveliness & utter
25 purity of new-fallen snow. It fell without force or sound; & all things huge & hasty & noisy were paralysed[4] in a moment. I walked along enjoying the wondrous lovely scene.

Glossary   1 & – and   2 exquisite tracery – beautiful, delicate pattern
3 The Strand – a busy central London street   4 paralysed – unable to move

Activity 2

Write another sentence comparing the points of view in Source A and Source B, using a different connective to the example on page 36 and including a quotation from each text.

- -

- -

- -

Comparison – features and effects

Objective

- Comment on features and effects

In Question 4, you are asked to compare how the writers present their points of view. Now you have understood the different points of view in the two texts on page 37, you need to look carefully at what features the writers use to present their views and what effect these features have on the reader.

Look first at the news article (Source A) on page 37. The writer has used a range of language features, such as facts and emotive language. The writer has also used structural features to present a point of view, such as a third-person perspective and a shift in setting.

Top tip

Try to include a balance of language and structural features in your answer to Question 4. Two of each would be a good idea.

Activity 1

Find two examples of each of the following features in Source A on page 37.

Feature	Examples
Fact	
Emotive language	
Third-person perspective	
Shift in setting	

The writer of Source A uses facts, such as 'The north and the Midlands were worst hit by the snow with 11cm (4.3in) falling in Leek, Staffordshire', to give accurate, precise and detailed information. The language is simple and clear and the effect is to make readers aware of the disruption and help them to decide if they should travel in the snow.

Activity 2

Fill in the spaces below to comment on the use of emotive language in Source A and its effect on readers. You could use phrases from the boxes on page 39.

> The writer of Source A uses emotive language, such as '_____'
>
> and '_____' to create a sense of _____
>
> _____. The language is _____ and _____ and the
>
> effect is to _____.

Fear and panic   Descriptive   Treacherous conditions   Dramatic

Make readers scared of travelling in the snow   Dangerous

Now look at Source B, the diary entry written in 1867, on page 37.
You need to explore the language and structural features in this text to
help you make a comparison.

Activity 3

Answer the following questions about the diary entry (Source B) on page 37.

1. How does the line 'Since midnight, snow had silently fallen' have an effect on readers?

----

2. The writer uses lists several times in the text. Choose one example and explain its effect.

----

3. Why do you think using a first-person perspective is effective in this diary entry?

----

4. How does the writer structure the text to create the sense of a journey?

Comparison – planning

Objective

● Plan a comparison

Question 4 on Paper 2 asks you to compare two texts. It is a challenging task for any student because there is so much to compare: ideas, points of view, language choices, structural features, etc. So it is really important to plan what you are going to write before you start. This helps you to think about what points you want to make and how you are going to organize them.

The task you are set here is:

> Compare how the writers of Source A and Source B on page 37 present their views on snow.

Activity 1

Look at the planning grid below. Using all you have learned in this section, complete the grid for Source A and Source B on page 37.

	Source A: Newspaper article	Source B: Diary entry
Theme/ Purpose		To describe the joy of snow
Point of view	Snow is disruptive	
Ideas presented	People abandon cars	
Language features		
Structural features		First-person perspective
My opinion		

Your planning grid contains all the points you will need to make in your comparison of the two texts. However, you must also remember to:

● use quotations to support all the points you make

● describe the effect the features have on the reader.

The planning grid will help you answer the question and organize your ideas into paragraphs. Each paragraph should include the points from one section of your planning grid.

> **Paragraph 1:** Compare the *theme* and *purpose* of both texts.
>
> **Paragraph 2:** Compare the *points of view* presented in both texts.
>
> **Paragraph 3:** Compare the *ideas* presented in both texts.
>
> **Paragraph 4:** Compare the *language features* and their *effects* in both texts.
>
> **Paragraph 5:** Compare the *structural features* and their *effects* in both texts.
>
> **Paragraph 6:** Give your *opinion* of which text is the most effective.

Activity 2

Using your planning grid, the paragraph plan and all the work you have done so far in this section, write your answer to the following question:

> Compare how the writers of Source A and Source B on page 37 present their views on snow.

Write your answer on separate paper.

Progress check

It's time to check your progress. For each Question, start at the bottom of the chart and decide if you think you have achieved that level. If you have, put a tick in the box and then read the text above. Have you achieved that level too? Do the same for all the Questions in the Reading section.

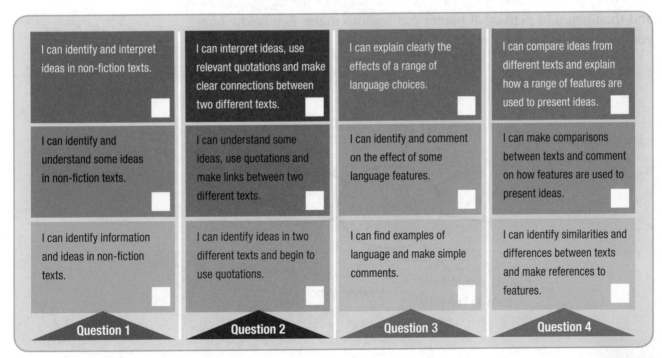

I can identify and interpret ideas in non-fiction texts. ☐	I can interpret ideas, use relevant quotations and make clear connections between two different texts. ☐	I can explain clearly the effects of a range of language choices. ☐	I can compare ideas from different texts and explain how a range of features are used to present ideas. ☐
I can identify and understand some ideas in non-fiction texts. ☐	I can understand some ideas, use quotations and make links between two different texts. ☐	I can identify and comment on the effect of some language features. ☐	I can make comparisons between texts and comment on how features are used to present ideas. ☐
I can identify information and ideas in non-fiction texts. ☐	I can identify ideas in two different texts and begin to use quotations. ☐	I can find examples of language and make simple comments. ☐	I can identify similarities and differences between texts and make references to features. ☐
Question 1	Question 2	Question 3	Question 4

Question 5

Writing non-fiction

Objectives

- Present a point of view
- Structure an argument
- Use language features to persuade
- Extend range of punctuation

For the Writing section of Paper 2, you will have one task to complete, Question 5. It is recommended that you spend 45 minutes on this task. Unlike the Writing section of Paper 1, you will not have a choice of tasks. You will be asked to write a non-fiction piece, presenting a point of view on a subject linked to the texts you have read in Paper 2 Section A: Reading. The question may ask you to argue or persuade; it may ask you to write a letter or an article for a magazine; it may ask you to write for students or for parents, but in all these tasks the purpose is to present your point of view clearly for the reader to understand.

An example of the type of question you may be asked is:

> A teacher at your school has made this statement: 'Fashion is pointless and a waste of money.'
>
> Write an article for your school newsletter in which you argue for or against this statement.

Your first task is to decide if you agree or disagree with the statement and then begin to plan what points you want to make. See below how you might organize your plan.

Structure

You will need to write a paragraph for each point you make to explain the point in more detail. You need to decide the order in which these points work best. It is a good idea to start with a simple, clear point and finish with your strongest and most convincing point. Your points should be either all agreeing or all disagreeing with the statement you have chosen, not a mix of both, or you may confuse the reader.

Activity 1

Choose the best four points from the plan opposite and put them in a list to show the sequence of your argument. This is the structure for your writing.

Point/Paragraph 1 _____

Point/Paragraph 2 _____

Point/Paragraph 3 _____

Point/Paragraph 4 _____

Discourse markers and topic sentences

To present your point of view, each paragraph should start with a different opening. These are called **discourse markers** and will help you structure the points you want to make. Below are some examples of discourse markers you could use to build your argument.

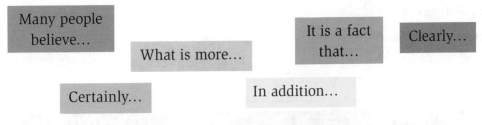

Often, the first sentence in each paragraph introduces the point you are going to make. This is called the **topic sentence**. See the examples below of how to use a discourse marker at the start of a topic sentence:

Clearly, the point of clothes is to keep you warm.

It is a fact that fashion is only for girls.

Many people believe that clothes should be made to last longer than one season.

> ### Key terms
>
> **discourse marker** a word or phrase used as an organizational tool to link ideas
>
> **topic sentence** the sentence that introduces or summarizes the main idea of a paragraph

Activity 2

Decide which of the discourse markers from page 43 you will use and write a topic sentence for the start of one of your paragraphs.

Language features

When writers are presenting their point of view, they often use a range of language features to make their points more persuasive. Some of the language features you may consider using in your argument are **repetition**, **rhetorical question**, list of three and **direct address**. See how some of these features are used to make a point more persuasive:

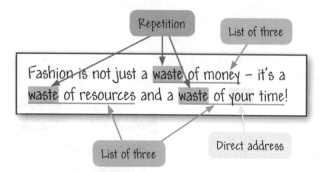

Key terms

direct address speaking directly to your audience, using 'you'

repetition repeating something

rhetorical question a question asked for dramatic effect where the answer is not required

Top tip

You don't need to use lots of features in the same sentence. This is just an example.

Activity 3

Write a sample sentence for your argument using each of the language features below.

1. Repetition _____

2. Rhetorical question _____

3. List of three _____

4. Direct address _____

Sentence structure

In addition to using language features in your argument, you should use interesting vocabulary and a wide range of sentence forms to keep the reader interested. To make an impact, for example, you could use some very short sentences, such as 'Fashion is foolish!' As you can see in this example, the sentence also uses an exclamation mark to make it even more dramatic. You should also try to use:

$$? - \text{" "}, : ; ( )$$

Activity 4

SPAG

Rewrite the following paragraph of an argument to make it more persuasive. Try to include:

- more exciting vocabulary
- varied sentence forms
- a range of punctuation
- some language features
- different discourse markers to start sentences.

> Clothes companies want young people to keep buying more clothes. This is why they keep making new fashions. It is a way to make more money. The people who lose out are the young people because they think they will get bullied if they don't wear fashionable clothes.

Activity 5

Using all you have learned about how to structure and write an answer to Question 5, complete the following task:

> A teacher at your school has made this statement: 'Smartphones are pointless and a waste of money.'
>
> Write an article for your school newsletter in which you argue for or against this statement.

You will have about 45 minutes to answer this question in the test so it is a good idea to give yourself a time limit. Write your article on separate paper.

Top tip

Remember not to use too many language features or you may confuse the reader.

Remember also to be polite – the reader will not be persuaded of your point of view if you are rude to them or suggest they are foolish.

Progress check

It's time to check your progress. For each Question, start at the bottom of the chart and decide if you think you have achieved that level. If you have, put a tick in the box and then read the text above. Have you achieved that level too?

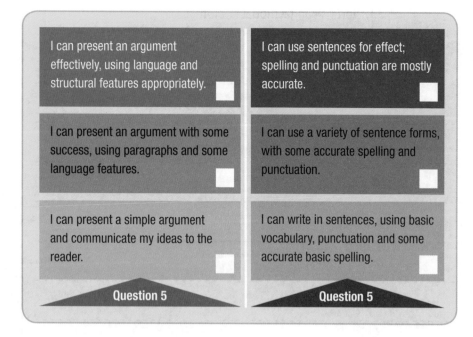

I can present an argument effectively, using language and structural features appropriately. ☐

I can use sentences for effect; spelling and punctuation are mostly accurate. ☐

I can present an argument with some success, using paragraphs and some language features. ☐

I can use a variety of sentence forms, with some accurate spelling and punctuation. ☐

I can present a simple argument and communicate my ideas to the reader. ☐

I can write in sentences, using basic vocabulary, punctuation and some accurate basic spelling. ☐

Question 5

Question 5

Key terms glossary

abstract noun   a word used to identify emotions, ideas and qualities, rather than physical things, e.g. 'bravery', 'happiness'

adjective   a word that describes a noun, e.g. 'happy'

adverb   a word that describes how an action is carried out, e.g. 'happily'

alliteration   when words start with the same sound to create an effect, e.g. 'snail slime'

autobiography   a personal account of someone's life, written by that person

climax   the most exciting point in a story

connective   a word used to connect words, phrases, clauses and sentences, e.g. 'and', 'but', 'however'

connotations   the underlying ideas and feelings suggested by a word

dialogue   conversation between two or more characters

direct address   speaking directly to your audiences, using 'you'

discourse marker   a word or phrase used as an organizational tool to link ideas

evaluation   a judgement about the value of something

exclamation   a word, phrase or sentence that expresses strong emotion, often ending with an exclamation mark (!)

explicit   stating something clearly and openly

falling action   the pace of events slows down and becomes calmer and more reassuring

first-person narrative   a story told from the point of view of a character involved in the action, using 'I'

flashback   a section in a text that is set before the events of the main story

future tense   a verb that describes something that will happen in the future, e.g. 'they will laugh'

imagery   descriptive language that creates an image in the reader's mind

implicit   suggesting something without stating it openly

metaphor   when one thing is described as being another to create an image, e.g. 'the sea was an ogre, wild and enraged'

narrative   a written story or account

narrative voice   the person telling the story from their point of view

narrator   the person who tells the story

non-fiction   writing that is factual, rather than fictional or made up

onomatopoeia   when the word sounds like the noise it describes, e.g. 'buzz'

past tense   a verb that describes something that happened in the past, e.g. 'they laughed'

perspective   a particular view of something

phrase   a group of words without a main verb

point of view   the way a character regards events or people

present tense   a verb that describes something that is happening now, e.g. 'they laugh' or 'they are laughing'

purpose   the reason for writing a text, e.g. to entertain, to describe or to persuade

question   a sentence that asks for information and ends in a question mark (?)

repetition   repeating something

rhetorical question   a question asked for dramatic effect where the answer is not required

rising action   the pace of events speeds up and becomes more dramatic and exciting

sequence   the order in which things happen

setting   where the events take place

simile   when one thing is compared to another, using 'as' or 'like', e.g. 'the fish darted from under the rock *like* silver bullets'

structural feature   a feature that helps to structure a text

structure   the organization of a text

suspense   a feeling of uncertainty about what might happen

third-person narrative   a story told by someone not involved in the action, using 'he', 'she' or 'they'

topic sentence   the sentence that introduces or summarizes the main idea of a paragraph

verb   'doing' or action words, e.g. 'ran', 'laughed', 'screamed'

OXFORD
UNIVERSITY PRESS

Great Clarendon Street, Oxford, OX2 6DP, United Kingdom

Oxford University Press is a department of the University of Oxford. It furthers the University's objective of excellence in research, scholarship, and education by publishing worldwide. Oxford is a registered trade mark of Oxford University Press in the UK and in certain other countries

British Library Cataloguing in Publication Data

Data available

ISBN 978-019-836880-9

10 9 8 7 6 5 4 3 2 1

Printed in Great Britain by Ashford Print and Publishing Services, Gosport

Acknowledgements

The author and publisher are grateful for permission to reprint extracts from the following copyright material:

Tim Bowler: *Storm Catchers* (OUP, 2001), copyright © Tim Bowler 2001, reprinted by permission of Oxford University Press.

Jamila Gavin: *The Eye of the Horse* (Mammoth, 1995), copyright © Jamila Gavin 1994, reprinted by permission of David Higham Associates.

Andrew Johnson: 'Travel chaos in England as snow and gales shut roads, harbours and airports', *The Guardian*, 27 Dec 2014, copyright © Guardian News & Media Ltd 2014, reprinted by permission of GNM Ltd.

No Strings International: about the charity in *Midnight Feast* edited by Nick Lake (Collins 2007), reprinted by permission of No Strings International.

Nigel Slater: *Toast: the Story of a Boy's Hunger* (Fourth Estate, 2010), copyright © Nigel Slater 2003, reprinted by permission of HarperCollins Publishers Ltd.

Mimi Thebo: *Hit the Road, Jack* (HarperCollins, 2004), copyright © Mimi Thebo 2004, reprinted by permission of HarperCollins Publishers Ltd.

Kate Thompson: 'The Dragon's Dream', copyright © Kate Thompson 2001, from *Mirrors* edited by Wendy Cooling (Collins, 2001, 2009), reprinted by permission of HarperCollins Publishers Ltd.

Although we have made every effort to trace and contact all copyright holders before publication this has not been possible in all cases. If notified, the publisher will rectify any errors or omissions at the earliest opportunity.

The author and publisher would like to thank the following for permission to use their photographs:

Cover: Steve Bloom Images/Alamy: **p20:** Edmund Lowe Photography/Shutterstock; **p23:** S.Borisov/Shutterstock

BRITAIN

in focus

Laurence Kimpton

HODDER AND STOUGHTON

LONDON SYDNEY AUCKLAND TORONTO

Acknowledgements

The author is grateful to the following for providing help and information:

Anglian Water Authority; Association of Agriculture; City of Birmingham Development Department; British Airports Authority (Stansted Airport); British Alcan Lynemouth Ltd.; British Coal; British Rail; Central Electricity Generating Board; Corby Industrial Development Centre; Cornwall County Council; Department of Trade and Industry; Keith Flinders; Ford Motor Company; Forestry Commission; David and Zillah Garth; A.C. Gurney; Highlands and Islands Development Board; Livingston Development Corporation; London Docklands Development Corporation; Metrocentre; Milton Keynes Development Corporation; M.H. Mulliner; Napp Laboratories; North West Water Authority; Norwich Union Insurance Group; Nilesh Pandya; Peak District National Park; Premier Brands; Rochdale Industrial Development and Advisory Centre; Royal Society for the Protection of Birds; Shell UK Limited; Swindon Enterprise; Welsh Development Agency; Yorkshire and Humberside Tourist Board.

Particular thanks are due to David Jones for his help and advice during the preparation of this book and to Rosalind Lomas for typing the typescript.

The publisher thanks the following for giving permission to reproduce photographs in this book:
Aerofilms (1.4 Fig. 2, 1.4 Fig. 3, 12.2 Fig. 1, 12.5 Fig. 4), Austin Rover (8.6 Fig. 4); Barnaby's Picture Library (4.4 Fig. 2, 12.1 Fig. 8); BBC Hulton Picture Library (4.3 Fig. 4, 4.6 Fig. 1); Birmingham International Airport (10.3 Fig. 4); Michael H. Black Photography (1.3 Fig. 5, 9.4 Fig. 8r); British Airways (10.3 Fig. 1); British Alcan Lynemouth Limited (8.2 Fig. 2); British Coal (7.2 Fig. 1); British Rail (10.1 Fig. 8, 10.1 Fig. 9); British Steel (8.5 Fig. 3); Central Electricity Generating Board (7.4 Fig. 3, 7.5 Fig. 2); The Creative Company/Milton Keynes Development Corporation (4.7 Fig. 2); F.A.O. (12.4 Fig. 9); Farmers Weekly (6.1 Fig. 5, 6.1 Fig. 6); The Felixstowe Dock and Railway Company (10.4 Fig. 2, 10.4 Fig. 4); P.N. Fitchett (1.3 Fig. 3); M.J. Fitchett (2.2 Fig. 2, 6.2 Fig. 4, 10.1 Fig. 3, 11.4 Fig. 3); Forestry Commission, Edinburgh (3.3 Fig. 3); D.P. Jones (3.4 Fig. 2); London Transport Museum (12.4 Fig. 1); Massey Ferguson (6.1 Fig. 4l); Metrocentre (9.1 Fig. 7); Network (4.1 Fig. 1b); North of Scotland Hydro-Electric Board (7.5 Fig. 6); Rhyl Suncentre (9.4 Fig. 7); J. Sainsbury plc (9.1 Fig. 6); Sea Fish Industry Authority (3.5 Fig. 2); Sevenoaks Leisure Centre (9.3 Fig. 2r); Shell (7.3 Fig. 3, 7.3 Fig. 4); Tyne and Wear P.T.E. (10.2 Fig. 4); University of Dundee (2.1 Fig. 5); Welsh Development Agency (T. Soames) (11.2 Fig. 5).

All other photographs were supplied by the author.

Contents

1. Britain's landscapes

1.1   The landscape

Britain has a great variety of landscapes, as you can see in Figures 1 to 6. The landforms in each of these scenes reflect the work of rivers, ice and the sea on a wide variety of rock types. Other natural features in the landscape include the soil and the natural vegetation, although many apparently wild landscapes have been greatly modified by people's activities. Figure 7 shows how the elements which form the landscape are related to each other.

Changing landscapes

Landscapes do not stay the same. Different human activities such as farming, mining, manufacturing and the building of villages and towns shape and change Britain's landscapes. Britain has been settled for thousands of years and the present day landscapes may consist of elements from many periods of history, as the photograph in Figure 8 shows.

Q1
Look at Figures 1 to 6. For each one, say whether natural or human influences appear to have affected the appearance of the landscape most. Give reasons for your answers.

Figure 1
Isle of Arran, Scotland

Figure 2
A Lake District valley

Figure 3
The Fowey Estuary, Cornwall

Figure 4
Edinburgh, an urban landscape

2

Figure 5
Fenland, Cambridgeshire

Figure 6
Berkshire Downs

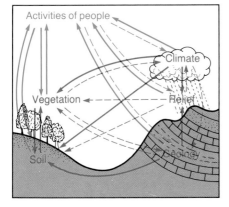

Figure 7
Relationships in the landscape

Figure 8
The landscape reflects both physical processes and many years of human settlement. Here a new industrial estate and a radio communications station has been superimposed on a field pattern over 500 years old.

Beautiful landscapes, ugly landscapes

People's opinions on how attractive a landscape is vary greatly. Figure 9 shows a way in which you can record your own opinions of a landscape.

Q2
(a) On a copy of the table in Figure 9, show your feelings about *two* of the landscapes in Figures 1 to 6. Use a different colour for each of the landscapes you choose.
(b) Compare your profiles (i) one with the other and (ii) with other people's profiles for the same landscapes.

Figure 9
The qualities of landscapes

How to record your opinion of a landscape
Place a tick on one of the five lines for each pair of adjectives to indicate your opinion. For example, if you think a landscape looks very attractive, place a tick on the line furthest to the left. If you think that both words of a pair equally describe a landscape or do not describe it at all, place a tick on the middle line. When you have put a tick for each pair of adjectives, join the ticks to form a profile of your opinions about a landscape.

Attractive	— — — — —	Unattractive
Interesting	— — — — —	Boring
Varied	— — — — —	Monotonous
Tidy	— — — — —	Untidy
Distinctive	— — — — —	Ordinary
Beautiful	— — — — —	Ugly
Colourful	— — — — —	Drab
Clean	— — — — —	Dirty
Well-kept	— — — — —	Badly kept
Healthy	— — — — —	Unhealthy
Safe	— — — — —	Dangerous

1.2 Geology and the landscape

Britain has a very varied geology with rocks from every geological period (Figure 1). The older rocks are mostly found to the north and west of a line joining the mouth of the river Tees and the mouth of the river Exe. The younger rocks are mostly found to the south and and west of this line.

Types of rock

The types of rock found in Britain are as varied as their ages. The three main groups of rocks are:

1 Sedimentary rocks are made up of layers (**strata**) of material. This may have been eroded from already existing land. Some sedimentary rocks are formed from the remains of animals (for example, limestone) or plants (coal). The existence of fossils enables the rocks to be dated and the geological time scale constructed.
2 Igneous rocks are formed from molten material (**magma**) which has cooled or solidified either on or beneath the earth's surface.
3 Metamorphic rocks are those which were formed originally as sedimentary or igneous rocks, but have been changed by heat and/ or pressure.

Highland and lowland Britain

The older rocks in the north and west of Britain tend to be more resistant to erosion and so form widespread areas of highland. The younger rocks in the south and east generally form areas of lowland. Thus the Tees/Exe line is also a division between highland and lowland Britain (Figure 2). Igneous and metamorphic rocks

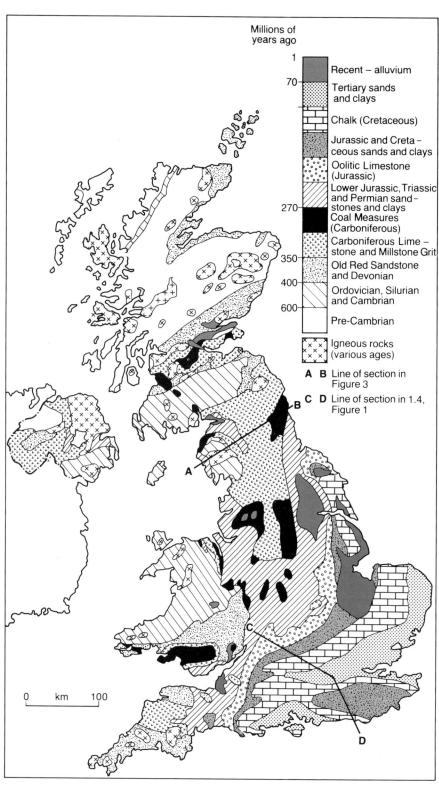

Millions of years ago

1	Recent – alluvium
70	Tertiary sands and clays
	Chalk (Cretaceous)
	Jurassic and Creta‑ ceous sands and clays
	Oolitic Limestone (Jurassic)
270	Lower Jurassic, Triassic and Permian sand‑ stones and clays
	Coal Measures (Carboniferous)
350	Carboniferous Lime‑ stone and Millstone Grit
400	Old Red Sandstone and Devonian
600	Ordovician, Silurian and Cambrian
	Pre-Cambrian
	Igneous rocks (various ages)

A B Line of section in Figure 3
C D Line of section in 1.4, Figure 1

0   km   100

Figure 1
Geology of Britain

4

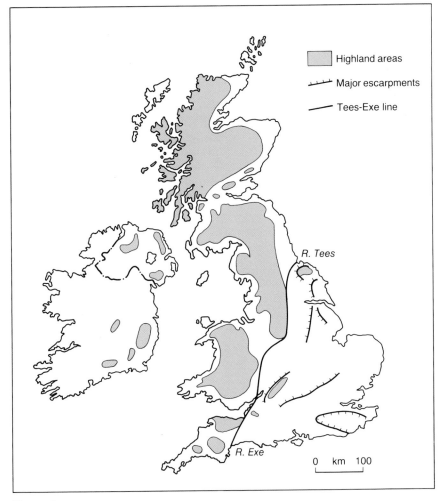

Figure 2
Highland and lowland Britain

Figure 3
Geological section across northern England

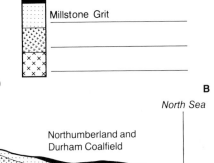

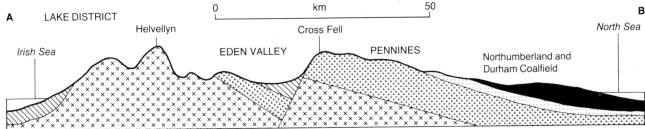

are mostly found in highland Britain. Their presence is often linked with major periods of mountain building in geological history and they form parts of many of Britain's highest mountain areas, such as the Cairngorms, the Lake District and Snowdonia.

Figure 2 shows that highland Britain includes some areas of lowland, normally occurring where rocks are relatively young (for example, the Cheshire Plain) or where blocks of land have

been lowered between geological faults (the Central Lowlands of Scotland). Within lowland Britain, the more resistant rocks, Jurassic limestone and the chalk, form hills such as the Cotswolds and Chilterns.

Shaping the landscape

The following pages show how different landscapes have been produced in Britain. Their

features have been influenced by a combination of the following factors:

● the resistance and character of the rocks

● weathering (the breaking down of rocks by chemical processes and freeze-thaw action)

● erosion by rivers, the sea and ice

● deposition by rivers, the sea and ice.

1.3 Highland landscapes

The landscapes of the mountains and landscapes in highland Britain range from rugged mountain areas with large areas of bare rock to wide expanses of plateau cut by a few valleys. These contrasts reflect differences in rock types and in the processes which have been at work in shaping the rocks.

Glaciated highlands

During the Ice Age, which ended only about 25 000 years ago, most of Britain was at some time covered by ice sheets. They rounded off sharp edges of uplands and deposited large amounts of boulder clay on the lowlands. The most dramatic glaciated landscapes are the result of the work of valley glaciers and are found in Britain's highest mountain areas in North Wales, the Lake District and the Highlands of Scotland (Figures 1 to 3). Large deep hollows known as **corries** or **cirques** (Figure 1) are striking features in the higher mountain areas. The corrie glaciers often merged to form major glaciers which moved along already existing river valleys. Such glaciers had tremendous erosive power. They straightened,

widened and deepened the valleys into great troughs with U-shaped cross-sections (Figure 3). The lower parts of tributary valleys were cut away so that their upper parts were left 'hanging' above the main valley. Overdeepening of valleys left hollows which, after the glaciers had melted, were occupied by lakes.

> **Q1**
> Make sketches of the photographs in Figures 1 and 3. On your sketches label as many glacial landforms as you can, by referring to Figure 2.

Limestone landscapes

Limestone gives rise to a particularly distinctive landscape (Figure 4). It is a permeable rock, allowing water to percolate along very marked **bedding planes**, (horizontal cracks between the rock layers or strata) and **joints** (vertical lines of weakness). Rainwater is a weak acid and dissolves the calcium carbonate of which limestone is composed. This process of **solution** occurs along the bedding planes and joints to produce features such as limestone pavements. Streams

Figure 1
Corrie, Snowdon, North Wales

Figure 2
Features of highland glaciation

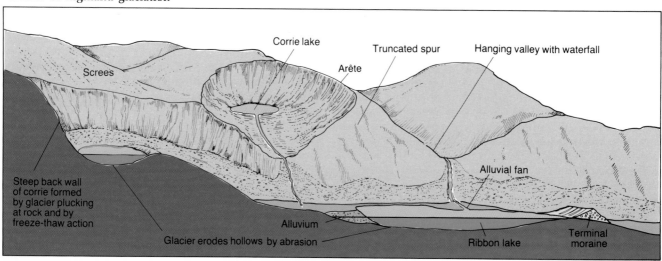

Screes

Corrie lake

Arête

Truncated spur

Hanging valley with waterfall

Steep back wall of corrie formed by glacier plucking at rock and by freeze-thaw action

Glacier erodes hollows by abrasion

Alluvium

Alluvial fan

Ribbon lake

Terminal moraine

Figure 3
Wastwater, Cumbria, a ribbon lake in a glacial valley

Figure 4
Limestone scenery, Malham Cove, Yorkshire

following lines of weakness dissolve the limestone to form swallow holes and cave systems. At the surface, the former courses of streams are shown by dry valleys.

Moorlands

Much of highland Britain consists of plateau areas or rolling uplands. Drainage is often poor and the plateau tops are covered by thick peat. In places, the underlying rocks of the moorlands are exposed as edges, (for example, Millstone Grit in the Pennines) or **tors** (for example, granite on Dartmoor, Figure 5).

The use of the highlands

The human and economic use of Britain's mountains and uplands may seem relatively limited because of poor soils, harsh weather conditions and rugged relief. However, as Figure 6 shows, they are of great importance. The impact of human use may in some cases be so great that activities have to be restricted, for example, through

the creation of National Parks. Figure 6 shows the other sections of this book where the use of these areas is looked at in more detail.

Q2
For each of the photographs in this section and those of highland areas in Section 1.1, make a summary table using the following headings: Location in Britain; Rock type (if known); Description of scenery; Existing and possible human use.

Figure 6
Human use of the highlands

HUMAN AND ECONOMIC USES	FURTHER DETAILS
Livestock and arable farming in valleys	Chapter 6
Extensive livestock grazing	Chapter 6
Recreation and tourism	Sections 9.4, 12.1
Mining and quarrying	Section 3.4
Hydro-electric power generation	Section 7.4
Military training	—
Forestry	Section 3.3
Water storage	Section 3.2
Industrial development based on local resources	—

Figure 5
Tor, Dartmoor

1.4　Lowland landscapes

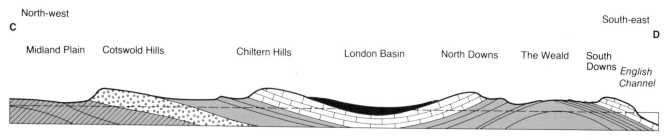

North-west

C

South-east

D

Midland Plain　Cotswold Hills　　Chiltern Hills　　London Basin　　North Downs　　The Weald　　South Downs　*English Channel*

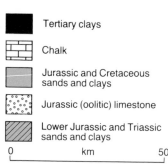

■ Tertiary clays

▭ Chalk

▨ Jurassic and Cretaceous sands and clays

▨ Jurassic (oolitic) limestone

▨ Lower Jurassic and Triassic sands and clays

0　　　　km　　　　50

Figure 1
Geological section across southern England

Scarp and vale

The geological map (Section 1.2, Figure 1) shows that in many parts of lowland Britain bands of resistant and less resistant rocks alternate. These are sedimentary rocks which have been gently tilted and folded. As a result of

Figure 2
The South Downs

differential erosion, the resistant rocks like chalk stand out as lines of hills, while less resistant clays form broad **vales**. The lines of hills have a steep **scarp** slope on one side and a gentle **dip** slope on the other; these features can be clearly seen on the geological section across southern England in Figure 1. Chalk is a highly permeable rock. As a result, chalklands have few surface streams, but many dry valleys. The chalk hills have smooth rounded contours (Figure 2).

Lowland river valleys

Many of Britain's major rivers flow for much of their course along or across the clay vales. Here the clays are usually covered by thick layers of river-deposited alluvium. Figure 3 shows an aerial view of the River Trent flowing northwards to the Humber Estuary. Notice the large meanders of the river and the wide flood plain. Figure 4 shows the important land forms associated with lowland river valleys; all owe their existence to erosion and deposition by the river.

> **Q1**
> Figure 5 lists some important ways in which lowland river valleys are used. Draw a sketch map, based on Figure 4 and label where the various uses are likely to be located.

Figure 3
The Trent Valley

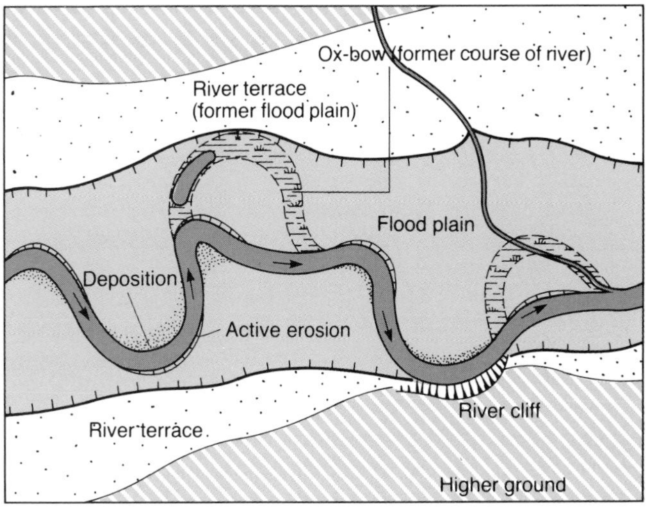

Figure 4
River valley landforms

Ox-bow (former course of river)

River terrace
(former flood plain)

Flood plain

Deposition

Active erosion

River terrace

River cliff

Higher ground

The Fens

In eastern England the Fens form another type of lowland landscape (see Section 1.1, Figure 5). The Fens were once a large area of marshland. The decay of reeds and sedges which grew in the marsh led to the building up of a thick layer of peat. Near the sea, silts were deposited over the peat when high tides flooded into the Fens. In Section 12.5 we will see how the natural fenland was drained from the 17th century onwards and transformed into a rich arable farming area. Today, therefore, the landscape of the Fens is more of a human than a natural landscape, as Figure 6 shows.

Glaciation in the lowlands

The effects here of glaciation are less spectacular than in the highlands. The ice sheets, as they melted, plastered deposits of **boulder clay** across the land. The boulder clay often gives rise to rather featureless landscapes. The soils which have developed on the boulder clay often prove to be particularly fertile for farming, such as over much of East Anglia where the boulder clay contains many fragments of chalk. The meltwater from the ice deposited sands and gravels which produce poor soils.

Figure 5
Human use of river valleys

- Farming
- Settlements
- Routes for roads, railways and canals
- Water transport
- Power stations
- Sewage works
- Sand and gravel pits
- Manufacturing industry
- Recreation (e.g. boating)
- Reservoirs

Q2
From Figure 6, draw a cross-section of the Fenland landscape, labelling the natural and man-made features in contrasting colours.

Figure 6
The Fens

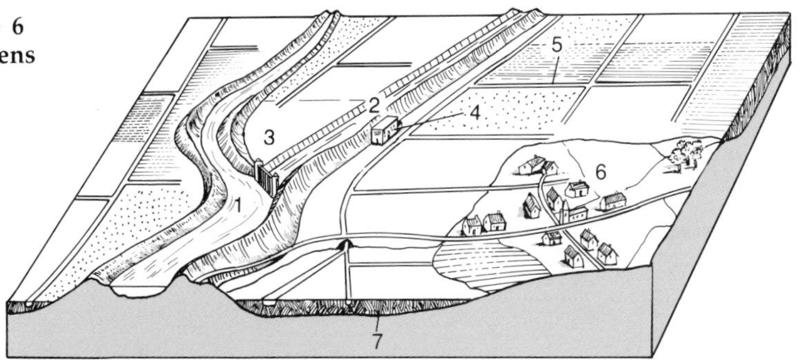

1 River (with banks raised to prevent flooding)
2 Main drainage channel
3 Sluice
4 Pumping station
5 Drainage ditch
6 Village on fen 'island'
7 Peat (shrinkage has resulted in its surface being lowered)

1.5 Coastal landscapes

The coastline of Britain has as great a variety of scenery as inland Britain. Most coastal scenery reflects erosion by the sea. The foaming breakers in Figure 1 clearly show that the sea holds tremendous power. Here, near Land's End in Cornwall, the land is particularly exposed to wave attack; 3000 kilometres of open sea stretch away to the west. In contrast, where a stretch of coastline is sheltered, the deposition of sand and silt leads to land being extended at the expense of the sea.

Along many stretches of coastline, there is a pattern of alternating bays and headlands. Usually this is the result of an alternation of resistant and weak rocks, as in the Isle of Purbeck, Dorset (Figure 2). Resistant chalk and limestone form the headlands, while the bays have been eroded out of weaker sands and clays.

Erosion by the sea

The sea erodes both by the force of the water itself (**hydraulic action**) and by waves hurling rocks against the base of cliffs (**corrasion**). Erosion at the base of cliffs leads to the collapse of the rock above. As cliffs retreat under attack by the sea, a wave-cut platform is formed. The sea attacks lines of weakness in cliffs and widens them to form deep recesses and caves. Where a cave is formed in a headland it might cut right through to form an arch. The collapse of the arch leaves an isolated stack which will eventually be worn into a stump. Figure 3 shows these features of a cliff coastline. If cliffs are formed of easily eroded clays or weak sandstones, their retreat may be very rapid. Parts of the Holderness coast, just north of the Humber Estuary are retreating at a rate of 2.75 metres a year.

Transport and construction by the sea

Spits such as Borth Spit in Central Wales (Figure 4) are important features of Britain's coastline. A spit is formed by the movement of sand and shingle along the coast by **longshore drift** (Figure 5). Behind the spit, silt is often trapped and a salt marsh develops. The sand dunes on Borth Spit are formed by the wind blowing sand inland from the beach.

Figure 1
The coast near Land's End

Figure 2
Isle of Purbeck, Dorset

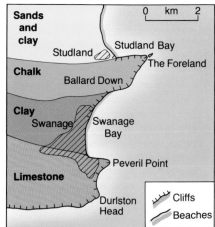

Figure 3
Features of coastal erosion. Stacks, Isle of Purbeck

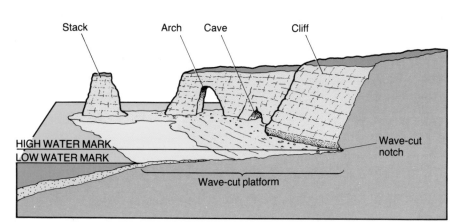

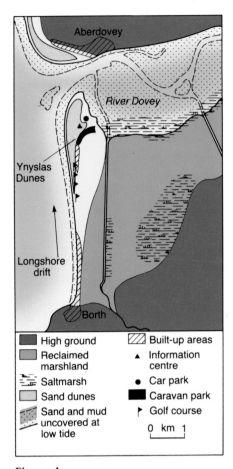

Figure 4
Borth Spit

Changes in sea level

Many large-scale features of Britain's coastline are the result of a general rise in sea level since the end of the Ice Age. In lowland areas, the flooding of broad river valleys has led to the forming of shallow estuaries with branching creeks, mud flats and salt marshes, such as the coast of Essex. In hillier areas, such as Cornwall, drowned steep-sided valleys form **rias** (see Section 1.1, Figure 3). In Scotland, glaciated valleys have been flooded to form **sea lochs**. Smaller scale features which are evidence of a rise in sea level are raised beaches and cliffs no longer under attack by the sea.

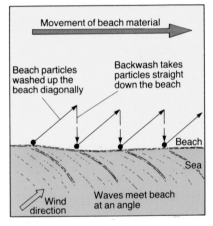

Figure 5
Longshore drift

Figure 6
The Gower Peninsula
Langland Bay looking west with
Oxwich Point in the distance

Q1
Figure 6 is a map of the Gower Peninsula in South Wales.
(a) What effect have the bands of easily eroded shales had on the shape of the coastline?
(b) List the features of (i) erosion and (ii) deposition which are found in this area.
(c) What evidence is there of sea level having fallen?

Q2
Borth Spit (Figure 4) is both a recreational area and a nature reserve (for plants, birds and animals).
(a) Draw the plan of Borth Spit. On your plan, (i) label the beach, caravan site, golf course, car park and nature reserve information centre; (ii) label the sand dunes and salt marsh as nature reserves; (iii) mark in with 'V's the areas which are likely to be most crowded with visitors on fine summer days.
(b) What conflicts might occur between the two main uses of Borth Spit? What measures can be taken to deal with them?

11

2. Weather and climate

2.1 Weather

Britain's weather is very variable from day to day and so weather forecasting is important for the efficient planning of farming, building work and many other activities. The knowledge of 'average' conditions of temperature and rainfall – the climate – is important for understanding geographical patterns such as the distribution of farming types or the pattern of water supply.

Air masses

Great masses of air above the earth's surface develop distinct characteristics: for example, air over the interior of a northern continent in winter will become cold and dry. Britain is affected by air masses from a number of origins (Figure 1), and this helps make the weather so variable.

Depressions and anticyclones

When a cold air mass from Polar regions mixes with a warm air mass from the Tropics over the Atlantic Ocean, the two types of air converge anticlockwise and

begin to rise into the upper atmosphere. A low pressure area or **depression** is thus formed (Figure 2). Depressions from the Atlantic Ocean bring unsettled weather. Figure 3 shows the patterns of weather associated with a depression. Notice how cloud and rain is a feature of the fronts where the cold and warm air masses meet. Rainfall associated with depressions is known as frontal or cyclonic rain.

A period of more settled weather is produced by an **anticyclone**. This is an area of high pressure in which air is sinking and spreading outwards from the centre. In winter, anticyclones usually bring cold, clear weather with frost and fog. Sometimes, however, a layer of low cloud leads to dull, cold weather. In summer, anticyclonic weather is very warm with long hours of sunshine.

POLAR MARITIME Cold, moist

ARCTIC MARITIME Very cold, moist (in winter)

POLAR CONTINENTAL Very cold, dry (in winter)

TROPICAL MARITIME Warm, moist

TROPICAL CONTINENTAL Hot, dry

Q1
The weather map in Figure 4 shows the weather conditions resulting from a depression moving across Britain.
(a) Describe the weather at (i) point X (Western Isles); (ii) point Y (London). (You need to mention temperature, wind direction and strength, cloud cover and precipitation.)
(b) Give reasons for the contrasts in weather between these two places.

Q2
(a) Figure 5 shows a satellite picture of cloud cover over the northeast Atlantic together with a map showing the pressure pattern. On a copy of the map, mark in the likely positions of a warm front, a cold front and an occluded front. Label the warm and cold sectors of the depression.
(b) Explain how weather satellites help in making weather forecasts.

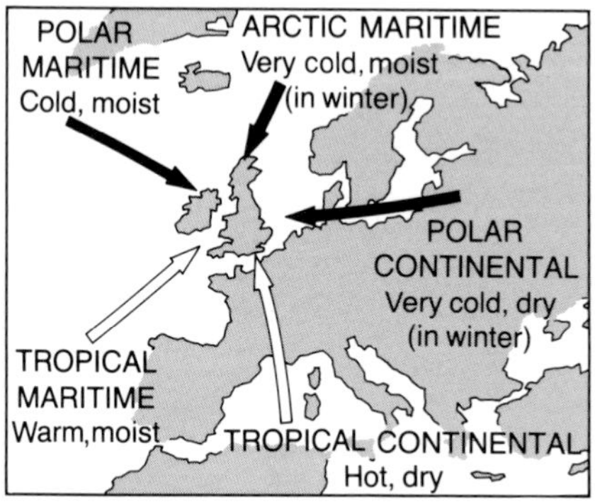

Figure 1
Air masses which affect Britain

Figure 2
How a depression develops

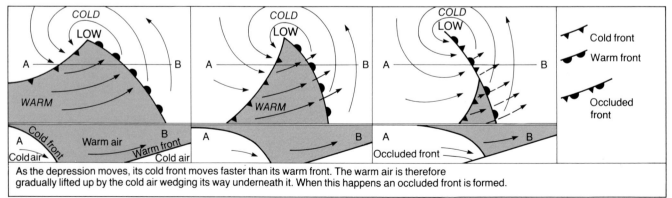

Cold front

Warm front

Occluded front

As the depression moves, its cold front moves faster than its warm front. The warm air is therefore gradually lifted up by the cold air wedging its way underneath it. When this happens an occluded front is formed.

Cold front
Cumulo-nimbus
Cumulus
COLD AIR
WARM AIR
Stratus
Nimbo-stratus
Alto-stratus
Cirro-cumulus
Cirrus
Warm front
COLD AIR
IRELAND
Irish Sea
WALES
ENGLAND
0 km 100

06.00 hours
4 November
LOW
976
980
984
988
992
990
1000
1004
1008
1012
1016
1020
1024
1028
X
Y
0 km 100
Fronts
Warm
Cold
Occluded
992 Isobar with pressure in millibars
Cloud amount (oktas)
0
1/8
2/8
3/8
4/8
5/8
6/8
7/8
8/8
Sky obscured
Wind speed (knots)
Calm
1–2
3–7
8–12
13–17
48–52 Tail gives wind directions
Add half-feather for each additional 5 knots up to 47 knots
Mist
Fog
Drizzle
Hail
Rain
Sleet
Snow
Rain shower
Snow shower
Thunderstorm

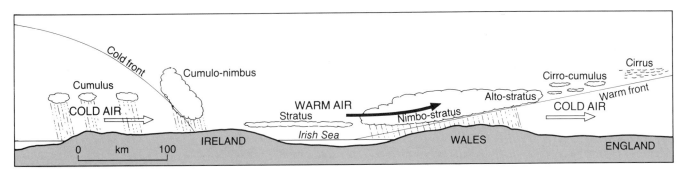

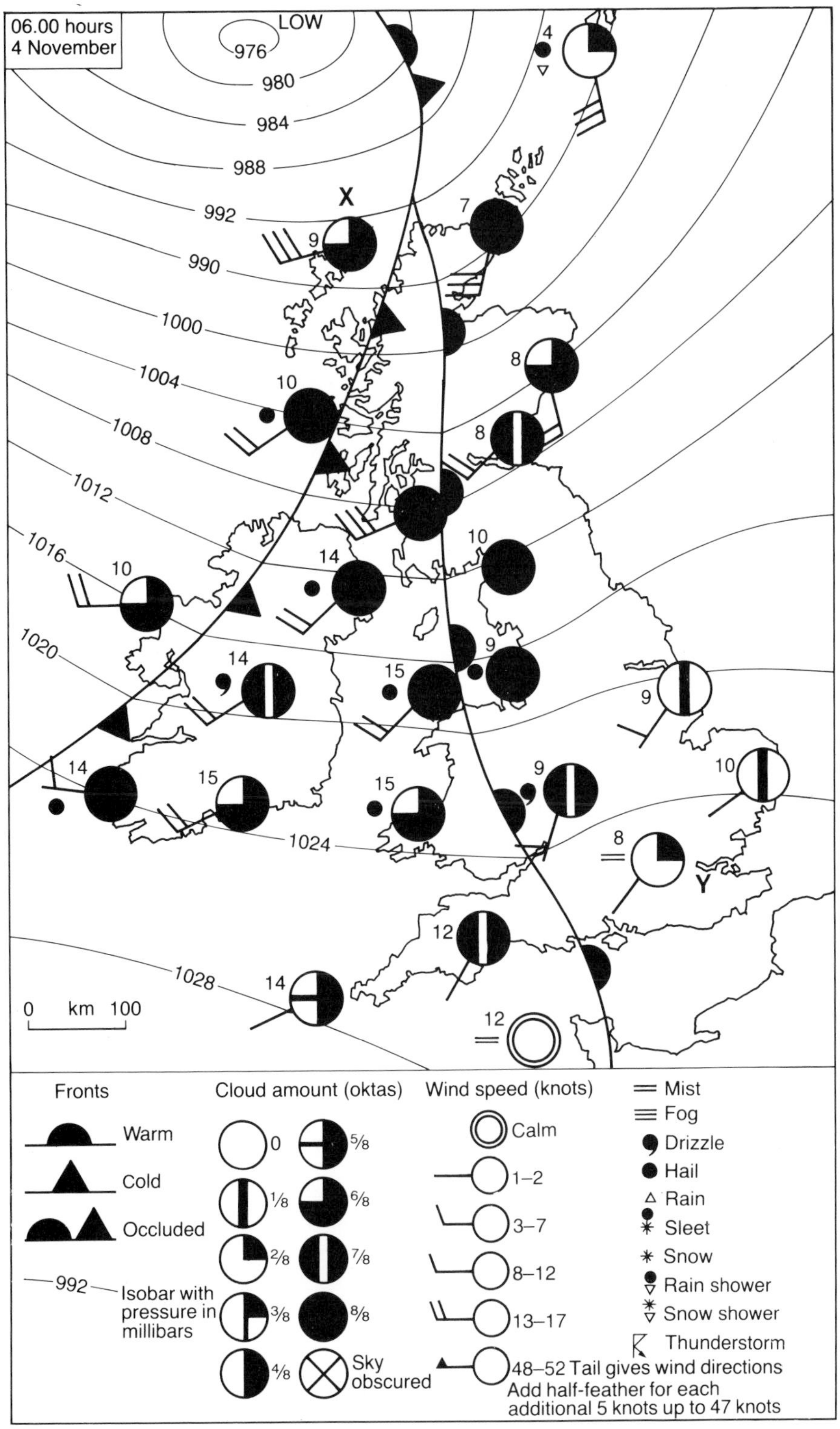

Figure 3
Cross-section of a depression

Figure 4
A weather map showing a depression to the north of Scotland

980
984
988
992
996
1000
1004
1008
1012
1016
1020

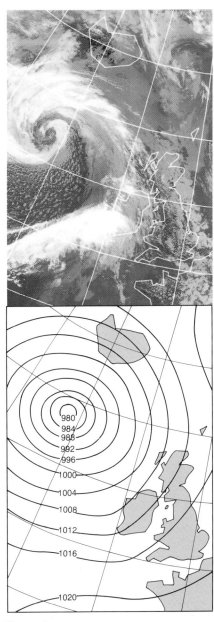

Figure 5
Satellite photograph and map of a depression over the northeast Atlantic

2.2 Rainfall patterns

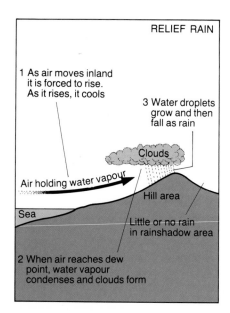

RELIEF RAIN

1 As air moves inland it is forced to rise. As it rises, it cools

3 Water droplets grow and then fall as rain

Clouds

Air holding water vapour

Hill area

Sea

Little or no rain in rainshadow area

2 When air reaches dew point, water vapour condenses and clouds form

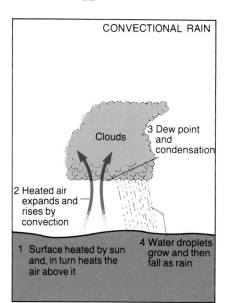

CONVECTIONAL RAIN

Clouds

3 Dew point and condensation

2 Heated air expands and rises by convection

1 Surface heated by sun and, in turn heats the air above it

4 Water droplets grow and then fall as rain

Figure 1
Relief and convectional rain

We have already seen that rainfall is associated with fronts in depressions. The clouds (made up of water droplets) have been formed by warm moist air being forced to rise above 'wedges' of denser cold air. When air rises through the atmosphere it moves into cooler and less dense layers and will therefore expand. When air expands it cools because heat is spread out through a greater volume of air. Cooler air cannot hold as much water vapour as warm air. When rising air is being cooled, a point will be reached when it is saturated with

water vapour – it can hold no more – and so condensation occurs and clouds are formed. Water droplets in clouds will grow in size and they eventually fall as rain. If temperatures are so low that water vapour turns into ice crystals then snow falls rather than rain.

Rainfall is not associated only with fronts. Moist air may be forced to rise, and rainfall caused, in two other ways as Figure 1 shows.

Figure 2
A fog-filled valley

Fog

If relatively warm, moist air close to the ground is cooled, the water vapour it contains will condense to form a layer of fog or mist. This cooling may happen in two main ways:

1 When the warm air moves horizontally across a colder surface, such as the sea.
2 When land rapidly cools on clear nights, the air in contact with it also cools.

Cooled air with fog is relatively dense and in hilly areas will concentrate in valleys (Figure 2).

> **Q1**
> Describe the problems caused by fog for road transport, air transport and shipping.

The distribution of rainfall

Figure 3 shows the pattern of average annual rainfall in Britain. Notice how the hill areas have high amounts of rainfall. The western slopes of these areas are especially wet, since most rainfall is brought by depressions which have developed over the Atlantic Ocean. The western hills shelter much of lowland Britain from the full impact of rain-bearing south-westerly winds. Thus the Midlands are in the **rain-shadow** of the Welsh mountains.

> **Q2**
> **(a)** What parts of Britain have particularly heavy rainfall? Give reasons for this pattern.
> **(b)** Why is eastern England the driest part of the country?

0 km 100
Over 1500 mm
1000–1500 mm
750–1000 mm
Under 750 mm

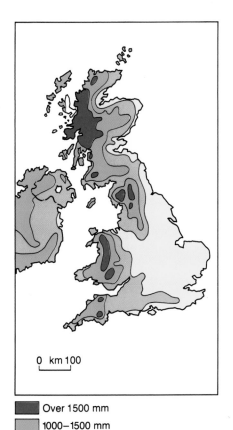

Figure 3
Rainfall distribution

The rainfall pattern as shown in Figure 3 helps to explain farming patterns in Britain. Relatively dry areas are particularly suited to arable farming while the higher rainfall areas are more important for livestock production. The rainfall pattern affects the planning of water supplies. Water is transferred from the water surplus areas of the West to the water deficient areas of the East and South (see Section 3.2).

Drought, floods and blizzards

For many people it is exceptional conditions that are important. Long dry periods combined with high temperatures in summer lead to major problems (Figure 4). Heavy rainfall can lead to flooding (see Section 12.5). Severe thunderstorms, especially if hailstones fall, can cause considerable crop damage. A relatively wet summer can hinder the growth of crops and cause cultivation and harvesting problems.

A hazard of winter weather is the occurrence of snowstorms or blizzards. Figure 5 illustrates the severe effects of just a short period of heavy snowfall and very low temperatures.

- Water supplies to homes, factories and other users disrupted
- Agriculture severely affected: reduction of crop yields, loss of some crops, poor grass growth leading to problems for dairy and other livestock farmers
- Forest and grass fires
- Reduction of river flows leading to problems for navigation and pollution control
- Subsidence of house foundations due to soil drying and shrinking

Figure 4
Effects of drought

Big Freeze-Up Will Spread Say Met Men

Britain was in the grip of sub-zero temperatures, heavy snow and biting easterly winds yesterday as the coldest weather for up to a century stranded passengers on snowbound trains, closed schools and caused chaos on the roads.

The Meteorological Centre reported that the lowest temperature recorded yesterday was −15.9 C at Aviemore in Scotland. Parts of eastern England reported overnight snowfalls of up to 3 feet.

In Kent, 300 rail passengers were stranded overnight on five trains halted by drifts and icy tracks, most minor roads were blocked, a quarter of the schools were closed and the Isle of Sheppey cut off.

Figure 5
Effects of heavy snow, January 1987

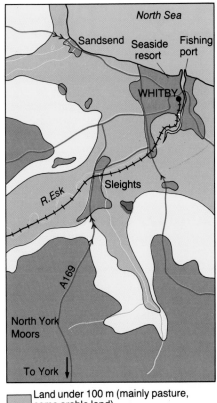

North Sea
Sandsend
Seaside resort
Fishing port
WHITBY
Sleights
R. Esk
A169
North York Moors
To York
Land under 100 m (mainly pasture, some arable land)
Land between 100 and 200 m (mainly pasture)
Land over 200 m (moorland used for rough pasture)
Built-up areas
Main roads
Steep hills on main roads
Railway
0 km 5

Figure 6
The Whitby area, North Yorkshire

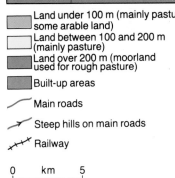

Q3
Figure 6 shows the Whitby area in North Yorkshire. Using evidence from the map, suggest what the likely effects on the area's life and economy will be of (i) a period of heavy snow and low temperatures; (ii) a long spell of dry, hot weather; (iii) a period of heavy rainfall in spring.

2.3   Temperature patterns

As with rainfall, average or mean temperatures are important in helping to explain geographical patterns. The average monthly temperatures for a winter month (January) and a summer month (July) are more useful than average annual temperatures.

Summer temperatures

Figure 1a shows average temperature conditions for July. (The lines which join points with the same temperature are known as **isotherms**). The map shows that southern areas tend to be warmer than northern areas (reflecting the effect of latitude) and that inland areas are warmer than neighbouring coastal areas (reflecting the cooling effect of the sea in summer). Clearly, these summer temperature patterns will influence farming. More significant for farming is the length of growing season, that is,

the time for which mean temperatures are above the value of 6°C (Figure 2). Figure 3 maps the average hours of sunshine for July. This pattern also helps to explain farming patterns (high sunshine totals are important for cereals and many fruits). It also shows that the seaside resorts of the South have a great advantage over those elsewhere.

Winter temperatures

Figure 1b shows average temperature conditions for January. The pattern of winter temperatures shows the warming influence of the North Atlantic Drift ocean current on the western parts of Britain. Winter temperatures are less of an influence on farming patterns than summer temperatures. However, it is clear that farmers in the South West will have an easier task in looking after livestock than farmers in the North East.

Local contrasts in temperature

Local contrasts in temperature are just as important to consider as broad patterns over the country. Figure 4 shows how altitude, aspect (the direction slopes face), relationship to the sea and urban development may all influence temperature.

Q1
Figure 5 shows the temperatures late in an early winter evening in the Whitby area (the same area as in Section 2.2, Figure 6). On a copy of the map draw in isotherms at 1°C intervals (The 1°C isotherm has already been drawn in Figure 5). Then by referring to Section 2.2, Figure 6, add labels to explain the pattern of temperatures.

Figure 1
July and January mean temperatures

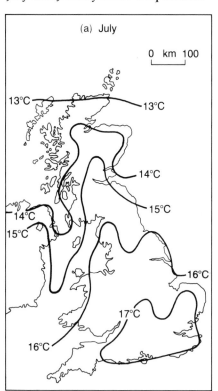

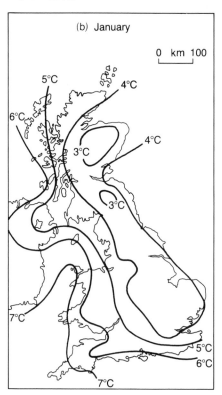

Figure 2
Length of growing season

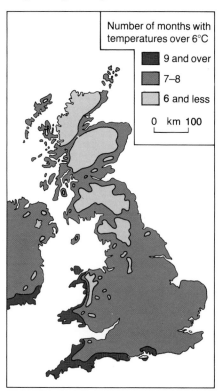

16

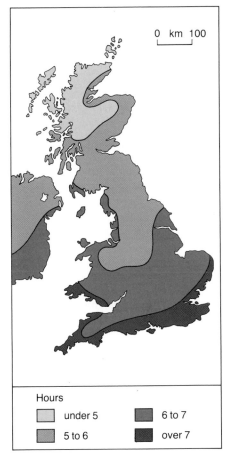

Figure 3
Hours of sunshine, July

Hours
- under 5
- 5 to 6
- 6 to 7
- over 7

0 km 100

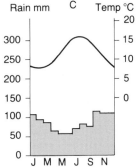

NORTH   SOUTH

Lower temperatures on high ground

South-facing slopes warmed by sun more than north-facing slopes

At night cold air sinks into 'frost hollow'

Warming influence of **buildings** in town creates a 'heat island'

Warming influence of sea in winter. Cooling breezes from sea in summer

Sea

Figure 4
Local temperature differences

Contrasting climates in Britain

A study of both rainfall and temperature patterns shows that Britain does not have a uniform standard climate.

Figure 6
Climate graphs of four different places

Q2
Figure 6 shows climatic graphs for Norwich, Falmouth, Dundee and Fort William, but not in that order. Find these places on an atlas map. For each graph:
(a) Describe the temperature pattern (mean maximum and minimum temperatures and mean annual range).
(b) Describe the rainfall pattern (total amount, seasonal distribution).
(c) State the name of the place, giving reasons for your choice. (You will need to refer to Figure 1 and to Section 2.2, Figure 3.)

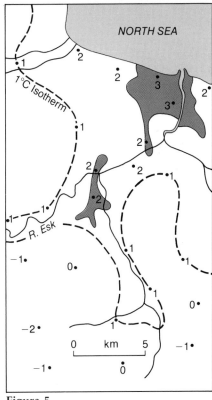

Figure 5
Temperatures on an early winter evening in the Whitby area, North Yorkshire

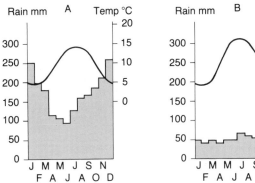

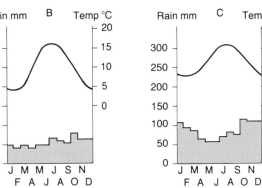

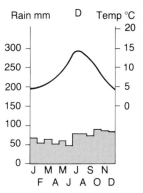

3.1 The nature of resources

Countries with a high level of technological and economic development make great demands on natural resources. Much of Britain's industrial development depended on importing resources that the country lacked. However, Britain has a wide variety of natural resources of its own.

Resources can be broadly grouped into non-renewable resources and renewable (or flow) resources (Figure 1). Fossil fuels are examples of non-renewable resources as the more people use, the less there is available for future use. Renewable resources vary greatly in type, as Figure 1 shows; they are resources which are continually available.

Non-renewable resources

Figure 2 shows low-quality iron ore being excavated near Scunthorpe. In 1960 Britain produced 17.4 million tonnes of iron ore; by 1986 only 0.29 million

tonnes was produced. From these figures, it might be expected that Britain's resources of iron ore were running out. In fact, this was not so; the decline in production was mainly due to the lower cost of high-grade imported iron ore. It became uneconomic to mine the low-grade British ore.

If demand for, say, a metal rises and prices rise as a result, then it will pay to develop a metal ore previously uneconomic to mine. Thus tin mining in Cornwall revived in the 1970s and early 1980s until a crash in prices in 1985 led to the collapse of the industry.

> **Q1**
> Under what circumstances might iron ore mining in Britain become important again?

Technological developments can lead to useful reserves of non-renewable resources being re-assessed. Thus, the exploitation of oil in increasingly deep waters off

the coast of Britain depends on the development of suitable methods (together with high oil prices to offset high production costs).

> **Q2**
> Consider the example of coal. Suggest what influence the following developments would have had on estimating future reserves: (i) the development of deep mining techniques; (ii) competition from cheap oil in the 1960s; (iii) the development of large-scale open-cast mining techniques.

Renewable resources

The continuous availability of renewable resources is not guaranteed. For example, overfishing has reduced the catch of several species around Britain's coast.

Figure 1
Classification of resources

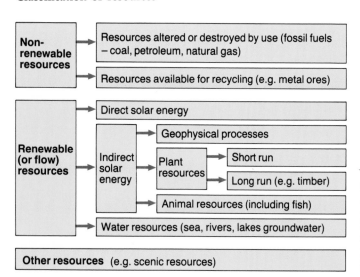

Figure 2
Iron ore mining near Scunthorpe

The renewable resources listed in Figure 1 include farm crops. This may seem surprising, as their production depends on the work of farmers. However, they would not be available without the continuous flow of solar energy or the maintenance of soil fertility. The development of 'scientific farming' is a good example of the attempt to increase the flow of a renewable resource.

Conservation and conflicts

When applied to resources, the term 'conservation' means using the resources wisely rather than not at all. A widely used definition of resource conservation is that the use of resources should be organized so as to provide the greatest yield for the greatest number of people over the longest period of time. This definition can easily be applied to renewable resources such as timber or fish. However, with non-renewable resources, alternatives have to be devised for when they run out.

The wise use of resources also aims at avoiding waste. Three approaches to avoid wasting resources are:

1 Use less of a particular resource to achieve the same end as before.
2 Use a by-product of a process which previously was wasted.
3 Recycle materials.

Q3
(a) Name examples of each of the three approaches to avoiding the waste of resources.
(b) Why is there a continuing search for new sources of energy and new materials?

The development of resources may well lead to conflicts. Different people will want to use resources in different ways or in varying amounts. Resource development may conflict with the preservation of an area as a scenic or recreational resource. Such issues are examined in Chapter 12.

At different times in history, the resources of an area are looked at in different ways. This reflects many of the factors mentioned already, such as the technology available. Figure 3 shows the resources being exploited in the North York Moors and Teesside area at three different times: the 1840s, the 1920s and the 1980s.

Q4
(a) Refer to Figure 3. For each map, list the resources which are being exploited. By each one indicate whether they are renewable (use a letter R) or non-renewable (use a letter N).
(b) Describe how the pattern of resource development in the Teesside/North York Moors area has changed over time. Suggest reasons for the changes wherever you can. (The maps include information to help you.)

Figure 4
Exploiting resources, North York Moors: the fishing village of Staithes and Boulby potash mine

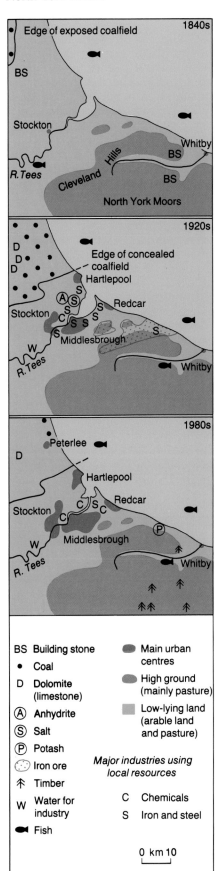

Figure 3
Resources from Teesside and the North York Moors

3.2 Water resources

In Britain 330 litres of water are consumed per person per day, an amount about twenty times the rate for 1830. The rise in water consumption is not only caused by an increase in population; rising standards of living and industrialization are also responsible. Domestic demand accounts for 140 litres per person per day, well under half the total. To meet the large demands for water, careful management of water resources is needed. The water companies which supply water are also responsible for disposing of sewage and industrial waste, pollution control and prevention, river management, flood protection, fresh water fisheries and water recreation facilities.

The movement of water

The hydrological cycle is of particular importance to people involved in water management. Figure 1 shows the movement of water within a drainage or river basin. (A drainage basin is the area drained by a river and its tributary streams.) The diagram shows that rainwater reaches the river in a number of ways and that some never reaches the river, as it is evaporated or transpired by the leaves of plants.

The graphs in Figure 2 show the flow of water in two different rivers which drain basins of the same size, following a period of rain. Such graphs are called **storm hydrographs**. The patterns of flow are quite different. There are many factors which affect water movement that could be responsible for this contrast. Figure 3 gives full details of these factors. Understanding the factors which affect the movement of water is very important in managing water, whether for water supplies or flood protection.

Figure 1
Water movement within a drainage basin

Q1

In Figure 4 there are details of three drainage basins which have the same area. Details of recently experienced weather are also given. Below the descriptions are three storm hydrographs. State which hydrograph matches each description and give the reasons for your choices.

The wet West and the dry East

The annual flows of rivers which drain similar areas in different parts of Britain vary greatly, largely because annual rainfall varies so much – from over 2 000 mm in the mountains of the North-West to under 600 mm in the South-East – but also because of all the factors which affect water movement in rivers, described in Figure 3.

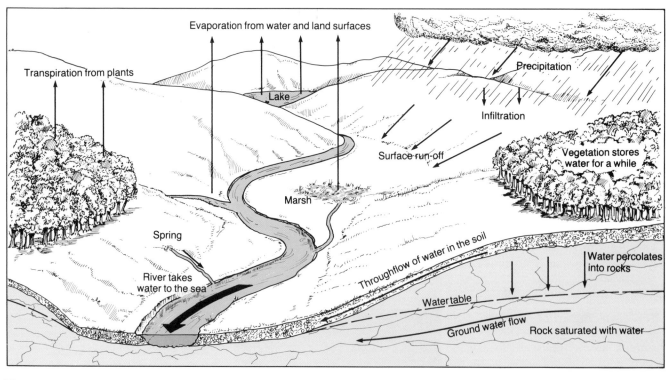

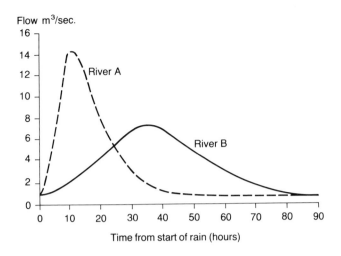

Figure 2
Two storm hydrographs

Figure 3
Factors affecting water movement in drainage basins

Drainage density	The closer streams are together the shorter the distance to be covered by runoff water flowing to them.
The shape of drainage basins	Water will take longer to flow through a long narrow drainage basin than through a shorter wider basin of the same area.
Slopes	Water runs off steep slopes quickly, so less water will soak into the ground than on gentle slopes.
Rocks	If rocks are impermeable, water will run off to streams. Where rocks are permeable, much rain water will soak in.
Soils	A deep soil with plenty of spaces will absorb a lot of water, but a thin soil or heavy clay soil will not.
Vegetation	Plants, especially trees, will temporarily hold rainwater and make runoff less rapid.
Temperature	The higher the temperature the more evaporation will occur.
Previous rainfall	If there has been recent rain the ground will be saturated so rain water will have to run off to streams. If rain follows a dry period there will be room for water to infiltrate the ground.

Q2

On average, 1 800 mm of the 2 000 mm of annual rainfall in northwest Scotland runs off the surface while in East Anglia only 125 mm of the 600 mm annual rainfall runs off. Suggest why a greater proportion of the rainfall becomes run-off in northwest Scotland than in East Anglia. (Consider amount of rainfall, slopes and geology.)

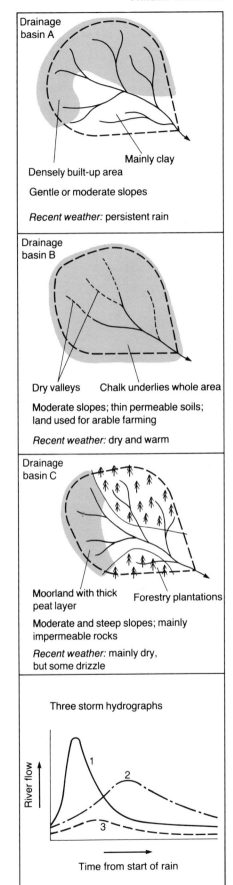

Figure 4
Three drainage basins

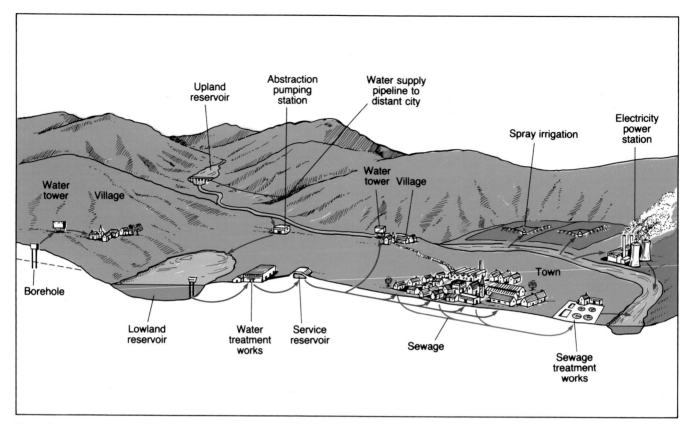

Figure 5
The water supply and disposal cycle

Problems of water supply

The water companies have to deal with four main problems in planning water supply:

1 In winter, the amount of rainfall is greater than the demand for water, but in summer the situation is reversed.
2 The areas of greatest demand are not the areas with the greatest supply. The high rainfall areas in the mountains of the West and North are sparsely populated, while the low rainfall areas include many major centres of population with a high demand for water.
3 Britain's rainfall varies considerably from average conditions. Periods of heavy rain may lead to floods. In some years major droughts can occur (for example, in 1959, 1976 and 1984) leading to major difficulties in supplying enough water.
4 Future demands are difficult to estimate.

Storing and supplying water

To deal with these problems, water has to be stored to meet demand when the natural supply is low and water has to be transferred from areas of plenty to areas where it is scarce. The storage and supply of water is, in effect, part of a man-made water cycle which fits into the natural cycle (Figure 5). The other part of the man-made cycle is the treating of polluted water or sewage before it is returned to rivers or the sea. Figure 5 shows that water may be obtained in a number of ways:

1 From rivers (**abstraction**), both for direct use and to fill lowland reservoirs.
2 Reservoirs in upland areas may be used to store run-off, water being channelled along rivers or piped to the points of demand.
3 From underground water-bearing rocks (**aquifers**) by means of boreholes.

Figure 6
Changing water demands

Domestic demand	This increased steadily up to the 1970s because of increasing population, improvements to houses (such as installing baths) and greater use of appliances such as washing machines.
Demand by electricity power stations	Electricity generation uses very large amounts for cooling, but 90% is returned to rivers. The demand has decreased since 1971 because more electricity is produced at coastal stations.
Industrial demand	Industries such as chemicals, steel and paper making use very large amounts of water. Cooling water is returned to rivers. Since 1971 demand has decreased because of more efficient use of water and the decline in industrial output.
Agricultural demand	Most of the water used by farms is for spray irrigation.

Growing demands for water

Demand for water rose steadily until the early 1970s. In England and Wales demand was 8.9 million cubic metres per day in 1955 and 14.1 million cubic metres per day in 1971. Since then the demand has grown only slightly to 15.0 million cubic metres per day in 1985. Because of different rates of population growth and industrial change, demand rises more rapidly in some areas than in others. Figure 6 gives details of changing demands for water.

It is very difficult to forecast future water demands. The water companies usually base their planning for the future on high estimates so as to provide enough water storage to meet years of severe drought. Figure 8 shows the location of major reservoirs and water transfer schemes in England and Wales. Many of these reservoirs are relatively new and were built to meet high future demands for water. However, the predicted high demands have not always come about; for example, most of the capacity of the very large Kielder Water in Northumberland has not been needed. Reservoir construction has met with increasing opposition in recent years on grounds that the water

companies are overestimating future demands, that they will lead to the loss of valuable land and that they interfere with the environment. In the uplands, the reservoirs have a major impact on valued environments; many suitable sites are within National Parks. In lowlands, as the reservoirs are shallow, much farmland is lost to store relatively limited amounts of water (Figure 7).

Other methods of storing water have been investigated. In South-East England and East Anglia experimental schemes involving the artificial storing of water underground have been carried out. In winter, surplus river water is pumped into aquifers like the chalk. During summer the stored water is pumped up, either for direct use or to add to river flows. The construction of barrages across estuaries such as the Wash and the Dee Estuary could provide large areas of fresh water storage, but at a high cost of construction.

Figure 8
Major reservoirs in England and Wales

Q3
(a) Refer to Figure 3 in Section 4.2 which deals with population change in Britain.
(i) Which areas are likely to have an increased demand for water in the future?
(ii) What problems will there be in meeting such demands?
(b) It has been suggested that a National Water Grid (like the National Grid for electricity), linking up the various supply schemes and major rivers, should be built. What advantages would such a grid have?
(c) In upland areas, what conditions and features in a valley would the water companies look for in deciding upon a reservoir site? (Consider the existing use of the land, the shape of the valley cross-section, types of rock, the possible site for the dam.)

Figure 7
Rutland Water, England's largest reservoir

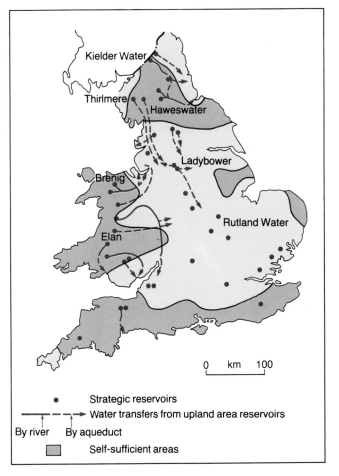

Strategic reservoirs
Water transfers from upland area reservoirs
By river   By aqueduct
Self-sufficient areas

3.3 Timber resources

British forests supply only 8 per cent of timber needs compared with 21 per cent for the countries of Europe. Most of Britain was once forested with broad-leaved deciduous trees such as oak and beech. As Britain was settled and as population grew, the forests were cleared. The clearance accelerated in the 19th century as the population grew rapidly and as industrial demand for timber rose.

The Forestry Commission

In 1919 the Forestry Commission was set up to begin a replanting programme, originally to provide a three year supply of timber in the event of war. The forests were developed on low-value land, mainly used for rough grazing. Ninety per cent of Forestry Commission forests are planted with quick-growing coniferous trees. The most common tree is the Sitka Spruce, a native of western North America. It has a growth rate over three times that of oak and twice that of beech. Coniferous wood is used for woodpulp, fencing posts, packaging, chipboard and in building construction. However, the processed timber has to compete with imports which may well be cheaper because of lower energy costs in the foreign saw and pulp mills.

The Forestry Commission now has almost one million hectares planted with trees. Privately owned forest areas occupy almost as large an area and account for most of the deciduous woodlands in lowland areas. In recent years private forest developments have expanded greatly. Grants for planting are available from the Forestry Commission, while wealthy individuals find investment in forestry reduces the amount of tax they have to pay.

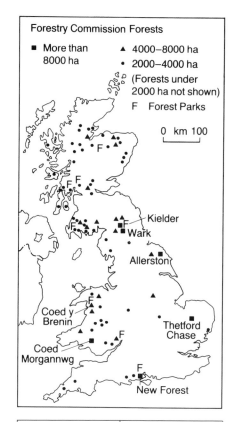

Forestry Commission Forests

- More than 8000 ha
- ▲ 4000–8000 ha
- • 2000–4000 ha
  (Forests under 2000 ha not shown)
- F Forest Parks

0 km 100

Kielder
Wark
Allerston
Coed y Brenin
Thetford Chase
Coed Morgannwg
New Forest

PRODUCTIVE FOREST AREA (thousand hectares)		WOOD PRODUCTION (thousand cubic metres)	
1947	1395	1973	3700
1965	1790	1977	4290
1970	1860	1981	4560
1975	1930	1983	4610
1980	1990	1985	5400
1985	2020	1987–9*	6300
		* estimated average annual amount	

Q1
(a) Look at the map in Figure 1. Describe and attempt to explain the distribution of Britain's main forested areas.
(b) Using the figures in Figure 1, draw a line graph to show the growth of the area under forests. Draw a second graph to show the growth in the output of forest products.
(c) Describe the patterns shown on your two graphs. Suggest reasons why the trend of the second graph does not exactly follow the trend of the first.

The impact of forestry

As Figure 2 shows, afforestation has had considerable effects on the uplands of Britain. Greater care is taken now than in the past to landscape forest areas to try to make them more scenically

Figure 1
Forestry in Britain

Figure 2
Effects of forestry in the uplands

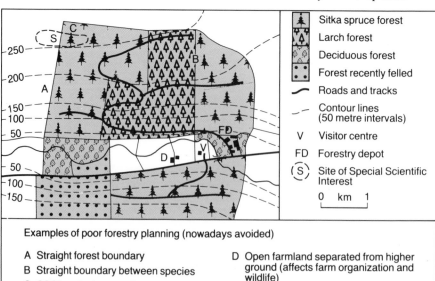

- Sitka spruce forest
- Larch forest
- Deciduous forest
- Forest recently felled
- Roads and tracks
- Contour lines (50 metre intervals)
- V Visitor centre
- FD Forestry depot
- (S) Site of Special Scientific Interest

0 km 1

Examples of poor forestry planning (nowadays avoided)

A Straight forest boundary
B Straight boundary between species
C SSSI partly destroyed

D Open farmland separated from higher ground (affects farm organization and wildlife)

attractive. Methods such as avoiding straight line boundaries and planting deciduous trees at the edge of coniferous plantations are now used.

It is important that forestry planning and management is linked with caring for the environment. The forests are also important recreational resources. Today, the Forestry Commission has extra responsibilities for safeguarding the environment, integrating forestry with farming and providing recreational facilities. Eight Forest Parks have been established to cater for visitors (Figure 1). Figure 4 shows the facilities which have been provided in the Coed y Brenin Forest in central Wales.

Despite the Forestry Commission's greater concern for the environment in recent years, new afforestation projects, especially private investment schemes, often attract much opposition. The expansion of forestry in the Flow Country of Caithness and Sutherland in the far north of Scotland has attracted particular opposition from the Royal Society for the Protection of Birds (Figure 5).

Figure 3
Felling a Douglas Fir in western Scotland

Q2
(a) It has been estimated that if all the potential forest land were to be planted with trees, timber production could meet about one quarter of Britain's needs. Considering the impact forestry has already had (see Figure 2):
(i) What are the arguments for more afforestation?
(ii) What are the arguments against more afforestation?
(b) Suppose that the Coed y Brenin Forest in Figure 4 were to be extended greatly in area. What might the views of the following be:
(i) a local hill farmer; (ii) a gamebird shooting group; (iii) a local unemployed 17 year old; (iv) the local Tourist Board; (v) the Royal Society for the Protection of Birds?

Figure 4
Visitor facilities in Coed y Brenin forest, central Wales

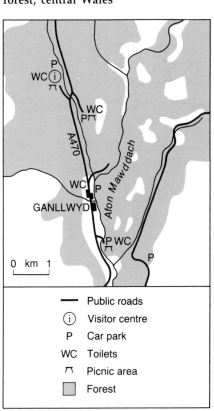

GANLLWYD

Afon Mawddach

A470

0 km 1

— Public roads
ⓘ Visitor centre
P Car park
WC Toilets
⊓ Picnic area
▢ Forest

The Trees of Wealth
Britain's last great wilderness at risk from the timber growers

The Flow Country of Caithness and east Sutherland is known to few beside the golden eagle and red deer. But now it is at the centre of a bitter conservation battle. Conservationists say that "green money machines" of Sitka Spruce and Lodgepole Pine – planted by rich private investors, including well-known names from television and show business – are damaging some of Britain's wildest places.

The Royal Society for the Protection of Birds point out that the Flow Country is the largest area of blanket bog in Britain. Greenshanks and golden plovers breed on the moorland, divers and geese on the lochs. At the present rate of planting, two-thirds of this land will be covered with trees by the year 2000. Nesting and feeding areas are destroyed. Ploughing and ditching alters the flow of streams and damages the spawning beds of salmon and trout. The RSPB dismisses the claims of 2,000 jobs for the area over 70 years as "pure imagination" and believes that forestry should be properly tied in with traditional land uses and activities such as farming, fishing and field sports to provide longer term jobs of greater benefit to the community.

Figure 5
Forestry in the Flow Country of northern Scotland

25

3.4 Minerals

Britain has considerable mineral resources. It can supply almost all the non-renewable energy needs and the minerals and rocks needed for building and construction, but needs to import most of its needs of metallic minerals. Igneous rocks provide metallic minerals, building stones and, in the case of granite, china clay. Metamorphic rocks also provide metallic minerals and building materials (for example, slate). Coal, limestone, clay, salts and some types of iron ore occur as sedimentary rocks. Oil and gas occur within sedimentary deposits. In some areas sedimentary rocks may contain veins of metallic minerals, a result of nearby igneous activity. River deposits provide gravels and sands. Figure 1 lists Britain's useful rocks and minerals. Coal, oil and gas are looked at in Chapter 7.

Figure 1
Useful rocks and minerals

- Fossil fuels (coal, oil, natural gas)
- Metallic minerals (e.g. iron ore, tin, copper)
- Clays (e.g. kaolin, brick clays, fireclay)
- Sands and gravels
- Limestone and chalk
- Building stones (e.g. granite, slate, millstone grit)
- Other minerals (salt, gypsum, potash, fluorspar, etc.)

Extracting rocks and minerals

A variety of methods is used to extract rocks and minerals. Quarries are dug to extract deposits at or near the surface. If

Figure 2
Quarries have a major impact on the environment

deposits occur at a greater depth, then mining is necessary. Within quarries and mines the differing nature of deposits means that many different methods of extraction have to be used, ranging from the blasting of rocks such as granite to the dredging of gravels out of flooded pits.

Problems for the environment

Quarrying and mining have a marked effect on the environment. Besides creating a large, unsightly hole which eats into surrounding farmland, a working quarry poses other problems, as Figure 2 shows. Although underground mining does not leave a surface hole, it gives rise to many of the same problems. In addition, subsidence of land might occur at the surface above mine workings. Spoil heaps of waste material may take up much land and mar the landscape. They are associated particularly with coal mining and the quarrying of china clay and slate (Figure 3).

Q1
(a) List the effects on the environment of quarrying.
(b) Suggest ways in which a quarry such as that shown in Figure 2 may be made less of an eyesore when quarrying has ended.
(c) How might (i) old gravel pits in river valleys and (ii) old coal spoil heaps be dealt with?

Mining, industry and settlement

Mineral exploitation has led to the growth of settlements to house the workforces of mines and quarries. In the 19th century when coal was the main source of power, industrial towns grew up on the coalfields. Other industries have also developed close to minerals, for example, cement making near deposits of chalk or limestone.

When mining ends because deposits are exhausted or it is considered uneconomic to continue, major difficulties occur for the local community. Unemployment and the decline of mineral-based industries are the most obvious effects (see Sections 7.2 and 8.3). Because many mining communities are isolated, it is often difficult to attract new industry.

Q2
(a) During the 20th century, minerals have proved to be less of an attraction to manufacturing industry than in the 19th century. Why would this be so?
(b) Name examples of industries based on local mineral deposits.
(c) Suggest why employment in mining and quarrying has declined in Britain during the 20th century.

Tin mining in Cornwall

Tin has been mined in Cornwall since Roman times. A century ago, over 300 tin and copper mines were in operation and Cornwall made England one of

Figure 3
Slate waste tips towering above houses in Blaenau Ffestiniog, North Wales

the world's leading producers of both these metals. Mining led to the population of the Redruth and Camborne area (Figure 4) increasing sixfold between 1770 and 1860. However, in the 1890s competition from cheap imported ores led to the closure of mines. By 1930 copper mining had ended and only two tin mines (Geevor and South Crofty) remained. But during the 1970s and early 1980s tin prices rose. Areas where difficult geological conditions make production costs high, such as Cornwall, could therefore produce tin at a profit. New mines were developed and the old-established Geevor mine was

greatly expanded in 1980. In October, 1985 the situation changed; the International Tin Council which regulated trade in tin collapsed and tin prices fell sharply. As a result, mines closed. Only South Crofty and Wheal Jane mines, both owned by the large international company Rio Tinto Zinc, survived. They produce at a loss and under the threat of closure, with the jobs of a thousand miners threatened.

Q3
Refer to Figure 4.
(a) Draw a cause and effect 'flow diagram' to show how the expansion of mining in western Cornwall in the 19th century led to the development of related industries and activities and to the growth of services to supply the growing populations.
(b) Draw a similar diagram to show the effects of a possible end to tin mining in western Cornwall.
(c) Explain why a heavy reliance on mining makes for an uncertain future for western Cornwall. Why might this area have difficulty in attracting new employment?

Figure 4
Tin mining in Cornwall

Figure 5
Geevor tin mine, Cornwall

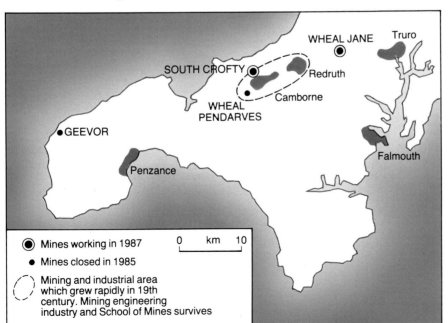

WHEAL JANE   Truro
SOUTH CROFTY   Redruth
WHEAL PENDARVES   Camborne
GEEVOR   Falmouth
Penzance

◉ Mines working in 1987   0   km   10
● Mines closed in 1985
⌒ Mining and industrial area which grew rapidly in 19th century. Mining engineering industry and School of Mines survives

3.5 Fishing

As an island, Britain occupies a prominent place in the waters of the northeast Atlantic. About 20 per cent of the world's catch of fish comes from this area. Fish are plentiful in this area because plankton, their chief source of food, thrive on the continental shelf (Figure 1).

There are two main types of fish caught in the northeast Atlantic: pelagic fish, such as mackerel and herring which feed close to the surface, and bottom-feeding demersal fish (white fish) such as cod, haddock, plaice, sole and coley. In addition, shellfish such as lobsters, crabs, oysters and cockles are found close to the shore and are of great importance to the inshore fishermen.

Figure 2
A modern purse-seiner fishing vessel

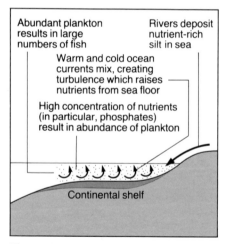

Figure 1
Cross-section of the continental shelf

Overfishing

The catch of fish in the northeast Atlantic is large, not only because of the large stocks but because of the large demand for fish from the countries of western Europe. In addition, countries from eastern Europe fish in these waters. Advanced fishing methods (Figure 2) and overfishing has led to a decline in the catches of some of the major species of fish, as Figure 3 shows. The catching

of young fish with small-mesh nets by some countries has further reduced stocks. In some coastal areas pollution has contributed to the decline of fish stocks. Many measures have been taken by individual countries and the EEC to combat the problem of overfishing (Figure 4).

Q1
(a) Describe the trends shown in Figure 3. Suggest why the catches of some species have declined or fluctuated more than others.
(b) Suggest why regulating the fishing industry of the North Sea with measures such as those in Figure 4 proves to be very difficult.

The decline of Britain's deep water fleet

The Humber ports of Hull and Grimsby were until recently Britain's most important fishing ports. Their prosperity was based

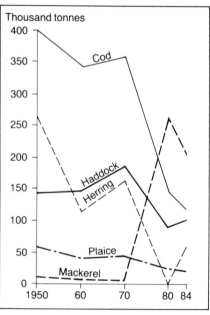

Figure 3
UK fish landings of major species

on their deep or distant water trawler fleets. In 1976 almost 100 000 tonnes of fish were landed by British trawlers at Hull. In 1981 only 8 000 tonnes were landed: most of the port's distant water fleet had been sold or scrapped. The fish markets of the two ports now depend on fish brought overland from other ports, on imported fish and on landings from foreign boats.

A major factor in this decline was the loss of fishing grounds around Iceland in the early 1970s

- Setting 'closed seasons' for catching certain species to allow numbers to recover.

- Controlling net mesh sizes so that small fish will escape and be able to reproduce.

- Setting quotas for the number of fish of different species that may be caught by different countries.

- Individual countries to set up limits close to the shore, within which fishing by other countries is tightly controlled.

- Encouraging the fishing industry to fish for species other than the traditional ones.

Figure 4
Measures to combat overfishing

and later off the coasts of Canada and Norway. These countries introduced 320 kilometre limits within which fishing by other countries was largely excluded. Other factors have also contributed to the decline of the deep water fleet: the high cost of fuel, low quotas, competition from foreign vessels selling fish in Britain and a lack of government aid. Unemployment rates in Hull and Grimsby became high (port and processing jobs have also been lost) and there were few alternative jobs available. In Aberdeen, Scotland's main deep water port, the oil industry provided alternative employment.

The middle water and inshore fleets

The fishing fleets operating nearer to Britain's coast have fared better than the deep water fleet, although similar problems have had to be faced. In November 1976 the EEC announced a plan for a 320 kilometre limit around the coast of its members (Figure 5). It took seven years of argument before an agreement was reached over each EEC member's share of the catch of

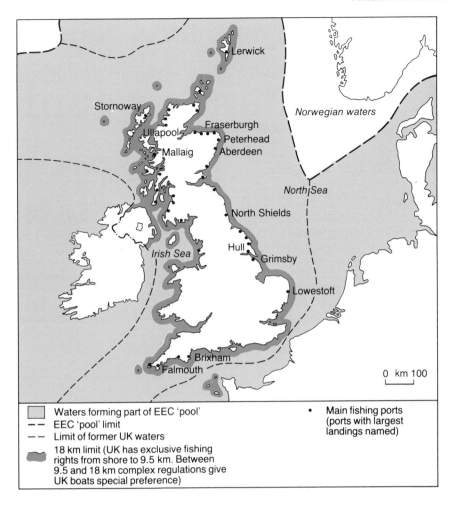

Waters forming part of EEC 'pool'
- - - EEC 'pool' limit
- - - Limit of former UK waters
18 km limit (UK has exclusive fishing rights from shore to 9.5 km. Between 9.5 and 18 km complex regulations give UK boats special preference)

- Main fishing ports (ports with largest landings named)

0 km 100

the main species of fish within this EEC 'fish pool'. Sixty per cent of the fish stocks are in traditional British waters, but under the EEC fishing policy introduced in 1983, the UK is entitled to only 37 per cent of the catch of the seven main species. Also, within the 'pool' the quotas and regulations listed in Figure 4 are in force. British fishermen have complained of overfishing and flouting of regulations by other EEC members.

Q2
(a) Figure 6 gives data on the changes in the UK fishing fleet and on employment in the fishing industry. Comment on the changes shown.
(b) Describe the problems of (i) the distant water fleet and (ii) the middle water fleet (fishing the EEC 'pool').

Figure 5
Fishing ports and fishing limits

Figure 6
Employment in fishing and the changing UK fishing fleet

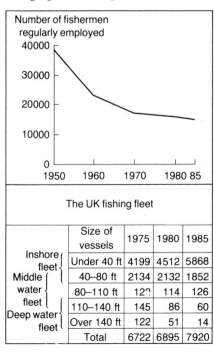

Number of fishermen regularly employed

The UK fishing fleet	Size of vessels	1975	1980	1985
Inshore fleet	Under 40 ft	4199	4512	5868
Middle water fleet	40–80 ft	2134	2132	1852
Middle water fleet	80–110 ft	12?	114	126
Deep water fleet	110–140 ft	145	86	60
Deep water fleet	Over 140 ft	122	51	14
	Total	6722	6895	7920

29

4. Population and settlement

4.1 Britain's people

Who are the British?

Britain's people come from a wide variety of origins. Most are descended from the many different groups who moved into Britain from the continent in prehistory and in early historical times (Figure 2). Others are descended from later immigrants from Europe and other parts of the world. These different groups are themselves the products of cultural and racial mixing.

During the Middle Ages, the development of trade between Britain and Europe led to the migration of small numbers of traders in both directions. In the 16th century, small numbers of refugees from religious persecution in the Netherlands and France settled in Britain. Industrial growth in the 19th and early 20th centuries attracted Germans, Italians, Poles and Russians to Britain. At the end of the 19th century, Jews who had suffered persecution in Russia came to Britain to join the small

Figure 1
Multiracial Britain

numbers already long established in the country.

There has also been a long history of Irish immigration to Britain and the emigration of English and Scots to Ireland. As industry and trade grew in the 19th century, the industrial port-cities of Glasgow and Liverpool were a particular focus of Irish immigration. The development of worldwide trade brought small numbers of people from outside Europe. They were mainly from China, Africa and the West Indies and they settled in the port districts of cities such as London, Liverpool and Cardiff.

During and immediately after the Second World War, many refugees from eastern Europe, especially from Poland, came to Britain. During the 1950s and 1960s there was considerable migration into Britain of people from countries which were formerly part of the British Empire, in particular from India, Pakistan and the West Indies. The peak years of this movement were 1958 to 1962 when 479 000 people entered Britain from the 'New' Commonwealth. In the 1970s and 1980s there have been three main groups of immigrants:

Figure 2
Early settlement of Britain

Picts — Celtic groups in British Isles
Scots — at time of Roman invasion
Irish — in 1st century
British

▨ Area of Roman Empire
   in 4th century

Movements of people to Britain
◄— 5th/6th centuries
◄— 7th/8th centuries
◄— 9th/10th centuries
◄— Norman invasion, 1066

0   km   500

Figure 3
Migration to and from Britain

I = Immigration (000s) E = Emigration (000s) B = Balance	1965			1985		
	I	E	B	I	E	B
'Old' Commonwealth						
Australia	20	85	−65	19	20	−1
New Zealand	7	16	− 9	12	7	+5
Canada	9	63	−54	8	6	+2
'New' Commonwealth						
West Indies	15	9	+6	4	3	+1
India, Pakistan, Sri Lanka, Bangladesh	27	9	+18	19	4	+15
Africa	21	16	+5	15	7	+8
Others	14	12	+2	23	16	+7
Other countries						
USA	23	27	−4	15	12	+3
South Africa	5	12	−7	16	5	+11
EEC countries	36	26	+10	54	29	+25
Others	41	29	+12	63	48	+15
Total	218	304	−86	248	157	+91

In 1965 the EEC countries were France, West Germany, Italy, Belgium, Netherlands and Luxembourg.

1 Dependants of people from the New Commonwealth already in Britain
2 People from EEC countries (people within the EEC are free to seek jobs in other member countries)
3 People from the 'Old' Commonwealth (Australia, New Zealand, Canada), South Africa and USA, most of whom are returning emigrants or are of British descent.

Migration from Britain

People have also migrated from Britain. Other than movements to Ireland, emigration on a large scale began in the 17th century when an estimated 80 000 people left for North America. As British influence in the world spread and a colonial empire was developed, emigration to North America continued, and in the 19th and 20th centuries migrants also left Britain for Australia, New Zealand, South Africa and other countries.

Q1
On an outline map of the world, mark in with arrows the main movements of people into and out of Britain since the beginning of the 19th century. Use different colours for movements before and after the Second World War. Name the areas which have sent and received migrants.

Q2
(a) Study Figure 3. For both 1965 and 1985, state (i) which countries supplied most of the immigrants; (ii) which countries were the main destination of the emigrants; (iii) the total population change resulting from migration.
(b) Describe the contrasts in the patterns of migration between 1965 and 1985.

Population distribution

Britain is a densely populated country with an average density of 2.4 persons per hectare. In Europe only the Netherlands has a higher density of population. However, as Figure 4 shows, people are distributed very unevenly over the country. Those districts with densities of 20 persons per hectare or more contain 34 per cent of the population but cover only 2.5 per cent of the land area. Densities vary from over 100 persons per hectare in two Inner London boroughs to 0.02 persons per hectare in Sutherland in the Scottish Highlands.

The most densely populated areas are urban areas which are either long-established centres of trade and industry or grew up as industrial areas on or near the coalfields in the 19th century. Rural areas vary greatly in population density. The areas of very productive farming with many villages, market towns and commuter towns in southern England contrast with the sparsely populated hill areas of the north and west of Britain.

Q3
Make a copy of the geological section of northern England, Section 1.2, Figure 3. Using the information in Figure 4, add labels to describe and explain the population density of the Cumbrian coastal plain, Cumbrian Mountains (Lake District), Eden Valley, the Pennines and the Northumberland and Durham Coalfield.

**Figure 4
Population
distribution**

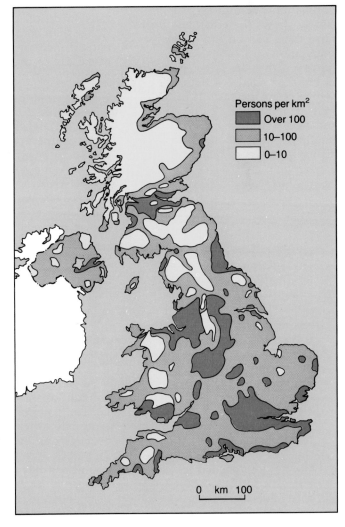

Persons per km²
Over 100
10–100
0–10

0   km   100

4.2 Population change

Great Britain has a population of just over 54 million. In addition, just over 1.5 million people live in Northern Ireland. As Figure 1 shows, the country's population increased rapidly in the 19th century. After the First World War population grew more slowly. Since 1971 the rate of increase has been very slight.

Population change reflects natural change and migration. Natural change is the difference between the number of births and the number of deaths over a period of time. Britain's population growth reflects the fact that for most of this century the number of births has exceeded the number of deaths. The recent very slow growth in population is due to a downward trend in birth rates since about 1965. The 1986 population pyramid (Figure 2) clearly shows the effect low birth rates have had on the country's population structure. Notice, however, that the larger number of children aged 0–4 than 5–9 indicates an increase in birth rates. Comparison of the 1986 pyramid with that for 1975 shows another important trend: the rising numbers of old people.

Q1

(a) Look at Figure 1. Describe how Britain's total population has changed since 1901. Why has the rate of growth slowed in recent years?

(b) Refer to Figure 2. Describe how the structure of the population of England and Wales has changed between 1975 and 1986.

(c) What effects would these changes have on (i) the size of the workforce; (ii) services needed for the old; (iii) services needed for children?

Figure 1
Great Britain: population change

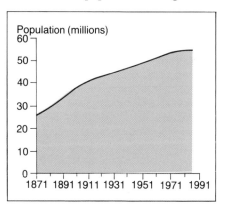

Contrasts in population change

Population changes at different rates in different areas. Migration, rather than contrasting rates of natural increase, is the main cause. Up to the late 1960s, there were two main migration trends:

1 A movement from older industrial regions in Scotland, northern England and Wales to more prosperous regions such as the South-East and the Midlands.
2 A movement from rural to urban areas.

Every ten years a **census** of population is taken. Figure 3 shows the pattern of population change in Britain between the censuses of 1971 and 1981.

Areas of population decline

1 Between 1971 and 1981 **Greater London** lost 739 000 people. Inner London's population declined especially quickly, in some boroughs by over 20 per cent. This decline in London's population has since stopped because of an increase in the birth rate and a reduction in the loss due to migration.

2 Most parts of Britain's six other **conurbations** (the largest urban areas) have also lost population. They include Britain's largest cities, Glasgow, Manchester, Birmingham, Liverpool and Leeds. Since 1981, with the exception of Liverpool, their population losses have slowed. Almost all of Britain's other **cities and large towns** have also lost population. The main reasons behind the population decline of the urban areas are:
(a) The redevelopment of old high-density housing in inner city areas and the resulting movement out of many people.
(b) Green Belts restrict building at the edge of most cities.
3 Small towns and villages in **old mining and industrial areas** have

Figure 2
Population pyramids, England and Wales

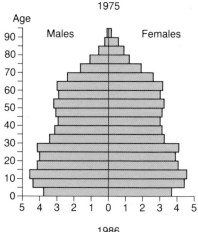

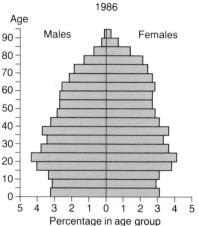

lost population as the old industries declined. These areas include parts of South Wales, Durham and Central Scotland.
4 Until 1971 many rural districts in Scotland, northern England and Wales were losing population. Since 1971, however, only a few **remote rural areas** have lost people.

Areas of population increase

1 Districts with **New and Expanded Towns** (see Section 4.7) have grown especially rapidly.
2 The population of **rural areas with small towns** has grown steadily since 1971. Reasons for growth in these areas include:
(a) The growth of new industries in small towns and, in northern Scotland, the growth of the North Sea oil industry.
(b) The wish of many people to live in attractive rural areas from which they can commute to the cities.
(c) The movement of people to rural areas for retirement.
(d) Housing development spilling over the boundaries of cities into neighbouring rural areas.
3 Many **coastal areas**, especially in the southwest, have attracted large numbers of retired people.

Q2
(a) Refer to Figure 4. Construct a graph with separate lines to show the changing population of each Standard Region between 1971 and 1986.
(b) Describe and attempt to explain the trends shown on your graph.

Q3
Considering the information on these pages, make a list of the main movements of people which have taken place since 1971.

Figure 5
Districts with large population changes, 1971–1981

Q4
Refer to Figure 5.
(a) Choose three districts which showed high population growth between 1971 and 1981. For each one suggest reasons for the rapid growth.
(b) Choose three districts which showed a large population loss between 1971 and 1981. For each one suggest reasons for population decline.

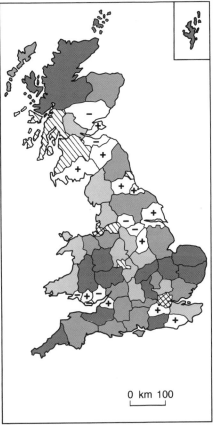

0 km 100

Figure 3
Population change, 1971–1981

Figure 4
Regional population change, 1971–1986

	1971 '000s	1981 '000s	1986 '000s
ENGLAND	**46 018**	**46 363**	**47 254**
North	3 142	3 104	3 080
Yorkshire and Humberside	4 856	4 860	4 899
East Midlands	3 633	3 819	3 919
West Midlands	5 110	5 148	5 181
North West	6 597	6 414	6 374
East Anglia	1 669	1 872	1 991
South East (excluding Greater London)	9 478	10 083	10 489
Greater London	7 452	6 713	6 775
South West	4 081	4 349	4 543
WALES	**2 731**	**2 791**	**2 821**
SCOTLAND	**5 229**	**5 131**	**5 090**

Increase over 10%

Increase 6 to 10%

Increase 2 to 6%

+ − Little change; decrease −2% to increase 2%

Decrease −6 to −2%

Decrease −10 to −6%

DISTRICTS WITH HIGH POPULATION GROWTH, 1971–81	%
Milton Keynes (Buckinghamshire)	86.0
Redditch (Hereford and Worcs.)	63.1
Tamworth (Staffordshire)	60.2
Shetland Islands	57.4
Gordon (Grampian)	38.5
Ross and Cromarty (Highland)	36.3
Cumbernauld and Kilsyth (Strathclyde)	36.0
Wimborne (Dorset)	33.0
Forest Heath (Suffolk)	31.3
Huntingdon (Cambridgeshire)	28.1

DISTRICTS WITH LARGE POPULATION LOSS, 1971–81	%
Glasgow City (Strathclyde)	−22.0
Inner London	−17.6
Manchester (Greater Manchester)	−17.5
Liverpool (Merseyside)	−16.4
Salford (Greater Manchester)	−12.9
Clydebank (Strathclyde)	−11.6
Knowsley (Merseyside)	−10.9
Newcastle-upon-Tyne (Tyne and Wear)	−9.9
Brent (Greater London)	−9.8
Nottingham (Nottinghamshire)	−9.5

33

4.3 Different cultures

Not everyone in Britain follows one particular 'British Way of Life'. People's way of life differs according to factors such as where they live, how they were brought up as children, their standard of living, their employment, their interests, their religious or other beliefs and their traditional **culture**. Culture involves people's behaviour learned from others around them as they grow up. It involves language, religious beliefs and traditions, together with the structure of the family and how children are brought up. Many people in Britain have particularly distinctive cultures. Some of these are very old-established, for example, the Welsh and Scots Gaelic cultures. Others are relatively recent to Britain, for example, the varied

cultures of people of New Commonwealth origin.

Wales, two cultures

Within Britain, the most distinctive traditional cultures are to be found where Celtic languages survive. In Scotland, the Gaelic language is important only in the extreme northwest of the Highlands and in the Western Isles. In Wales, the Welsh language is much stronger. In parts of Wales more than 80 per cent of the people can speak Welsh (Figure 2). In the more densely populated south the proportion is much lower, reflecting long-standing English influence and immigration.

The Conquest of North Wales by Edward I in the late 13th century established English rule over all of Wales. Gradually, the English language replaced Welsh

in the extreme south and in the east-facing valleys of central Wales. The 19th century growth of coal mining and industry in South Wales led to the immigration of people from England. In North Wales English people settled on the coalfield and in coastal resorts such as Rhyl and Llandudno. Areas in the west were shielded from English influence by the Welsh mountains. Much of this Welsh language 'heartland' consists of sparsely populated mountains, but there are two areas with greater numbers of people: the western part of Gwynedd in the northwest and much of Dyfed in the southwest.

Much has been done to keep the Welsh language and culture alive through teaching Welsh in schools (in some it is the main language of teaching), through cultural events and through radio and television. However, some Welsh speakers see the movement

Figure 1
Different cultures (a) a Scottish pipe band (b) West Indian carnival (c) an Asian shop, Bradford (d) Chinatown, Liverpool

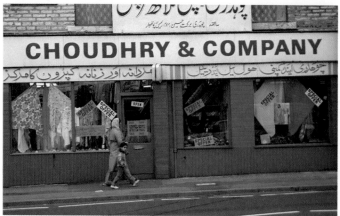

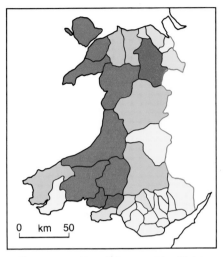

Figure 2
Wales; Welsh-
speaking areas

Figure 3
Welsh language
and culture under
threat? A Welsh
Language Society
poster

Percentage of population speaking Welsh

- 60.0 and over
- 40.0–59.9
- 20.0–39.9
- 10.0–19.9
- 0–9.9

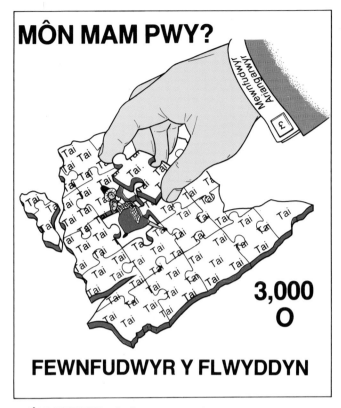

MÔN MAM PWY? = Anglesey, whose mother? (Anglesey is known as the 'mother of Wales'.)
3000 O FEWNFUDWYR Y FLWYDDYN = 3000 immigrants a year

Tai = house
Mewnfudwyr = immigrants
Ariangarwyr = 'lovers of money' (the housing developers)
The woman in traditional costume represents the Welsh people.

into rural Wales of people from England as a threat to their language and way of life. This movement has been large enough to reverse the decline in the population of most of North and central Wales. Figure 3 illustrates this issue in the island of Anglesey, a major centre of Welsh culture.

Q1

(a) Figure 3 shows a poster which was posted up on empty houses, old and new, in Anglesey by the Welsh Language Society. Explain the comments on the poster.
(b) What are the advantages and disadvantages of the movement of people into areas such as Anglesey?
(c) Do you consider the part of Britain that you live in to have a distinctive traditional culture? If so, what are its characteristics?

Migration from the Commonwealth

In Section 4.1 we saw that many of the more recent immigrants to Britain were from countries that were once part of the British Empire. During the 1950s and early 1960s there was a labour shortage in services such as public transport, catering and the health service and in industries such as textiles. People from the West Indies, India, Pakistan and other countries were encouraged to come to Britain to make up this labour shortage (Figure 5).

**Figure 4
West Indians arriving in Britain in the 1950s**

35

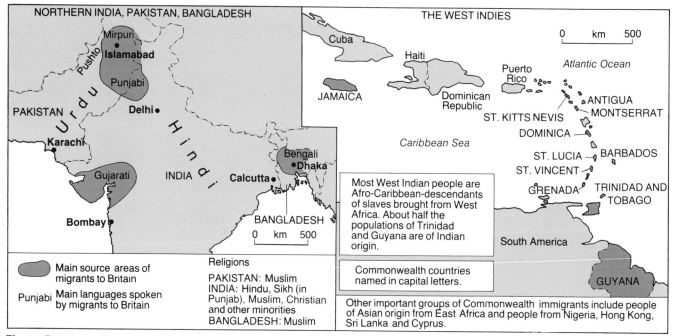

Figure 5
Migration from the New
Commonwealth and Pakistan

They saw in Britain better opportunities for employment and brighter futures for their children than in their home countries. Many people from the West Indies looked on Britain as their 'mother country'. The 1962 Commonwealth Immigrants Act and later acts of Parliament restricted the number of people entering Britain. An important immigrant group who continued to enter the country after 1962 were holders of British passports, mostly people of Asian origin from East African countries. In 1971–2 many of these people came to Britain as refugees, following their expulsion from Uganda. During the 1980s almost all immigration from the New Commonwealth has consisted of the dependants of people already living in Britain.

Q2
(a) Refer to the maps in Figure 5. Why is it a mistake to assume that all West Indians and all Asians share a similar culture and background?

Ethnic minorities in Britain's cities

Earlier immigrants to Britain such as the Jews from eastern Europe, the Irish and the non-Europeans who settled in ports, first lived in the older, poorer parts of the cities where accommodation was cheap and unskilled work was near. Later arrivals tended to go to the same areas to be close to people from the same background especially, as in the case of the Jews, if they had to face prejudice and hostility from others. Figure 6 shows how over 70 years later than the main period of Jewish immigration to London, Jews have tended to move out to the suburbs.

The New Commonwealth immigrants settled in the cities in those parts of Britain which needed their labour: London, the West Midlands conurbation and the textile towns of Lancashire, West Yorkshire and the East Midlands. As with earlier immigrant groups, being relatively poor, usually unskilled workers, they could only afford housing that was cheap to buy or rent. This housing is concentrated in older, inner city areas. Again, later arrivals moved to the same areas to be close to relatives or to people from the same

Figure 6
Jews in London

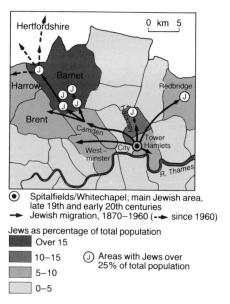

● Spitalfields/Whitechapel; main Jewish area, late 19th and early 20th centuries
→ Jewish migration, 1870–1960 (--→ since 1960)

Jews as percentage of total population
▓ Over 15
▒ 10–15
▒ 5–10
░ 0–5
Ⓙ Areas with Jews over 25% of total population

background. Figure 7 uses an approximate measure (population in households whose head was born in New Commonwealth or Pakistan) to show the distribution of people belonging to ethnic minorities in England and Wales.

Although many immigrants and their British-born children have moved out of inner city areas, most remain. Reasons for this include:

1 A relatively high proportion of

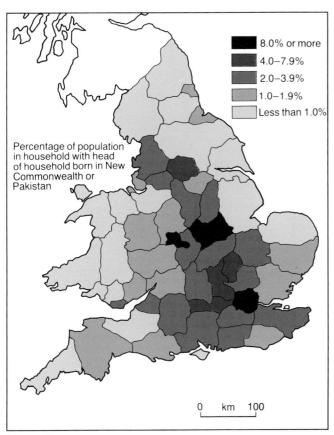

Percentage of population in household with head of household born in New Commonwealth or Pakistan

- 8.0% or more
- 4.0–7.9%
- 2.0–3.9%
- 1.0–1.9%
- Less than 1.0%

0   km   100

Figure 7
England and Wales; distribution of people belonging to ethnic minorities

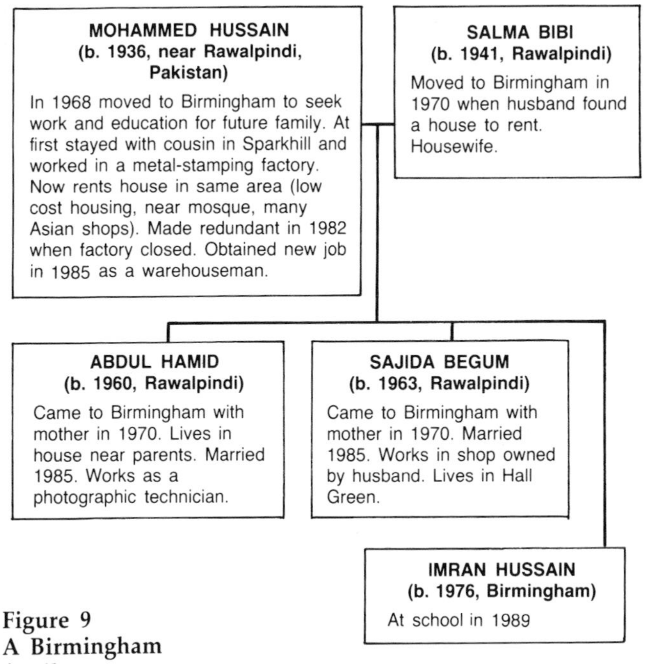

MOHAMMED HUSSAIN
(b. 1936, near Rawalpindi, Pakistan)

In 1968 moved to Birmingham to seek work and education for future family. At first stayed with cousin in Sparkhill and worked in a metal-stamping factory. Now rents house in same area (low cost housing, near mosque, many Asian shops). Made redundant in 1982 when factory closed. Obtained new job in 1985 as a warehouseman.

SALMA BIBI
(b. 1941, Rawalpindi)

Moved to Birmingham in 1970 when husband found a house to rent. Housewife.

ABDUL HAMID
(b. 1960, Rawalpindi)

Came to Birmingham with mother in 1970. Lives in house near parents. Married 1985. Works as a photographic technician.

SAJIDA BEGUM
(b. 1963, Rawalpindi)

Came to Birmingham with mother in 1970. Married 1985. Works in shop owned by husband. Lives in Hall Green.

IMRAN HUSSAIN
(b. 1976, Birmingham)

At school in 1989

Figure 9
A Birmingham family

---

them work in lowly paid, unskilled or semi-skilled jobs. Also they have been particularly hard hit by unemployment (Figure 8). Low incomes mean people cannot afford to move to areas of better housing.
2 Many people wish to remain near to others from the same ethnic or cultural background. When racial prejudice is met with, this wish is strengthened.
3 Discrimination in housing (by people selling houses or by council officers); this is illegal but usually hard to prove.

Figure 8
Unemployment is higher among Britain's black and Asian population

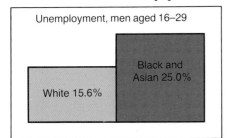

Unemployment, men aged 16–29

Black and Asian 25.0%

White 15.6%

The multicultural society

The New Commonwealth immigrants and their children have, to varying extents, become absorbed into British society, but many cultural differences remain. When cultures are brought from other countries to Britain, they may well be modified. Many individuals, especially the children of immigrants, wish to keep some parts of their original culture, but adopt aspects of the ways of life to be found in Britain. Conflict develops between parents and children in some cases.

The existence of different cultures in Britain means that it has grown to become a multicultural society. Such a society should involve people respecting those from different cultures, with everyone having equal rights, responsibilities and opportunities. However, differences, especially racial differences, are unfortunately used as an excuse for prejudice

and discrimination by individuals and organizations. The Commission for Racial Equality was set up to enforce the laws which make racial discrimination in, for example, housing and employment, illegal and to promote harmony between people from different backgrounds. The laws are difficult to enforce, as it is often impossible to prove beyond doubt that racial discrimination occurred in a particular case. Also laws cannot force people to change their attitudes. Some members of ethnic minority groups have set up their own pressure groups to support their claims for fairer treatment.

Q3
Figure 9 gives details of a family who live in Birmingham. The older members of the family were born in Pakistan
(a) List the reasons given for migration to Britain.
(b) Why did this family settle in Birmingham?
(c) What factors have influenced where (i) the parents, (ii) the older children live in Birmingham?

4.4 People in Northern Ireland

The 1.5 million people of Northern Ireland are a divided population. The division is religious and political. The majority Protestant population wish Northern Ireland to remain part of the United Kingdom; they are therefore also known as Unionists or Loyalists. Thirty-five per cent of the population are Roman Catholic; most of them wish to join with the Irish Republic to form a united Ireland.

The partition of Ireland

The origins of a divided Ireland and the division between Protestants and Catholics lie back in the 17th century. Then, the English rulers of Ireland encouraged many Scots farming families to settle in Ulster, the northern part of Ireland. The settlers were Protestant by religion, in contrast to the native Irish who were Catholics. The descendents of these settlers opposed the movement for Irish independence. In 1922 Ireland was partitioned following the Protestants' refusal to join the newly independent Irish state. The boundary was drawn so that a Protestant majority would exist in Northern Ireland, although as Figure 1 shows, Catholics are more numerous in some areas.

The 'Troubles'

News of Northern Ireland on television and in newspapers is dominated by reports of conflict and violence. The current 'Troubles', as the Northern Irish call the political and religious conflict, began in the late 1960s. The Catholic population, besides

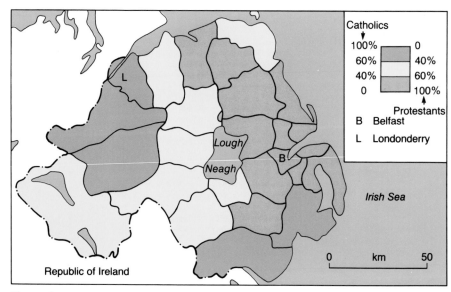

Figure 1
Northern Ireland; population segregation

wishing to join the Irish Republic, had other grievances: they claimed that since 1922 they had been discriminated against in employment, housing and education. Also they complained of being excluded from political power. Many Protestants felt threatened by the demands of the Catholics and the existence of the Irish Republic to the south. In 1969 the grievances and suspicions erupted into violence. Continuing trouble led to the UK government sending in the army to prevent conflict between the two communities. Some Republicans turned to violence and terrorism to force the issue, the IRA (Irish Republican Army) using bombs and bullets against Protestants and the British army. Extremists on the Protestant side have also used violence to further their aims.

The Troubles have resulted in many deaths and injuries and in huge economic cost for Northern Ireland (Figure 3). As yet there appears to be no solution in sight, with large numbers of

Figure 2
Political slogans, Belfast

Compensation for deaths, injuries and damage to property	£1 010 m
Extra security (policing, army operations, etc.)	£4 195 m
Loss of output, loss of income from tourism	£3 680 m

Figure 3
The economic cost of the 'Troubles', 1969–83

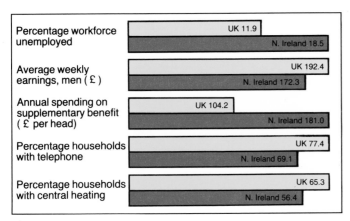

Figure 4
Standards of living in Northern Ireland are lower than in the rest of the UK

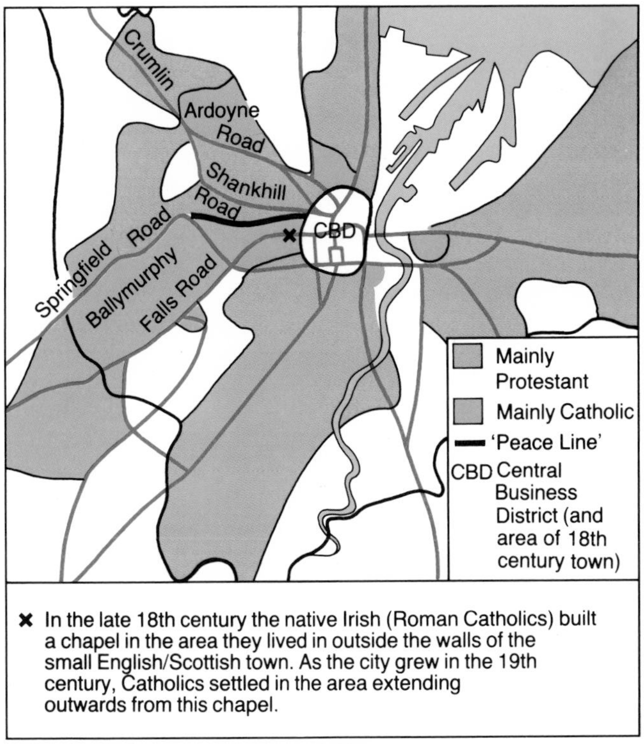

Figure 5
Segregation in Belfast

✘ In the late 18th century the native Irish (Roman Catholics) built a chapel in the area they lived in outside the walls of the small English/Scottish town. As the city grew in the 19th century, Catholics settled in the area extending outwards from this chapel.

people on both sides refusing to compromise. However, the level of violence has decreased in recent years and some areas have been little touched by the Troubles. Many people go about their lives in a similar way to those elsewhere in the UK, taking little notice of the political and religious conflict.

Q1
(a) Why do most Protestants in Northern Ireland wish to remain in the United Kingdom? Why do most Catholics wish for a united Ireland?
(b) Protestants and Catholics go to different schools, live in separate areas and seldom mix socially. What are the disadvantages of this situation?
(c) What effects have Northern Ireland's problems had on the rest of the UK?

Belfast

Figure 5 shows how the city of Belfast is divided by religion. The inner city working-class areas and council estates on the west side are the most strictly segregated. In the inner areas, poor housing and unemployment rates as high as 40 per cent have encouraged the growth of conflict. The so-called Peace Line is a barrier built by the British army to separate the two communities. The higher-quality housing areas are much less segregated and are little affected by violence.

Q2
(a) Look at Figure 5. Describe and explain the distribution of Catholic areas in Belfast.
(b) Segregation in Belfast has become even more marked since 1969. Why would this be so?

The economy

Standards of living in Northern Ireland are lower than in the rest of the UK (Figure 4). Traditional industries such as textiles and ship building have long been in decline while newer industries such as artificial fibres, attracted by government aid in the 1960s, have also contracted. Agriculture, dominated by small livestock farms, is also in a depressed state. Government schemes to encourage new industries have not attracted sufficient jobs to replace those lost. In attracting new employment, Northern Ireland has several handicaps:

● Energy costs are high as it lacks its own power resources.

● Its population of 1.5 million provides only a small market.

● Its location is remote from the rest of Britain and Europe, the sea crossing adding to transport costs.

● The political troubles discourage overseas investors.

4.5 Settlement patterns

Britain's people live in a great variety of settlements, ranging in size from hamlets and villages to towns and cities. Most of these settlements have long histories. Although Britain was settled well before Roman times, very few present day villages and towns date back so long. In lowland Britain, most villages were established by the Anglo-Saxons between the 6th and 10th centuries, sometimes using the sites of ancient settlements. Many villages in the North and East were established by the Vikings. As Figure 1 shows, place names provide evidence for the origins of settlements.

Sites and situations

When settling an area, people have had to find settlement sites which are convenient for meeting their various needs. Factors such as location of water supply, availability of land suitable for farming, local supplies of building materials and the availability of land free from floods influenced decisions on where to site villages. Usually the sites chosen were **minimum-energy** sites where all these things could most easily be obtained. The villages in North Yorkshire in Figure 2 are examples of such sites.

Q1
Refer to Figure 2.
(a) What do the village name endings suggest about their origins?
(b) Describe the sites of Sherburn and Yedingham.
(c) Explain how the sites of most of the villages on the map could be described as minimum-energy sites.

Many towns owe their early importance to advantages of site. Examples include natural defensive sites, bridging points, and natural harbours. More important in explaining the growth and importance of a town than its site is its **situation**, that is, its position in relation to the surrounding area. Thus a port may develop at the site of a natural harbour, but will expand only if it has a productive hinterland (trading area).

Patterns

The patterns settlements make divide between **nucleated** settlement (houses grouped into hamlets and villages) and **dispersed** settlement (single houses or farms scattered over the countryside). Reasons for nucleation or dispersal in an area may be historical, cultural or linked with physical geography. In Anglo-Saxon times, when the land was worked in strips, the people built their houses in a central village with the open fields around it. Between the 14th

	ELEMENT	MEANING
Celtic origin	Llan-	church
	Aber-	mouth of river
	Tre-, Trev-	homestead, village
Roman origin	-caster, -cester, -chester	camp or fort
	-port	gate, harbour
Anglo-Saxon origin	-ing	the people of
	-ham,	homestead, village
	-ton	homestead, village
	-bridge	bridge
	-ford	ford
	-borough, -bury	fortified place
	-ley	clearing
	-stead	place
	-wick, -wich	outlying hut, salt pan
	-den	pasture in wood
	-hurst	copse
Scandinavian	-toft	homestead, clearing
	-by	homestead
	-thorpe	daughter settlement
	-thwaite	clearing
	-garth	enclosure
	-ergh	outlying hut

Figure 1
Place name origins

Figure 2
Settlement in the Vale of Pickering, North Yorkshire

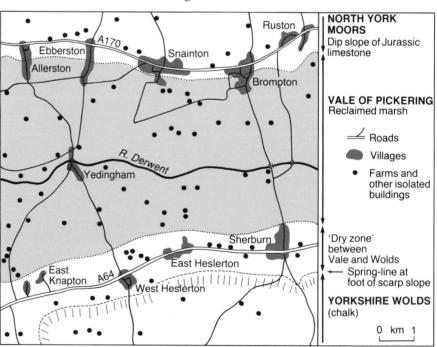

40

and early 19th centuries, the enclosure of land resulted in the development of individual farms and therefore the dispersal of settlement. As a result, a mixture of villages and small farms is typical of the settlement pattern of much of lowland Britain. In contrast, dispersed settlement dominates many upland parts of Britain where the difficult physical geography can support only a low-density, scattered population. Many settlement patterns exist within the basic patterns of nucleated and dispersed settlement. In Figure 2, the villages are arranged in distinct lines at the edge of the Vale of Pickering and they show a variety of shapes.

Q2

Refer to Figure 2.
(a) Suggest why the low-lying land of the Vale of Pickering is mainly an area of dispersed settlement.
(b) Describe the shapes or layouts of Ebberston and Brompton.

Market towns

At first, rural settlements were self-sufficient. As needs became more complex, trade developed and some villages grew into market towns or service centres providing a centre for people from neighbouring villages to sell their surplus produce and buy goods they could not provide for themselves. Although the action of landowners who obtained charters to hold markets and the enterprise of merchants was important in the development of market towns, the successful settlements were usually those that were most accessible from the others. Warwick (Figure 3) had the natural advantage of a defensive site guarding a crossing point of the River Avon. The town grew up around the castle and a charter to hold a market was granted by the King in 1086. As with most market towns today, Warwick's function as an

agricultural market town is now only one of many functions. It is a centre for shopping and other services (although less important than neighbouring Leamington), is an important tourist centre and has some manufacturing industry.

Q3

(a) Give reasons to explain why Warwick developed successfully as a market town.
(b) Draw a labelled sketch map of Warwick to show the advantages of its site for a medieval market town. On your map mark in the area of the medieval town and the modern town. Add a label to explain why most land by the River Avon was not built on.
(c) Suggest why Warwick has become an important tourist centre.

The settlement hierarchy

Figure 5 shows the pattern of settlements in the Hereford region. The city of Hereford is the main regional centre. There are several market towns and a large number of villages. The map has

classified the settlements on the basis of population size into a number of levels of importance or a **hierarchy**.

The importance of settlements is closely bound up with the services they provide. Services and shops that are used frequently are known as low order services; they are said to have a low **range** because people are usually unwilling to travel far for them. Services and shops that are used infrequently are known as high order services and have a high range. A newsagent is an example of a low order service while a furniture store is an example of a high order one. Some services or functions can act as indicators of a place's importance in the hierarchy of settlements. Thus the presence of no more than a post office/general store and a public house would indicate a hamlet, while the presence of, for example, certain large stores and regional offices of organizations would indicate a city which was a high order service centre. (Such an important centre would have many low order services as well.) Figure 6 shows the occurrence of some selected functions for the main settlements in the Hereford region. So that a similar approach can be used easily for other areas, only those functions whose presence can be established from a telephone directory have been included in the table.

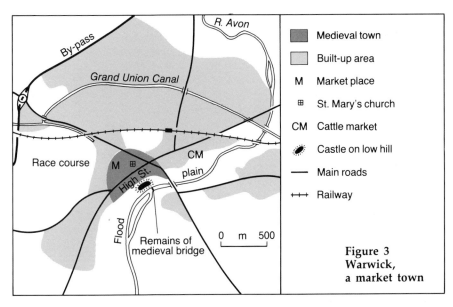

Medieval town
Built-up area
M   Market place
⊞   St. Mary's church
CM   Cattle market
      Castle on low hill
—   Main roads
+++ Railway

Figure 3
Warwick,
a market town

Figure 4
Warwick: the Castle, guarding a crossing point of the River Avon, and the High Street

Settlement patterns are always changing. The development of industrial areas with towns close together gave rise to more complex patterns of service centres. Improved communications have led to smaller market towns being passed by for larger ones.

Changing villages

During the early 20th century many villages lost population, as the farming labour force fell. Village trades, crafts and small industries also declined. This decline continued in most of the country immediately after the Second World War. Since the early 1960s the main changes in villages have been as follows:

● A continued decline of employment in farming and traditional trades.

Q4

Refer to Figure 6.
(a) Which functions mark Hereford off as a city separate from the other settlements?
(b) Suggest which functions should be used to indicate a town as distinct from a village. (The presence of *every* indicator function is not needed for a place to qualify as a town).
(c) What functions could be used to indicate major villages (which would serve neighbouring settlements) from minor villages?
(d) Draw a hierarchy diagram of the Hereford region. Put Hereford at the top, the market towns on a line below and the major villages on the next line. On the fourth line, write across the page 'minor villages or hamlets'.

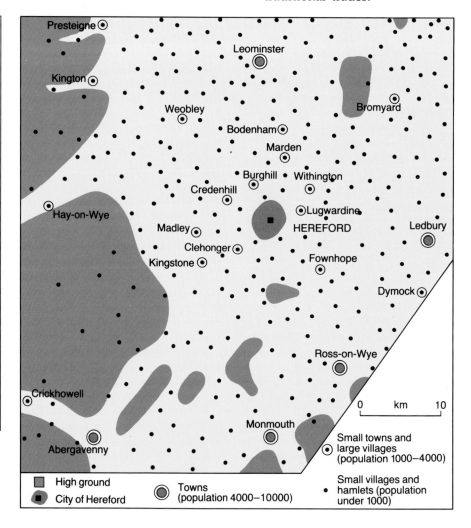

Figure 5
Settlement pattern of the Hereford region

42

- A steady movement from the towns of people who see villages as pleasant places to live and can afford to commute to the towns for work. Prosperous retired people have also settled in villages.

- The growth of second home ownership in areas of attractive countryside.

- A decline in services such as shops, primary schools and public transport.

- The rapid expansion of villages close to towns and cities as commuter settlements.

- A continued population decline in some small villages in remote areas.

- Some villages have attracted modern industry or have developed as tourist centres.

Figure 7 shows how one village – Hinxton in Cambridgeshire – has changed. Many of the trends listed above can be seen at work in this village. (Section 11.3 takes a closer look at some of the issues involved with these changes.)

SETTLEMENTS WITH OVER 1 000 PEOPLE	POPULATION	Marks & Spencer	Woolworth	Boots Chemist	W.H. Smith	Supermarket (national chains)	Electricity Board showroom	Bank	Building Society	Hospital	Newspaper office
Hereford	47 800	1	1	1	1	3	1	10	13	4	3
Abergavenny	9 427		1	1	1	3	1	4	5	1	1
Leominster	9 127		1	1		2	1	4	4	1	1
Monmouth	7 503		1	1	1	1	1	4	5	1	1
Ross-on-Wye	7 160		1	1	1	3	1	4	3	1	1
Ledbury	4 549		1	1		2	1	4	3	1	
Credenhill	2 417										
Kington	2 067							2	1	1	
Crickhowell	2 011						1	1			
Bromyard	1 698							3		1	
Clehonger	1 626										
Presteigne	1 501							2			
Burghill	1 400										
Hay-on-Wye	1 302						1	3			
Dymock	1 285										
Marden	1 144										
Bodenham	1 112										
Lugwardine	1 094										
Fownhope	1 091										
Weobley	1 080										
Kingstone	1 031								1		
Withington	1 027										
Madley	1 016										

Figure 6
Some functions of the larger settlements in the Hereford region

Q5
Look at Figure 7. Consider which of the changes listed above apply to Hinxton. Then write an account of the changes which have taken place in Hinxton, giving evidence from the map.

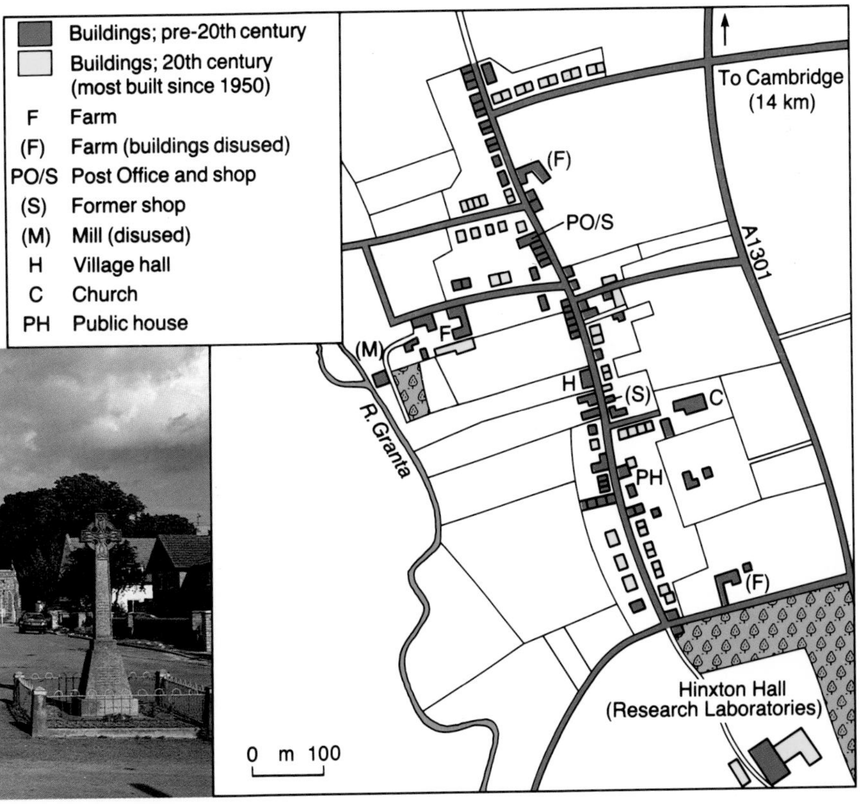

Figure 7
Hinxton, Cambridgeshire

Buildings; pre-20th century
Buildings; 20th century (most built since 1950)
F Farm
(F) Farm (buildings disused)
PO/S Post Office and shop
(S) Former shop
(M) Mill (disused)
H Village hall
C Church
PH Public house

To Cambridge (14 km)

(F)
PO/S
A1301
(M)
F
R. Granta
H (S) C
PH
(F)

0 m 100

Hinxton Hall (Research Laboratories)

4.6 Towns, cities and conurbations

Until the mid-18th century only about 20 per cent of the population lived in towns. Eighteenth century developments such as the smelting of iron with coke, the steam engine and new textile machinery led to the Industrial Revolution which involved large-scale manufacturing. Industrial towns rapidly developed, especially on or near the coalfields (Figure 1). Urban growth continued in the 20th century, although since the 1950s most large urban areas have lost, rather than gained population.

Figure 1
Sheffield in the 19th Century

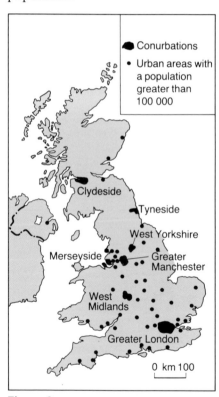

Figure 2
Conurbations and large urban areas

Britain's conurbations

Where towns were close together their growth led to them merging into one another to form **conurbations**. Figure 2 shows the location of Britain's seven conurbations. All have a major city as their focal point, but also contain other important cities or towns. Their growth over a long period of time and their large size has led to major planning problems, such as the renewal of poor housing (see Section 5.3) and organizing transport systems (see Section 10.2).

The West Midlands conurbation

The West Midlands conurbation is dominated by the city of Birmingham. Besides Birmingham, many other towns, mostly in the Black Country, acted as focal points of the conurbation's growth (Figure 3). The Metropolitan County of the West Midlands extends beyond the conurbation to include Coventry. The early growth of this conurbation was based on coal mining, metal smelting and metal working; much of its 20th century growth was based on the motor industry, although many other types of industry have also grown up. Birmingham is also a major centre for administration, shopping and commerce. Since the late 1970s the conurbation has been badly hit by the industrial recession and thousands of jobs have been lost. Within the conurbation, industrial decline in the old core areas contrasts with new developments at the edge.

Greater London

Britain's largest conurbation was formed by the spread of suburbs outwards from central London. The outward spread, often in the form of 'tentacles' following railways and major roads, merged with and engulfed small towns and villages (Figure 4). The growth from central London reflected the importance of the central area for government, commerce and finance. The importance of London as an industrial centre and port was also responsible for the conurbation's growth. For over 40 years further expansion has been restricted by the Green Belt.

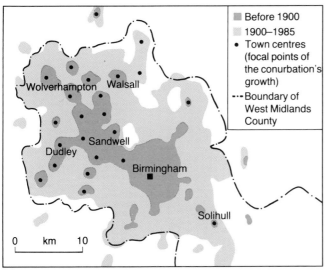

Figure 3
The West Midlands Conurbation

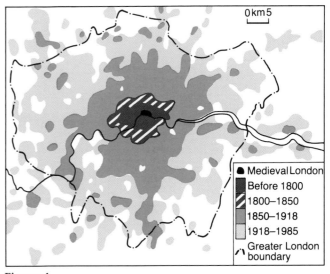

Figure 4
The growth of London

Q1

(a) (i) Draw simple sketch diagrams to show how the West Midlands and Greater London conurbations have grown in different ways.
(ii) What are the reasons for these differences?
(b) How has London's position within Britain helped it to become so important for government, commerce and industry?

Q2

(a) Refer to Figure 5. For each town describe the pattern of employment, mentioning any particular specializations.
(b) Cambridge is usually described as a university town, Blackburn an industrial town and Bournemouth as a seaside resort. Do the employment figures suggest that these are accurate descriptions? Give reasons for your answers.

Towns and cities outside the conurbations

Many towns and cities grew up specializing in particular functions; thus a town or city may be referred to as a port, an industrial town or a seaside resort. Some towns have specialized in a particular manufacturing industry. Today most British towns and cities have over half their working population employed in the Tertiary Sector, that is, in service occupations. They have a wide variety of functions and most of those which were dependent on one industry have now diversified. However, towns and cities usually owe much of their character to the functions which were once dominant and the specializations they still have.

EMPLOYMENT GROUP	PERCENTAGE OF LABOUR FORCE		
	Cambridge	Bournemouth	Blackburn
Agriculture, forestry, fishing	0.8	0.5	0.5
Mining and quarrying	—	—	0.1
Total primary	0.8	0.5	0.6
Metals, metal goods	0.2	0.5	2.6
Mechanical engineering	0.5	1.6	7.3
Electrical and electronic eng.	6.1	0.5	4.5
Instrument engineering	2.4	0.3	0.2
Chemicals	0.1	3.0	4.5
Motor vehicles, transport equipment	0.4	0.6	1.0
Food, drink, tobacco	1.0	1.6	3.6
Textiles	0.1	0.3	5.5
Footwear and clothing	0.2	0.4	2.2
Paper, printing and publishing	2.9	1.3	6.9
Other manufacturing	1.7	2.3	3.7
Total secondary	15.6	12.4	42.0
Construction	6.6	6.8	5.4
Energy and water industries	0.7	0.7	1.4
Wholesaling	3.0	4.4	3.4
Retailing	11.5	16.4	10.6
Hotels and catering	3.5	9.4	3.5
Transport and communications	6.1	8.0	5.6
Banking, insurance, business services	8.7	13.6	4.6
Public administration, defence	6.7	5.2	3.9
Medical and health services	7.9	4.9	6.0
Education	17.6	5.6	6.0
Miscellaneous services	11.3	12.1	7.0
Total tertiary	83.6	87.1	57.4

Figure 5
Employment structure in three towns

4.7 New Towns and Cities

In 1945, at the end of the Second World War, London and Britain's other major cities faced a severe housing crisis. Many thousands of people lived in overcrowded slum housing and there had been severe wartime bomb damage. At the same time, London was facing the prospect of continued outwards sprawl, so adding to the congestion of people and traffic. To meet these problems, slum housing was replaced with new, Green Belts were created around cities to stop their growth and New Towns were built to relieve the overcrowding and provide homes for people displaced by slum clearance schemes.

New Towns

Of the fifteen New Towns begun before 1955, eight were planned to take London's surplus or **overspill** population (Figure 1). Their 'target' populations ranged from 30 000 to 140 000. The New Towns were designed to be 'self-contained and balanced communities for work and living' and therefore new industry was encouraged and attempts were made to provide a wide variety of houses to rent and buy. Many new ideas in urban planning were introduced. These included pedestrianized central shopping areas, houses grouped into self-contained neighbourhoods with their own local service centres, through traffic routed away from housing areas, cycle path networks, factories grouped into industrial estates and large areas of planned open space.

Many of the new planning ideas and aims proved to be successful, but problems were encountered. The London New Towns did not become as self-contained as was hoped because they were close enough to the capital for people to commute to work. On moving from London, many people found New Town life difficult to cope with, as social

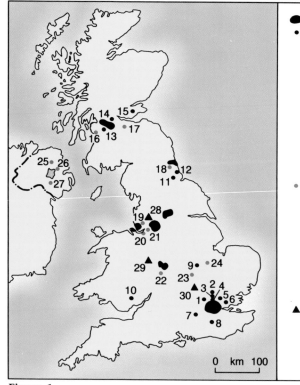

Figure 1
Britain's New Towns

- ● Conurbations
- ● First generation New Towns
  - 1 Hemel Hempstead
  - 2 Stevenage
  - 3 Welwyn Garden City
  - 4 Hatfield
  - 5 Harlow
  - 6 Basildon
  - 7 Bracknell
  - 8 Crawley
  - 9 Corby
  - 10 Cwmbran
  - 11 Aycliffe
  - 12 Peterlee
  - 13 East Kilbride
  - 14 Cumbernauld
  - 15 Glenrothes
- ● Second generation New Towns
  - 16 Irvine
  - 17 Livingston
  - 18 Washington
  - 19 Skelmersdale
  - 20 Runcorn
  - 21 Warrington
  - 22 Redditch
  - 23 Northampton
  - 24 Peterborough
  - 25 Ballymena
  - 26 Antrim
  - 27 Craigavon
- ▲ New Cities
  - 28 Central Lancashire
  - 29 Telford
  - 30 Milton Keynes

0   km   100

and recreational facilities were poorly developed and they were away from friends and relatives in the capital.

Not all New Towns had the main purpose of housing the overspill population from the large cities. For example, Peterlee was built to provide new homes and new jobs on the Durham Coalfield.

Q1
List the advantages and disadvantages which people would have found when moving to New Towns from the large cities.

Expanded Towns

Many existing well-established towns also took overspill people from London and some other conurbations. New housing estates and industrial areas were built with both national and local government money. Expanded Towns such as Swindon and Basingstoke are now as large as many New Towns.

New Cities

The most recent new urban developments have larger target populations: they are the New Cities of Telford, Central Lancashire and Milton Keynes. All three include within their areas a number of existing settlements. Telford was an expansion of an already existing New Town development. Central Lancashire already had a population of 235 000. Milton Keynes (Figure 2) had the aim of being a new 'growth pole' midway between London and Birmingham, while taking overspill from London and other parts of the South-East.

- In 1967 the government announced plans to build a new city of 250 000 people around the towns of Bletchley, Stony Stratford and Wolverton, an area with a population of 40 000. 1987 population: 133 000.

- Sited by M1 motorway and main London–Glasgow railway line, 80km from London, 105km from Birmingham.

- Major roads, in the form of a grid, act as a framework for development. There is a separate system of cycleways and footpaths.

- Employment areas are scattered throughout the city to spread traffic. 65 000 jobs created.

- Housing areas are built in a variety of styles and have their own community centres.

- Central Milton Keynes includes a large indoor shopping centre, office and leisure developments.

▅▅▅	Motorway
▅▅▅	A class roads
──	Other important roads
╌┼╌┼╌	Railway (with station)
▓	Open space
▓	Employment areas
□	Other development (mainly housing)

Q2
Refer to the information on Milton Keynes in Figure 2.
(a) Describe and explain the pattern of main roads.
(b) Describe the location of (i) 'employment areas' and (ii) open space.
(c) In what ways has Milton Keynes been planned differently from earlier New Towns?
(d) What advantages has Milton Keynes for attracting industry and other businesses?

**Figure 2
Milton Keynes**

The New Towns in the 1980s

As Britain's population growth dropped during the early 1970s, the need to house people in New Towns became less. The target populations of most of the New Towns was reduced and some planned developments will not now take place. In recent years, some of the New Towns outside the South-East found it difficult to attract sufficient new jobs to provide employent for their new population. For example, Telford has an unemployment rate of over 20 per cent. Many people now believe that the regeneration of declining inner city areas is a much more important priority for the future.

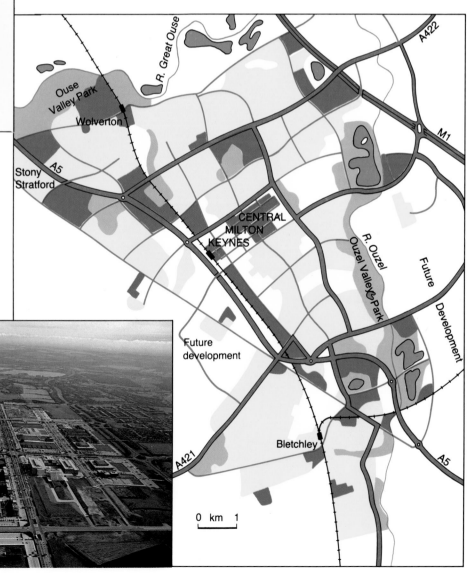

5. Inside Britain's cities

5.1 Patterns in cities

Some of Britain's cities have long histories stretching back for hundreds of years, while others only became important urban centres during the Industrial Revolution or even in the present century. These differences in history, together with contrasts in local settings and in functions, give each city its own character. However, there are many similarities in the way cities have grown and similar types of areas can be identified in most cities.

Age-growth zones

Cities grew outwards from their original sites along roads and railways, leaving a pattern of concentric age-growth zones as shown in the map of Exeter in Figure 1.

Land use patterns

Within each age-growth zone there is a variety of land uses: housing, factories, warehouses, shops, offices, open space, transport and a number of more specialized uses such as hospitals and schools. Figure 2 maps the pattern of urban growth and land use in a typical British city.

Q1
Look at Figure 2. Describe and explain the location of the following types of housing: (i) 19th century terraces; (ii) low-density, high-cost housing; (iii) private semi-detached housing; (iv) council estates; (v) new private estates. (The direction of the prevailing wind and the dirty nature of 19th century industry are points to bear in mind when suggesting some explanations.)

The Central Business District
At the heart of cities is the Central Business District (the CBD). Being the most accessible

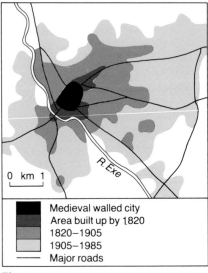

Figure 1
The growth of Exeter

Medieval walled city
Area built up by 1820
1820–1905
1905–1985
— Major roads

Figure 3
Land values and land uses

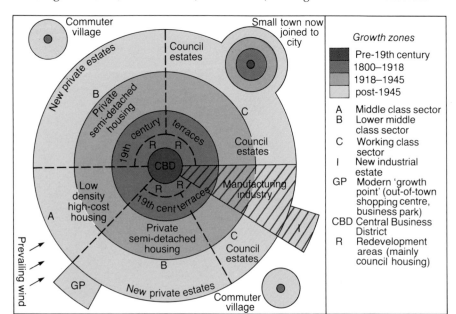

Growth zones

Pre-19th century
1800–1918
1918–1945
post-1945

A   Middle class sector
B   Lower middle class sector
C   Working class sector
I   New industrial estate
GP Modern 'growth point' (out-of-town shopping centre, business park)
CBD Central Business District
R   Redevelopment areas (mainly council housing)

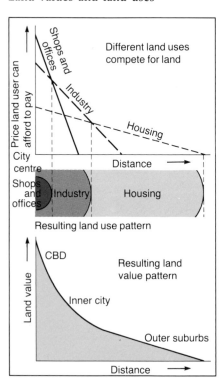

Figure 2
Model of growth and land use in a British city

48

place in a city, it attracts shops and offices. In addition it will contain theatres, cinemas and other places of entertainment, public buildings and major railway and bus stations.

There is high demand for sites in the CBD so land values are the highest in the city. As shops and offices make large profits in relation to the areas they occupy, they can afford expensive CBD rents which reflect the high land values. Figure 3 shows how land values vary within a city and how they have an effect on urban land use patterns. Because of competition for space, the use of valuable land is made more economical by building tall blocks which give extra floor space and therefore more rent. Shops and those offices which require particular ease of access to customers (for example, banks and insurance offices) occupy high-rent ground floors beneath lower-rent upper floors.

In the CBDs of the larger cities especially, specialized zones develop. For example, major shops occupy the most accessible areas which have the highest rents. Figure 4 shows the specialized zones within Cardiff's CBD; notice how there are distinct shopping, financial, administrative, and market areas.

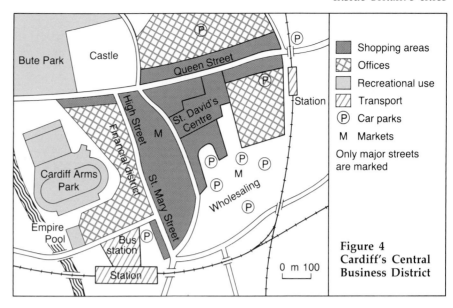

**Figure 4
Cardiff's Central Business District**

Q2

(a) Explain why the land uses in Figure 4 are found in the CBD.

(b) Describe how maximum use is made of valuable land in the CBD.

(c) Suggest reasons for the development of distinct zones in a large CBD such as that of Cardiff. (Different land values are only one factor to consider.)

Industrial areas

Within the older areas of Britain's cities, some industry consists of small factories and workshops mixed up with housing. Larger factories such as those involved in heavy industry and textile mills

were usually built on low-lying land, lining canals, navigable rivers and railways as they ran out from the city. In ports, factories using imported materials would be close to the docks. Old industrial areas have often been redeveloped, not always with new factories; some have become areas of open space or housing.

In those parts of cities developed since the 1920s, an important location for industry is along major roads. Such developments include industrial estates, with both factories and warehouses in addition to large single-factory sites. Originally, many of these industrial areas were on the edge of cities where large plots of low-cost land were available.

Residential areas

Much of the older housing in Britain's cities consists of closely packed terraces built to house the large numbers of people who moved into the cities in the 19th century. As people needed to live within walking distance of their places of work, their houses were built close to the factories. Areas with the worst housing have usually been cleared since 1945 and replaced with new flats and houses, but wide areas remain with overcrowded, run-down housing. In Scotland, the housing built in the 19th century for industrial workers was usually in

the form of tenement buildings (Figure 5). Not all 19th century housing was of poor quality. The managers of industry and professional people lived in large houses, usually on that side of the city centre which was furthest away from the industrial areas, upwind from the smoke of factories. Many of these areas have remained exclusive. Sometimes though, the character of such areas has been changed by the subdivision of old houses into flats and bed-sitters.

The areas of housing developed between the two wars are usually dominated by estates of semi-detached housing. Also at this time the first large council estates

**Figure 5
Tenement housing, Edinburgh**

were built, often next to the 19th century working-class housing. Those parts of cities developed since 1945 vary greatly in their type of housing. The most expensive private housing is often found on the same side of the city centre as the large 19th century houses or is clustered around the centres of one-time villages, engulfed by the urban sprawl. Large areas at the edges of many cities are occupied by council estates which housed many people displaced by inner city redevelopment.

Land use patterns in Nottingham

Figure 6 shows the pattern of land use in Nottingham. Much of this pattern closely reflects the model of urban structure and

Figure 6
Land use in Nottingham

growth in Figure 2. The more complex pattern of land use towards the edge of the city reflects the fact that Greater Nottingham is a small conurbation. As Nottingham spread outwards, it joined up with and engulfed villages and small industrial towns such as Bulwell and Beeston. To the west, Nottingham is joined in places to the small industrial towns of the Erewash Valley.

Q3 (a) Study the map of Nottingham in Figure 6. Describe and attempt to explain the location of (i) industrial areas; (ii) areas of high-cost housing; (iii) council estates.
(b) Draw a diagrammatic map to show how Greater Nottingham has grown from both a major centre and a number of smaller centres.

You will need to draw the outline of the built-up area, the centres from which growth has taken place and arrows to show the directions of growth.
(c) Use the information in Figures 6 and 7 to make a summary table of the distinctive urban zones in Nottingham. Figure 8 shows how to set your table out.

Figure 7
Urban zones in Nottingham

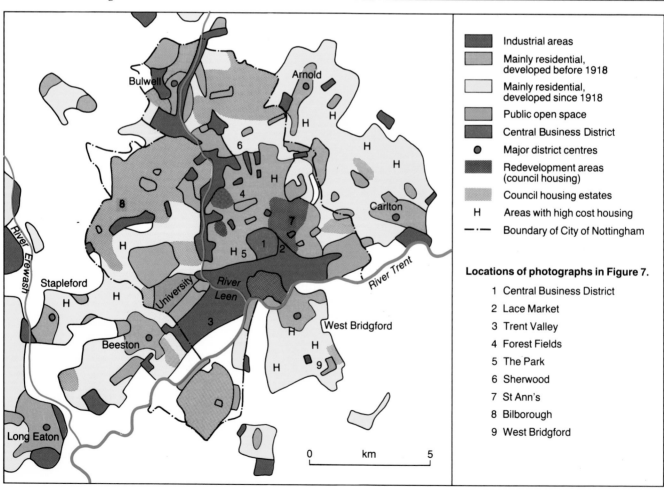

Industrial areas
Mainly residential, developed before 1918
Mainly residential, developed since 1918
Public open space
Central Business District
● **Major district centres**
Redevelopment areas (council housing)
Council housing estates
H **Areas with high cost housing**
–·– **Boundary of City of Nottingham**

Locations of photographs in Figure 7.

1 Central Business District
2 Lace Market
3 Trent Valley
4 Forest Fields
5 The Park
6 Sherwood
7 St Ann's
8 Bilborough
9 West Bridgford

0   km   5

1 Central Business District

2 Lace Market

Early 19th century factories and warehouses

3 Modern industry, Trent Valley

Modern factories built on Trent flood plain

4 Forest Fields

Old inner city
3 E S U P

5 The Park

Prosperous inner city
1 S

6 Sherwood

Suburb – private housng
1 2 P

7 St. Ann's

Redeveloped inner city
3 E U P

8 Bilborough

Suburb – council housing
2 3 U P

9 West Bridgford

Prosperous suburb
1 P

Relatively high proportion of:
1 Professional and managerial
2 Skilled manual workers
3 Unskilled & semi-skilled manual
E Ethnic minorites
S Single people
U Unemployed
P Pensioners

		Type of area	Distance from CBD	Population characteristics	Types of housing and other buildings	Street plan pattern	Age of buildings
1	CBD	Commercial					
2	Lace Market	Industrial					
3	Trent Valley	Industrial					
4	Forest Fields	Old inner city					

Figure 8
Table of urban zones in Nottingham

5.2 Social contrasts

Figure 1
Housing contrasts

Cities are places of contrast. For example, housing can vary greatly in appearance and quality, depending on its age, its tenure (whether council or privately owned), its size, its type (for example, flats, semi-detached, etc.) and how well it has been maintained (Figure 1).

> **Q1**
> Make labelled drawings to show and explain contrasts in housing in the area near your school.

Social and economic contrasts in Birmingham

Contrasts in Britain's cities go deeper than the appearance of housing areas and the impression of poverty or wealth they might give. Figure 2 maps data for several indicators of social and economic conditions in Birmingham. The maps show the marked contrast between the inner city areas and the rest of Birmingham. Closer inspection of the maps reveals some other important features:

1 The inner ring of poor areas is broken in the southwest by the prosperous 19th century suburb of Edgbaston.
2 In some respects, parts of the outer city share the problems of the inner city areas: these are the large council estates built in the 1930s or in the post-war period.

> **Q2**
> **(a)** On a map showing the ward boundaries of Birmingham, put a large dot in each ward where (i) the car ownership rate is less than the Birmingham average; (ii) overcrowding is worse than average; (iii) unemployment is worse than average for Birmingham. Thus, for example, Shard End ward would receive two dots for items (i) and (iii). Give your map a suitable title and key.
> **(b)** Figure 3 gives more data for Birmingham's wards. On a second map (i) shade in areas where more than 15 per cent of households are headed by a person born in the New Commonwealth or Pakistan; (ii) mark with a 'P' all wards where 15 per cent or more of the population are in professional and managerial occupations; (iii) mark with a 'U' all wards where 30 per cent or more of the population are semi-skilled and unskilled manual workers. Give your map a suitable title and key.
> **(c)**(i) Describe the pattern shown on your first map.
> (ii) Refer also to your second map. Which groups of people are more likely to live in poor housing conditions and be less prosperous?

52

Figure 2
Contrasts in Birmingham

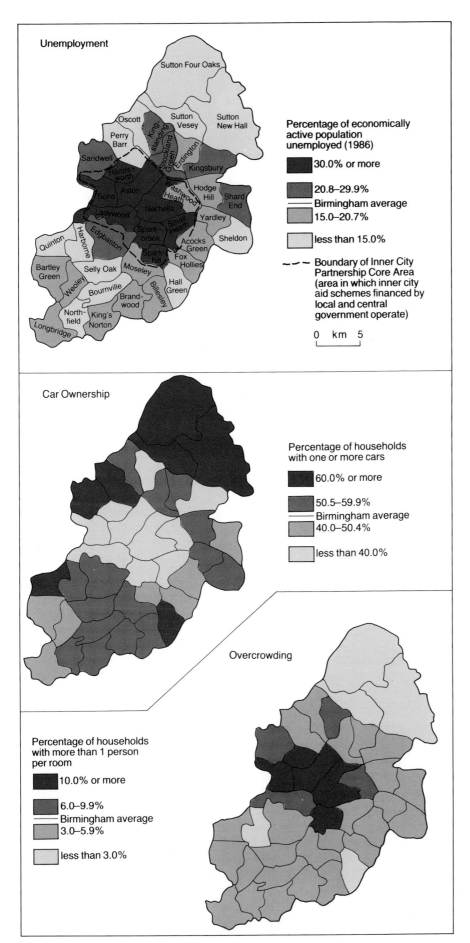

	NCP	P/M	S/U
Acock's Green	6.8	7.5	29.7
Aston	38.4	4.1	40.4
Bartley Green	3.4	8.4	33.3
Billesley	3.3	8.4	30.0
Bournville	4.6	13.6	27.4
Brandwood	4.5	9.6	27.3
Edgbaston	15.7	26.0	18.6
Erdington	5.6	10.5	23.8
Fox Hollies	6.8	6.1	36.1
Hall Green	4.5	16.3	17.9
Handsworth	53.2	5.4	38.1
Harborne	4.2	17.9	22.4
Hodge Hill	3.3	9.0	30.0
Kingsbury	3.4	5.1	38.2
King's Norton	3.4	10.8	30.7
Kingstanding	3.5	5.7	37.7
Ladywood	31.5	7.6	33.8
Longbridge	3.2	6.1	33.7
Moseley	19.7	17.8	18.8
Nechells	35.3	4.0	40.5
Northfield	2.4	11.4	27.5
Oscott	2.3	7.7	29.4
Perry Barr	5.3	11.6	22.8
Quinton	3.6	13.7	23.9
Sandwell	38.0	14.0	21.8
Selly Oak	7.9	14.3	24.5
Shard End	2.3	4.7	34.1
Sheldon	2.1	8.2	25.5
Small Heath	43.0	5.1	36.8
Soho	61.8	2.5	32.0
Sparkbrook	50.4	3.8	40.4
Sparkhill	47.8	7.9	34.0
Stockland Green	12.7	7.6	28.7
Sutton Four Oaks	1.6	33.5	11.3
Sutton New Hall	2.1	17.7	19.6
Sutton Vesey	2.0	26.2	12.0
Washwood Heath	21.8	4.2	35.6
Weoley	3.4	8.5	32.9
Yardley	4.5	7.9	27.2
Birmingham	15.1	10.5	28.8

NCP: Percentage residents in households headed by a person born in New Commonwealth or Pakistan
P/M: Percentage residents in professional and managerial occupations
S/U: Percentage residents in semi-skilled and unskilled manual occupations

Figure 3
Social contrasts in Birmingham

5.3 The inner cities

Just under four million of Britain's people live in inner city areas. Many of these people experience social and economic hardships in surroundings which are unattractive, depressing and even in a state of decay. The difficulties of these areas were sharply brought to public attention by riots in 1981, 1982 and 1985 in several cities. Many people believe that the condition of the inner city areas is the most important social and economic issue facing the country.

Comprehensive redevelopment

In the 1950s and 1960s the problem of bad housing in inner city areas was tackled by large scale **comprehensive redevelopment**. Slum housing was cleared and replaced by new housing, often in the form of flats. Also, derelict land was cleared, public open space created and new shopping centres, schools and other facilities built.

Britain's most deprived areas

Despite comprehensive redevelopment of large areas of poor housing, the inner cities remain Britain's most deprived areas. A survey made of the Inner London Borough of Lambeth identified the following problems: poor council housing (including flats built in the 1950s and 1960s), poor privately rented housing, extensive dereliction, inadequate social services, declining industries, low incomes, falling populations, large concentrations of old and young people, many single parents, many children in care, poor schools, poor recreational facilities, increasing levels of unemployment, particularly among the young, the black and the unskilled, many people suffering from low morale, stress and a feeling of hopelessness, high levels of vandalism and crime and a lack of open space.

Q1
Refer back to the maps of Birmingham in Section 5.2. What evidence is there for the inner areas of Birmingham having problems like those described in Lambeth?

Population decline

Comprehensive redevelopment has led to inner city areas losing many people. New housing was at a lower density than the old and more room was made available for schools and open space. As a result, only about one-half to two-thirds of the original population could be rehoused in the same area. People have also left areas not redeveloped to find better housing, better jobs and a more pleasant environment. Thus, between 1961 and 1981, the population of Inner London declined by almost a million from 3 493 000 to 2 498 000.

Industrial decline

The inner city areas have shown dramatic job losses over the last 30 years or so. For example, between 1952 and 1976 Inner London had a net loss of 644 000 jobs (a 24 per cent decline). Inner city factory sites usually lack room for expansion, have high rates and poor road access. Buildings are often unsuited to modern industry (Figure 2). In port cities, many jobs were lost in the docks.

Figure 1
Dingle, inner Liverpool, an area of poor housing, high unemployment and declining population

Figure 2
Inner city industry, Birmingham

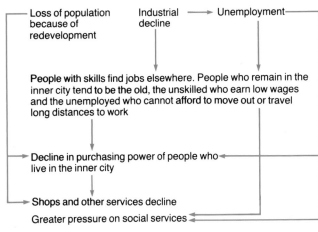

Figure 3
The effects of population loss and industrial decline in inner city areas

Unemployment and pressure on services

Figure 3 shows the 'knock-on' effects of the loss of population and industrial decline in inner city areas. The most serious impact is high unemployment. For example, parts of inner Birmingham have unemployment rates of about 30 per cent.

Over half of Britain's people who belong to ethnic minorities live in inner city areas. The future of these areas is therefore of particular concern to them. They have been particularly hard hit by unemployment because many were working in unskilled and semi-skilled jobs (most jobs lost have been of this type).

Q2
(a) Why do people move out of inner city areas? Which groups of people in particular tend to leave?
(ii) What effect does this movement have on the population structure of inner city areas?
(Population structure refers to the balance between different age, social/economic and ethnic groups.)

(b) Suggest why the following are typical features of many inner city areas:
(i) many people suffering from poor health; (ii) great pressure on the social services provided by councils; (iii) a high crime rate; (iv) declining shopping facilities.

Figure 4
Inner city aid schemes

Help for inner city areas

Tackling the problems of inner city areas requires huge amounts of money. Central government provides over £350 million a year of aid for inner city areas through the **Urban Programme**. Almost three-quarters of this sum is spent in **Inner City Partnerships** and **Inner City Programmes**. Figure 4 shows the location of

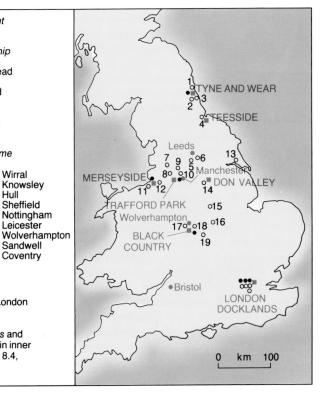

■ *Urban Development Corporations*
● *'Mini' – UDCs*
● *Inner City Partnership Authorites*
Newcastle/Gateshead
Liverpool
Manchester/Salford
Birmingham
Hackney ⎫
Islington ⎬ London
Lambeth ⎭

○ *Inner City Programme Authorities*

1	North Tyneside	11	Wirral
2	South Tyneside	12	Knowsley
3	Sunderland	13	Hull
4	Middlesbrough	14	Sheffield
5	Bradford	15	Nottingham
6	Leeds	16	Leicester
7	Blackburn	17	Wolverhampton
8	Bolton	18	Sandwell
9	Rochdale	19	Coventry
10	Oldham		

Brent ⎫
Hammersmith/ Fulham ⎬ London
Tower Hamlets
Wandsworth ⎭

Some *Enterprise zones* and *Freeports* are located in inner city areas (see section 8.4, Figure 2)

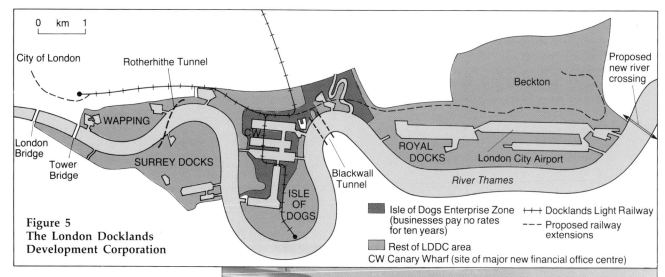

Figure 5
The London Docklands
Development Corporation

Isle of Dogs Enterprise Zone (businesses pay no rates for ten years)
Rest of LDDC area
CW Canary Wharf (site of major new financial office centre)
┝┿┥ Docklands Light Railway
--- Proposed railway extensions

these schemes in which central government, local authorities and business interests combine together and receive special grants for social, industrial and other projects. All these schemes are restricted to England.

In 1986 the government began to set up **City Action Teams** in small areas of inner cities which were suffering from very severe social and economic problems. These teams aim to attract private investment, involve the local people, and set up projects such as training unemployed people in new skills.

Large-scale schemes

In 1976 Britain's largest urban renewal scheme was begun in Glasgow. This scheme known as the GEAR project (Glasgow Eastern Area Renewal) involved housing development, creating new jobs, reclaiming derelict land and many other schemes.

More recent large-scale schemes, the **Urban Development Corporations** (UDCs), have put a much greater emphasis on attracting investment from private business. The government provides money for the UDCs to purchase land and improve the **infrastructure** (for example, transport and the environment) in large decaying areas. The aim is then to attract private companies to develop manufacturing, service industries and housing. The first

Two sides of the Docklands developments

1 Between 1981 and 1987 £257 million was invested in Docklands by LDDC and £2242 million of private investment was attracted.
2 Infrastructure developments include the Docklands Light Railway, London City Airport, road improvements and the reclamation of derelict land.
3 7000 housing units completed by 1987; 20000 units to be built by 1994. New housing includes converted riverside warehouses.
4 10000 new jobs created by 1986, with another 40000 expected by 1991.
5 New business developments include the Canary Wharf financial centre, the plants of most national newspapers, light industry and new shopping centres.
6 Major leisure developments such as the marina in the Surrey Docks and the Docklands Sports Centre.

● "These new jobs have gone to outsiders. We haven't got the skills." (Unemployed ex-docker)

● "My scrapyard's been closed down. They say it doesn't fit in. I've had to make fifteen men redundant." (Ex-scrapyard owner)

● "We've rented this house for twenty years. Now it's been compulsorily purchased and we're being thrown out. The LDDC doesn't have to rehouse us." (Resident, Isle of Dogs)

● "We need a house with a garden for the kids. We'll never get enough points for a better council flat and we can't afford homes at over £100000." (Council tenant living in tower block)

two UDCs were set up in 1981 in London Docklands and Merseyside. In 1987 the government announced the setting up of five more large UDCs and four 'mini-UDCs' (Figure 4).

Q3

Figure 5 gives details of developments in London Docklands.
(a) How does the approach of an Urban Development Corporation differ from that of an Inner City Partnership?
(b) Describe how the LDDC is improving the infrastructure.
(c) Why are the Docklands proving attractive to:
(i) developers of offices;
(ii) house building companies?
(d) Developments in the Docklands are leading to gains for some people and organizations, losses for others. Who gains? Who loses? Explain the answers you give.
(e) Suppose that an UDC was being set up in another large inner city area. If you were the government minister responsible for approving plans, what changes in approach, if any, would you make? What conditions, if any, would you impose on developers?

Improving the environment

Most of the money spent on inner city projects is used for improving housing, improving the environment and providing employment. The next section (5.4) looks at housing in particular detail. Derelict buildings and vacant land have been a constant problem for the inner cities. For example, in Liverpool about 12 per cent of the inner area is wasteland that has been awaiting redevelopment for twenty years or more. Here the Merseyside Development Corporation completed in 1984 the largest single piece of inner city reclamation ever attempted in Europe: 100 hectares of docks and refuse tips were reclaimed (Figure 6).

Providing employment

Many people believe that reducing the level of unemployment is the key need in inner city areas. All of the schemes in Figure 4, aim to create jobs. However, progress is often difficult because:

● Old-established industry continues to decline.

● Many firms do not see the inner cities as attractive environments in which to locate.

● Many of the new jobs which have been created in inner city areas are filled by people from outside these areas, because local people often lack the necessary skills.

A number of inner city projects have been concerned with helping local people, especially those from ethnic minorities, to develop their own businesses and so create employment. An increasing number of people believe that involving local people is important, not just in creating new job opportunities, but in improving housing conditions and tackling many other problems.

Q4
(a) (i) What causes land to become derelict in inner city areas?
(ii) Why is the reclamation of derelict land so important?
(b) List the possible 'knock-on' effects of creating new jobs in inner city areas.
(c) What are the advantages in involving people who live in inner city areas in (i) detailed planning decisions; (ii) work on improving housing and the environment?

Figure 6
Developments by the Merseyside Development Corporation: the Albert Dock development (shops, restaurants and museums occupying old warehouses) and reclaimed waterfront land, formerly a waste tip

5.4 Housing

Housing is a basic human need. Good housing helps people to lead more satisfying, less stressful and healthier lives. Despite the slum clearance and redevelopment schemes of the 1950s and 1960s, poor housing remains a major task for planners to deal with. Much old inner city housing remains in poor condition. In addition, much pre-war council housing has deteriorated, while many post-war flats have proved to be costly mistakes.

Figure 1
A street in a Housing Action Area in Small Heath, Birmingham. Here the interiors of houses were modernized with the aid of improvement grants while the exteriors were improved at no cost to the owners – an 'envelope scheme'

Housing improvement

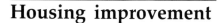

During the 1970s and 1980s the replacing of old with new housing has continued, but more slowly and usually with houses rather than flats. There has been more emphasis on improving existing houses, with grants being made available to house owners. Areas with particularly severe housing and social problems may be declared **Housing Action Areas**.

Improving old housing lets existing communities of people stay in the same area and provides reasonable quality housing at a lower cost than new housing. However, some critics have said that improvement schemes have only put off the day when housing will have to be replaced. Also, many people with low incomes have difficulty in affording their contribution towards improvements, a problem worsened by cutting the size of improvement grants.

An unintended effect of improvement grants is a process called **gentrification**. This involves larger 19th century housing which had declined in quality and had been subdivided into flats or let at low rents. The houses are bought up and restored by relatively wealthy people, taking advantage of grants (Figure 2). The housing has been improved, but the increase in house prices drives out poorer people.

Figure 2
'Gentrification' of a house in Bristol

Figure 3
Liverpool; flats awaiting demolition and flats being refurbished

Figure 4
Tile Hill Estate, Coventry. Well-kept houses and gardens contrast with run-down public areas

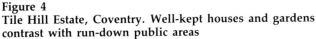

Q1

(a) (i) What are the advantages of housing improvement over complete redevelopment? What are the disadvantages?
(ii) Refer to Figure 1. What advantages have 'envelope works' over separate improvements to the outside of houses?
(b) (i) Explain what is meant by 'gentrification' and suggest why this process takes place.
(ii) What are the advantages and disadvantages for an area being gentrified?

Council housing

About 30 per cent of Britain's homes are rented from local authorities. Much pre-war council housing is now showing its age. Even housing built in the 1950s and 1960s has given rise to major problems, especially where 'industrial' building methods were used. Particular problems have been experienced with tower blocks and other flats (Figure 3). Demolition has been the only practical solution for the worst of these. On many post-war council estates run-down public areas

contrast with areas of well-kept houses and gardens (Figure 4).

In the 1980s far fewer council houses have been built each year than in previous decades. Also, many have been sold. As a result, housing waiting lists are long. However, most new council housing is in the form of houses with their own gardens.

Q2

(a) What are the problems of living in tower blocks? Which groups of people are particularly affected? How can these problems be dealt with?
(b) What are the arguments for and against selling council houses to their tenants?

New private housing

Most new private housing is built by large building companies on estates at the edge of towns and cities. The shortage of land in some areas has led to pressure to release Green Belt land for development. Usually, private builders have not been keen to build on inner city sites, as greater profits could be made in the outer suburbs where land was cheaper and demand was higher.

Recently, however, the building companies have begun to build houses for sale in the inner cities, often in association with building societies, themselves often reluctant to lend to people in these areas. In some cities, blocks of council flats have been sold to developers for renovation and sale to first-time buyers. Also, there has been more involvement in inner city areas by housing associations (non-profit making organizations which rent out housing) and housing co-operatives (housing schemes jointly owned and run by their residents) in building new and improving old housing.

Q3

(a) Why are suburban sites more profitable than inner city sites for builders?
(b) Look at an advertisement in your local newspaper for a new housing development.
(i) Describe how the builder is attempting to promote the development. Consider both the houses themselves and the advantages claimed for the location of the estate.
(ii) Do the advantages claimed for the location of the estate match up to reality? Explain your answer fully.

6. Farming

6.1 The changing face of farming

Farming is extremely important to Britain's people, economy and landscape. Although only 2 per cent of the British workforce work on farms, they produce about two-thirds of Britain's food needs. Many of the foods which are imported are tropical and warm temperate crops which cannot be grown in Britain. Britain also exports important amounts of agricultural produce, usually in a manufactured form. Industries connected with farming, such as the processing of crops and the manufacturing of machinery and other goods needed by farms, employ about 7 per cent of the workforce, so agriculture makes an important contribution to employment. British farming is very efficient and its workforce is highly productive. Such efficiency and productivity depends on good organization, large capital investment in equipment and buildings and large subsidies from the government and the EEC.

The farm system

Figure 1 shows how a farm can be seen as a system, with the inputs being converted into outputs in the form of various crops and animal products. The farmer uses his knowledge, experience and skills to harness the inputs to produce his crops and animal products at a profit. The flow of money in the diagram is very much simplified. Because farmers have to wait some time before they see money coming in from their investments in inputs, they need to take out loans which are repaid with the money received from the sale of outputs. Money is also received from the government through subsidies and other grants (see Section 6.2).

Q1
(a) Refer to the farm system diagram in Figure 1.
(i) Which inputs are natural (or environmental)? Which inputs are human and economic?
(ii) Describe how some outputs are recycled into inputs.
(b) Why will loans cost the farmer money? What dangers are there when a farmer borrows heavily to invest in new equipment and then finds that prices for his outputs fall?

Feeding Britain

In the 1950s and 1960s it was government policy to keep food prices low and to make the country as self-sufficient as possible. The government therefore supported the production of many food products through a system of subsidies paid to farmers. Cheap imports of products such as wheat and butter also helped to feed the nation economically. At the same time, the government encouraged farmers to produce food more efficiently by adopting new methods.

Figure 1
The farm system of a mixed farm

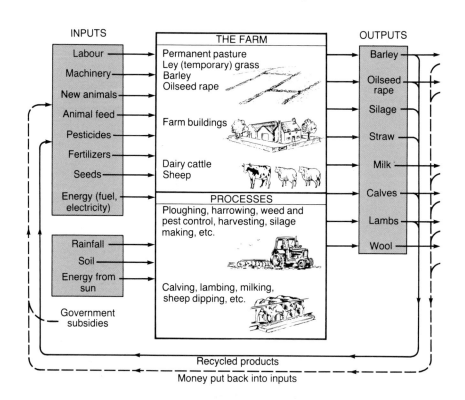

Farming and the EEC

Since 1973 Britain has been a member of the European Economic Community (EEC). The EEC countries have agreed a Common Agricultural Policy (CAP) to support farming. Imports of cheap food from outside the EEC are controlled by high import duties and by quotas, to protect EEC farmers from competition. The CAP subsidizes farmers by the means of **intervention prices**. Each year, for important farm products, the EEC sets a price at a level some way below current market prices. If the market price drops to this set price – the intervention price – the EEC will buy the surplus produce at that price. Therefore, farmers receive guaranteed prices for their production, even if it is surplus to the market's needs. This system, combined with increasingly efficient farming methods, has led to surpluses of many products building up: examples include skimmed milk, butter, meat and cereals. Surpluses can be sold to countries outside the EEC but because EEC prices are higher than world prices, **export subsidies** are needed to reduce prices.

The CAP is very expensive to run and has caused much disagreement between the EEC countries. It is partly paid for by the import duties on farm produce from outside the EEC. The consumer also has to pay for the CAP through taxes and by

paying relatively high prices for food. Concern over the building up of surpluses and the huge sums of money spent on intervention prices, export

subsidies and storage has, since 1985, led to a move to lower many prices and to limit the production of some products.

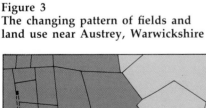

NUMBER AND SIZE OF FARMS

	1961	1981
Under 20ha *	205600	55410
20–100ha	93000	88660
100–200ha	17000	22170
Over 200ha	4500	19250

* Most small units are worked part-time and contribute very little to total farm output

Figure 2
Changes in farming

Figure 3
The changing pattern of fields and land use near Austrey, Warwickshire

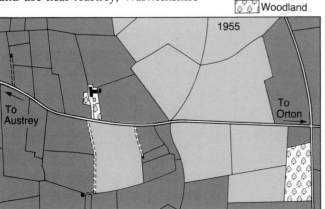

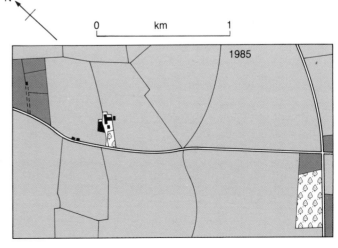

Figure 4
Modern farm machinery

Q2
(a) What are the objections to the CAP, involving the building up of surpluses?
(b) Should the consumer pay for subsidizing food production through taxes or higher priced food? Give reasons for your answer.
(c) Describe how the CAP differs from government policy for farming before Britain joined the EEC.

Changes in farming

Government and EEC policies, new methods and the application of science to farming have led to dramatic changes taking place over the past 40 years or so. The statistics and graphs in Figure 2 show how great many of these changes have been.

Bigger farms and fields

Over the post-war period the average size of all types of farm in Britain has increased greatly. Farms have been combined and large farms have taken over neighbouring smaller ones. A large farm makes it possible for the cost of machinery and labour to be spread over a large area and thus produce crops more efficiently. On arable farms, hedgerows have been removed and small fields combined into large ones to enable machinery to be used more efficiently (Figure 3). The creation of such huge fields creates problems, however:

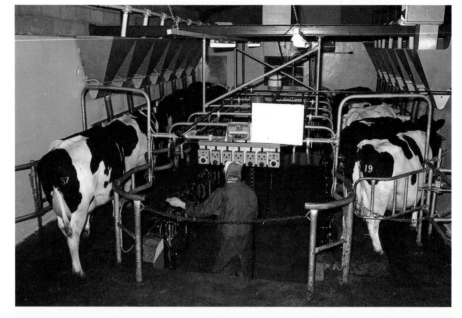

● Larger dairy herds (average size of herd in 1985 was 130 compared with 45 in 1970)

● Use of high-yielding breeds (Friesian and Holstein)

● Use of artificial insemination so as to breed from top quality bulls

● Scientific approach to feeding cows including careful use of concentrates

● Use of efficient milking parlours such as the herringbone type (see photograph) with automated milking methods and push-button controlled feeding

Figure 5
Trends in dairy farming

wind erosion of light soils, the destruction of wildlife habitats and the creation of a monotonous landscape.

Increased use of chemicals

A major factor behind the rising yields of crops has been the increased use of chemicals in farming. Artificial fertilizers are used to maintain soil fertility and provide the correct balance of minerals for a particular crop. They enable cereals to be grown year after year in many areas (monoculture or continuous cropping). Chemical sprays are widely used to kill weeds (herbicides), insect pests (pesticides) and crop fungus diseases (fungicides). In recent years there has been increasing concern over the widespread use of chemicals in arable farming (see Section 6.4).

New strains of crops

Plant breeding has led to the introduction of new high-yielding or disease-resistant strains of crops. The introduction of high-yielding varieties of wheat in the 1970s has led to the crop being grown more widely and the successful growth of 'hard' wheat used in bread-making. Previously Britain had to rely on imported hard wheat.

Mechanization

Mechanization has been a feature of arable farming in Britain for many years. Very rapid progress has been made over the past 30 years with the development of more powerful tractors, the introduction of larger and more specialized machines, the use of hydraulic systems, the application of electronics and improved comfort and safety for operators (Figure 4). Many new cultivation methods have been developed such as the limited cultivation of land with various types of tined (pronged) instruments.

Changes in livestock farming

As with arable farming, livestock production has seen dramatic changes over the post-war years. Dairy farming is a good example to illustrate the nature of these changes. Between 1960 and 1980 the milk yields of cows increased by about 50 per cent. A high-yielding cow can produce 40 litres of milk in 24 hours. Figure 5 lists the factors which have led to higher yields and great efficiency on dairy farms.

The intensive methods used to rear pigs and poultry are so different from traditional farming practices that they are often known as **factory farming**. In both poultry and pig units, temperature, light and amounts of feed are automatically controlled (Figure 6). The controversy which surrounds factory farming methods are looked at in Section 6.4.

Q3

Refer to Figure 2.
(a) Describe and explain the changing yields of wheat and barley from the graphs shown.
(b) Draw bar graphs to show how the number of dairy herds has gone down while the average size of herd has gone up. Give reasons for these changes.
(c) Suggest reasons for the steady decline in the number of farm workers in Britain.

Q4

Look at Figure 3.
(a) Calculate the approximate average size of field in 1955 and 1985 in the Austrey area.
(b) About what proportion of the hedgerows has been lost between 1955 and 1985?
(c) Write an account of the changes which have taken place in farming in the Austrey area between 1955 and 1985. Suggest reasons for the changes in your account. (The changes in land use are closely linked with many of the other changes.)

Less farmland

The increased production of crops and animal products has been achieved from a decreasing area of land. Farming has to compete with many other forms of land use. During the 1960s and early 1970s about 17 000 hectares of farmland was lost each year, mainly to housing, but also to motorways and roads, other urban land uses and forestry. Since about 1975 the industrial recession combined with a decline in house building has led to less farmland being lost. Most of the loss of land from farming has been in a belt stretching from Lancashire through the Midlands to the South-East and has involved much good quality land.

Q5

(a) Why has Britain's better quality farmland usually been under greater threat from urban development than poorer quality land?
(b) Suppose that land were to be taken out of production to prevent surpluses of farm products building up.
(i) What quality of land would most likely be involved?
(ii) Why would this land usually not be the same as that under threat from urban development?
(iii) What other uses could be made of such land?

Figure 6
Intensive pig rearing

6.2 Factors influencing farming

The farmer's decisions

To be successful a farmer needs to choose crops and livestock wisely. Physical or environmental factors set limits on the choices which can be made. Within such limits the farmer has to consider various human and economic factors when considering what farming activities will be profitable. Farmers usually aim to make the maximum profit they can from their land, but it needs to be remembered that they have different personal preferences for types of animal or crop and have different knowledge and skills. Also, one farmer may well be satisfied with making a lower profit than another if it means less effort or less risk. Figure 1 shows the many factors at work in influencing a farmer's decisions.

The various factors in Figure 1 will affect patterns on a variety of scales: on the individual farm, within an area or region and over the whole country. The importance of the factors varies according to the scale of study. The broad pattern of farming land use over the whole country reflects the major contrasts in climate and relief. Human and economic factors are more important at a local level.

Physical factors

When considering the physical factors which influence farming it is useful to think of each crop as having a set of ideal or optimum conditions for its successful growth. Away from the area with optimum conditions, yields will be lower and the risks of crop failure greater.

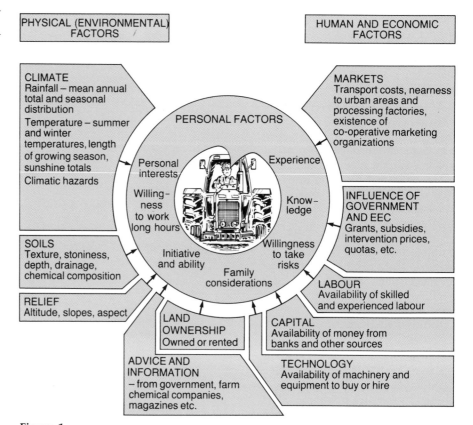

Figure 1
Factors influencing a farmer's decisions

Climate

Climatic factors are very important in shaping the farming map of Britain shown in Figure 2. The total amount and seasonal distribution of rainfall set limits on many farming activities. Aspects of temperature are also important: the length of the growing season, summer maximum temperature and the risk of frost.

Mean annual rainfall in Britain ranges from under 700mm to over 2000mm (section 2.2, Figure 3). Where annual rainfall is over 850mm it is risky to grow cereals: crops may have to be sown late because the land is too wet, while the grain may not ripen properly before autumn rains set in. In areas of very low rainfall irrigation is necessary if good yields of crops such as potatoes are to be obtained. On the other hand, successful grass growth depends on higher amounts of rainfall although if rainfall becomes excessive, as in many western hill areas, the quality of pasture becomes poor.

The higher summer temperatures of the South and East (Section 2.3, Figure 1) give these areas particular advantages for growing crops. Where temperatures are higher in winter, the critical temperature for plant growth (6°C) is reached earlier in the year. Figure 2 in Section 2.3 shows how the growing season begins earlier and lasts longer in western coastal areas. Fruit growing is particularly successful in areas with high sunshine totals, high summer temperatures and the absence of spring frosts.

Farmers are concerned about exceptional weather conditions as well as average conditions. Late frosts, summer thunderstorms, drought, periods of very heavy rain and heavy snow can harm various farming activities. In some cases farmers can reduce the damage, for example, using irrigation equipment to sprinkle potatoes can prevent frost damage.

Local climatic differences can influence how a farmer plans the use of his land. Local differences in altitude and relief affect critical temperatures and therefore the success of crops. For example, fruit growers reduce risks of spring frost damage by not planting trees in the frost hollows of valley floors.

Soils

The texture, drainage, depth and chemical composition of the soil affect farming. **Texture** refers to the size of particles which make up a soil. Clay soils are made up of very fine particles which stick together and so they may easily become waterlogged. Sandy soils have a coarse texture and water will drain through them easily. A soil made up of a mixture of clay particles, silt (medium-sized) particles and sand is known as a loam and is particularly well-suited to arable farming. Some soils contain many stones and may therefore be of little use for root crops. Soils on steep slopes are usually much thinner than those on lowlands and therefore less suitable for cultivation.

The fertility of a soil depends on its chemical composition which largely reflects the type of underlying rock. For example, soils on granite are acid and may need liming for successful cultivation.

Relief and altitude

Flat or gently sloping land is well-suited to the use of machinery, providing it is well-drained. Dairy cows which have to be milked twice a day are more easily managed away from rough, steeply sloping land.

Figure 2
Main types of farming in Britain

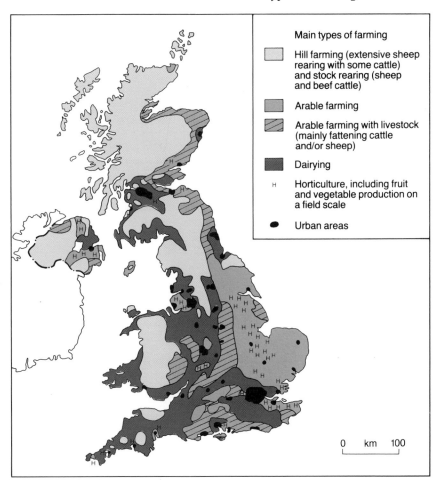

Main types of farming

Hill farming (extensive sheep rearing with some cattle) and stock rearing (sheep and beef cattle)

Arable farming

Arable farming with livestock (mainly fattening cattle and/or sheep)

Dairying

H   Horticulture, including fruit and vegetable production on a field scale

●   Urban areas

0   km   100

Fen peat soil, with a crop of sugar beet

Chalk soil, just sown with spring barley

Figure 3
Contrasting soils

Many hill areas of Britain are only suitable for sheep rearing because of their difficult terrain (Figure 4). Steep slopes and thin soils will only support rough pasture. Many upland plateau areas suffer from bad drainage, acid soils and because of their altitude, from low temperatures.

Human and economic factors

Within the physical limits, two factors have a particularly great influence on whether an activity will be profitable or not: markets and the influence of government.

Markets
Farm produce is sold in a variety of ways: to processing factories, in the case of milk to a government marketing organization, to wholesalers and merchants, by auction and sometimes directly to the public. The location of the market may influence a farmer's choice of activity, especially if he has to pay transport costs himself. Nearness to a processing factory is important if the product is perishable (for example, peas for freezing) or if the product is bulky and has a high waste content (for example, sugar beet). Decisions on whether to grow

vegetables or fruit for sale as fresh produce may depend on the nearness of urban areas or the existence nearby of a co-operative organization which packs and markets the produce for farmers. Production of poultry and pigs often depends on a contract with a nearby factory which provides much of the capital needed and buys the animals for slaughter and processing.

Q4
(a) Name examples of farm products sold in each of the ways named above.
(b) Look at advertisements in local newspapers of farms which operate 'pick-your-own' systems or farm shops. (June and July is the best time to look.) Map their locations and any others you know about. Describe and explain the pattern shown on your map.

Government influence
Government and EEC policies have been very important influences on British farming. The intervention prices and other policies of the EEC have influenced the decisions of farmers over how to use their land and in turn have affected

patterns on a national scale. Thus, the high level of support for arable farming in the late 1970s and early 1980s led to the expansion of arable farming westwards and northwards at the expense of livestock production. The increase in the growing of oilseed rape (Figure 5) and a rise in the numbers of sheep are direct results of raising intervention prices.

The government and the EEC also help farmers by providing grants for modernizing farm buildings, improving pasture and draining land. In some cases, government policy may bring farmers into conflict with conservationists. Recently, some farmers have received government money for *not* undertaking new developments because of the potential damage to the environment and wildlife. Chapter 12 takes a closer look at such issues in the countryside.

The EEC provides help to farmers in those parts of the country which it defines as Less Favoured Areas (Figure 6). These areas are in danger of depopulation, where physical conditions are harsh, farm income is low and most land is suitable only for extensive livestock rearing. EEC help in these areas aims to make sure that farming is continued, farms modernized, minimum population levels maintained and the countryside conserved.

Figure 4
Sheep on a hill farm

Figure 5
Oilseed rape

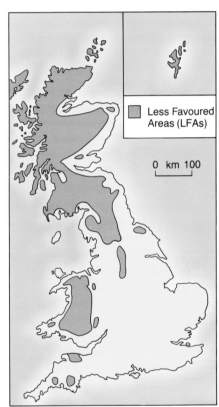

Figure 6
Less Favoured Areas (LFAs)

Less Favoured Areas (LFAs)

0 km 100

Q5

(a) (i) How does the system of intervention prices work? (Refer back to Section 6.1.)

(ii) Explain why high intervention prices may lead to the expansion of the area under a particular crop.

(iii) Why might a farmer who changed from livestock to arable farming in recent years be worried about the future reduction of intervention prices?

(Consider the investments in new equipment he will have made.)

(b) Describe and explain the distribution of Less Favoured Areas shown in Figure 6.

---

foodstuffs. Machinery for arable farming is very expensive, for example, £85000 for a large combine harvester. Most of the capital farmers need is borrowed from banks and other financial institutions.

Land ownership

In 1900 only 25 per cent of British farms were owner-occupied, the remainder being worked by tenants of country landowners and institutions such as the Church. Now 64 per cent of farms are worked by their owners, with much of the remaining 36 per cent being owned by financial institutions such as insurance companies and pension funds. Ownership of his land can enable the farmer to plan for the future with more certainty. However, many former tenants have had to borrow large sums of money to buy the land they farm.

Q6

Larger farmers and managers of farms owned by institutions are usually able to produce crops very efficiently and are more easily able to make major changes in their farming activities. Why is this?

Capital

An individual farmer's decisions are affected by many other human and economic factors, as Figure 1 shows. It is worth having a closer look at two of these factors: capital and the ownership of the land. Successful farming depends on large amounts of money or capital being invested; it is a **capital-intensive** activity. High quality arable land costs over £5000 a hectare while even poor hill land can cost £1000 a hectare. To start a dairy herd of 80 cows would need the investment of £45000 for cows and a further £60000 for machinery, equipment and

6.3 Farming patterns and contrasts

Changing crop patterns

Changing farming practices and changing influences on farming have affected patterns of crop production. Figure 1 shows how the relative importance of the different arable crops has changed. The rapid growth in the area under barley during the late 1950s and the 1960s reflected the increased demand for animal feed and the development of high-yielding varieties which made it very profitable. In the 1970s the area under wheat expanded.

In contrast to the two main grain crops, the areas under sugar beet and potatoes have changed little.

Since Britain joined the EEC, high prices have led to the great expansion of the area under oilseed rape. It is useful as a 'break' crop (to interrupt a run of cereals) and can be handled with the same machinery as cereals. The demands of vegetable freezing and canning factories has led to the increased importance of field crops of peas, beans and carrots. In the 1980s some farmers have experimented with crops such as linseed which can be processed for oil and animal feedstuffs.

Figure 2 shows where the main arable crops are grown in Britain. Notice the importance of the drier East. All sugar beet is grown under contract to the British Sugar Corporation. It is a heavy crop with a high waste content and so transport distances must be kept as short as possible. Its distribution therefore reflects the location of the sugar factories, besides physical factors. Most potatoes are produced in the East, but irrigation is often needed early in the growing season.

Q1
(a) Describe and explain the changes in the areas under barley, wheat and oats shown in Figure 1.
(b) Referring to examples, explain how changing eating habits may affect crop production.

Contrasts in arable farming

Figure 3 shows a large arable farm near King's Lynn in Norfolk. Its large area, large fields, heavy investment in machinery and equipment and small labour force are typical of modern arable farming. The large wooded area and the employment of a gamekeeper is rather unusual and

Figure 1
Changes in areas under major crops

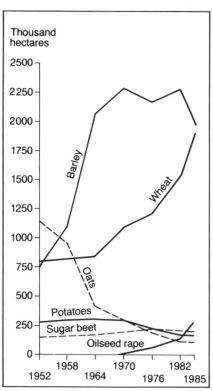

Figure 2
Major crops

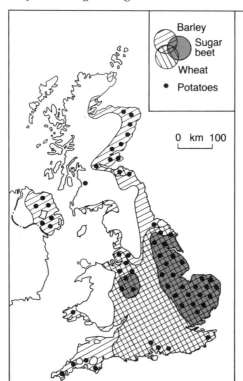

WHEAT
Needs a dry climate (preferably under 750mm of rain a year) and warm, sunny conditions to ripen. Gives highest yields in deep, fertile, quite heavy soils.

BARLEY
Needs a dry climate (preferably under 1000mm of rain a year). It will ripen in a cooler, less sunny climate than wheat and is grown on both light and heavy soils.

SUGAR BEET
Needs dry conditions (under 900mm of rain a year, sunny summers and deep, light, well-drained soils.

POTATOES
Require a dry climate, yet plenty of rain early in the year. Early potatoes are grown in the west (mild winters, few spring frosts). Need deep, light soils.

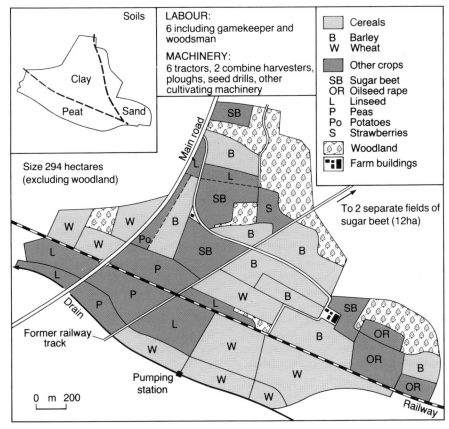

Figure 3
Mount Lynn Estate, Norfolk, a large arable farm

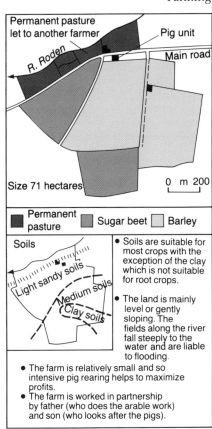

Figure 4
Edgebolton Farm, Shropshire

reflects the wish of its owner – a businessman in industry – to organize shooting parties. Large amounts of artificial fertilizers and sewage sludge are used to maintain fertility. There is also a limited rotation of crops: sugar beet, peas, oilseed rape and linseed provide breaks from cereal growing. Rotation also helps to prevent the build-up in the soil of plant diseases and pests.

Arable farming is not the same everywhere in Britain. Figure 4 shows the land use of a smaller arable farm in Shropshire which produces barley and sugar beet but also has a pig unit.

Horticulture

Horticulture involves four main specialist activities: vegetable growing, fruit growing, glasshouse production and the cultivation of flowers, pot plants and garden plants. In the past, all of these activities were usually

practised on small, very labour-intensive market gardens. Now, most vegetables are grown on larger farms. This is because costs can be kept low with mechanized production and large-scale production makes grading and marketing easier. The market gardens now concentrate on high-value vegetables which still require much hand work and on glasshouse products, including pot plants and flowers. Large amounts of capital need to be invested in glasshouses with automated ventilation and heating systems, irrigation systems and other specialized equipment.

Selling the produce

Most market gardeners and fruit farmers belong to co-operative growers' associations which pack and market the produce. Where urban areas are nearby, some growers operate 'pick-your-own' systems and farm shops (Figure 5).

Q2
(a) Draw a systems diagram of the Norfolk farm in Figure 3. (Refer back to Section 6.1, Figure 1, if necessary.)
(b) Describe how soils have affected land use planning on this farm. What other factors would the farm manager consider when planning land use?
(c) What climatic advantages does East Anglia have for arable farming? (Refer to Figure 2 and to Section 6.2.)

Q3
For the Shropshire farm in Figure 4: (i) describe the physical factors and (ii) describe the human and economic factors which have influenced its farming activities. (You will need to read through Section 6.2 again.)

During the past 30 years or so, many small market gardeners have gone out of business, unable to compete with larger producers or imports from Europe. Glasshouse tomato growers have been badly hit by high heating oil prices and competition from Dutch growers who have lower fuel costs. Growers of orchard fruit have also faced severe competition from the EEC; the warmer and sunnier conditions of France and Italy give higher yields and the French have organized strong marketing campaigns.

Areas of production

The areas which produce fruit and vegetables in Britain (Section 6.2, Figure 2) overlap areas important for other types of farming. The main areas are usually favoured by one or more of the following factors:

● Nearness to large urban markets (for example, around London).

● Climatic advantages such as early springs in the sheltered valleys of southern Cornwall and Devon, or high sunshine totals needed for ripening fruit as in Kent.

● Soils that are deep and fertile such as in the Fens, or are light, easily worked and warm up quickly in spring, as in the Vale of Evesham.

Q4
(a) (i) What are the advantages of growers belonging to co-operative organizations?
(ii) What are the advantages to growers of 'pick-your-own' systems and farm shops?
(b) Why are advertising and promotion campaigns very important for fruit growers?

Figure 5
A farm shop

Contrasts in livestock farming

Livestock are kept on both specialist livestock farms and on mixed farms. Figure 6 gives details of the output of the main livestock products. There are five main types of livestock production in Britain:

1 Dairy farming.
2 Hill farming in which sheep, and sometimes cattle, are reared on rough upland grazing and permanent pasture.
3 Rearing beef cattle and sheep on farms which grow some fodder crops and are found mainly on the edges of hill farming areas.
4 Fattening beef cattle and sheep, using fodder crops or pasture.
5 Intensive pig and poultry production.

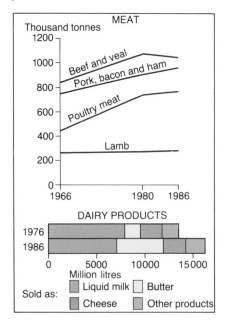

Figure 6
Changing production of meat and dairy products

Dairy farming

Dairy farming is mainly found in the lowland areas of western Britain where moderately high rainfall, mild winters, a long growing season and relatively cool summers favour a good supply of grass. Some dairy farms are found in the East where there is good access to major urban areas. The local factors which affect the suitability of a farm for milk production are listed in Figure 7. The Cheshire dairy farm in Figure 8 has such advantages. It also has a herd of sufficient size to operate successfully at a time when dairy farmers face problems such as milk quotas (see below) and high feed costs.

● Good water supply to farm and fields

● Grazing for cows within easy reach of the milking parlour

● Farm easily accessible to milk collection tankers

● Good quality buildings to house cows in winter

● Room to construct a slurry lagoon (a pit to store manure which is spread on the fields in summer)

● Soil which will retain moisture, yet is not so heavy and wet that the cows' hooves will turn it into mud in wet weather or will become waterlogged

---

Figure 7
Local factors favouring dairy farming

Q5
(a) What physical factors favour Cheshire for dairy farming?
(b) What local advantages has the farm in Figure 8 for dairy farming? What features of the farm enable it to produce milk efficiently? (Refer back to Figure 5 in Section 6.1 for details of modern trends in dairy farming.)

Liquid milk consumption in Britain at 4.5 pints (2.56 litres) a head per week is higher than in other European countries, partly because only Britain has a doorstep delivery system. An increasing proportion of milk production is processed into butter and other products. This reflects a decline in liquid milk consumption from even higher previous levels and the reduction in butter imports from New Zealand and other Commonwealth countries. Surplus milk production in the EEC as a whole led to production limits (quotas) being imposed on dairy farmers. Some small farmers received quotas which were too small for economic production. They have had to go out of business or change to other farming activities.

Hill farming

Wide areas of northern and western Britain are unsuitable for growing crops or for intensive forms of livestock farming. Figure 9 gives details of a typical hill farm in Cumbria. It covers a very large area, but income is not high because most of the land is low quality and can support few animals per hectare. Farms such as this have only survived because of government help. Despite being located in a Less Favoured Area and so qualifying for EEC help and despite higher EEC lamb prices since 1980, the farmer has had problems in

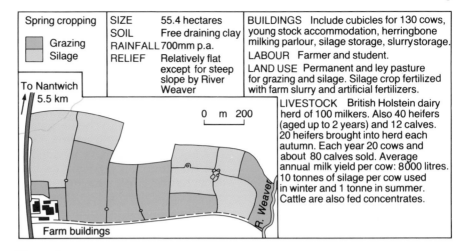

Figure 8
Austerson Hall, near Nantwich, Cheshire, a dairy farm

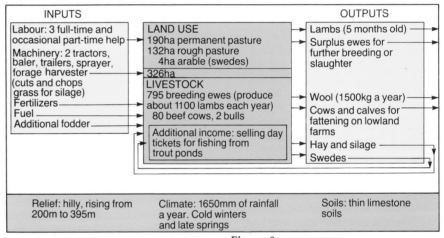

Figure 9
The farm system of a hill farm in Cumbria

making a good profit. Prices for fuel and animal fodder have been high. In areas where the tourist industry is important, some hill farmers earn additional income by providing services for the visitors (Figure 10).

Figure 10
A camp site on a hill farm

Q6
(a) Describe (i) the environmental and (ii) the economic problems that hill farms face.
(b) (i) Suggest why hill farmers need additional sources of income.
(ii) List the ways in which they might earn money by providing for the needs of visitors.
(c) Why is it important that the government continues to support farming in the hill areas of Britain?

6.4 Farming and the future

Farming in Britain faces many issues and questions. Often they have become subjects of great controversy, with people holding views ranging from one extreme to another. The major questions are these:

1 Should policies which encourage the production of large surpluses of food, in particular cereals, be continued?
2 Should the government continue to subsidize farming more heavily (in relation to output) than manufacturing?
3 Should farmers in poorer areas be specially subsidized so as to preserve the local economy and landscape?
4 Should there be greater controls on how farmers use their land?
5 Should farmers receive more help to conserve the countryside?
6 Should good-quality farmland near cities be used for building?
7 Should intensive livestock production be more carefully controlled (or even abolished)?
8 Should the amounts of chemical fertilizers and pesticides used in farming be lessened, even if production and profits were to be reduced?

The important environmental questions involving the impact of farming on the countryside are of very great concern and are looked at in more detail in Section 12.3. The answers to some of the wider questions are already being given, for example, 'No' to question 1. The EEC countries have decided that the Common Agricultural Policy is too costly and that intervention prices and other subsidies should be reduced. The British government has decided to follow two approaches in order to lower food production:

1 Grow less food on existing farmland.
2 Take some farmland out of production and encourage alternative economic activities in the countryside (see Section 12.3).

Factory farming

Figure 1 shows some of the wide range of views which people have on the intensive production of livestock, that is, factory farming. Notice that the farmer is not the only commercial interest involved. Consumers have to balance their concern for the welfare of animals with the wish for food at a reasonable price. Recently, there has been a small move away from the most intensive methods: an increasing number of pigs are being reared outside and a rising demand for 'free-range' eggs, even if at a higher price, has led to an expansion of this type of egg production.

> ### Q1
> **(a)** List the arguments for and against factory farming.
> **(b)** What is your opinion on this issue? How should the issue be dealt with in the future? Justify your views

Chemicals and farming

The use of chemical fertilizers and pesticides is a key feature of modern farming. Their most significant effect on the environment has been to reduce the numbers of wild plants and insects in intensively farmed areas. The effects are not just on the plants in the fields and on the insect pests. The reduction in numbers of wild flowers has led to a marked decrease in the butterfly and moth population. Spraying of flowering oilseed rape affects bees which are taking the nectar from the flowers. Spray drift affects hedges and trees at the edge of fields.

In addition, there are several other concerns: uncertainties about the side-effects of new chemical products, the build-up in soils of chemicals which do not quickly decompose, the presence of chemicals in fruit and vegetables and the contamination of water supplies by nitrate fertilizers in water draining off fields (Figure 3).

Critics of the widespread use of chemicals in farming say that 'organic farming' should be more widely adopted. Organic farming is based on concern about the soil; agricultural chemicals are

Figure 1
Different views on factory farming

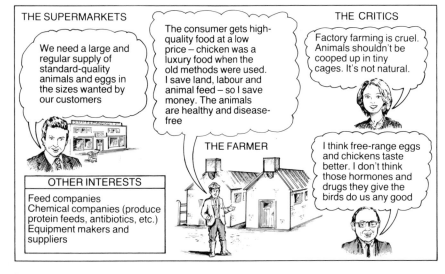

THE SUPERMARKETS

We need a large and regular supply of standard-quality animals and eggs in the sizes wanted by our customers

OTHER INTERESTS
Feed companies
Chemical companies (produce protein feeds, antibiotics, etc.)
Equipment makers and suppliers

The consumer gets high-quality food at a low price – chicken was a luxury food when the old methods were used. I save land, labour and animal feed – so I save money. The animals are healthy and disease-free

THE FARMER

THE CRITICS

Factory farming is cruel. Animals shouldn't be cooped up in tiny cages. It's not natural.

I think free-range eggs and chickens taste better. I don't think those hormones and drugs they give the birds do us any good

Figure 2
Crop spraying

seen as disrupting the sensitive soil ecosystem and as causing a loss of soil fertility. But by adding organic matter in the form of compost and animal manure, the balance of the soil is not disturbed (Figure 4).

Some critics of modern farming see many of the issues we have looked at as forming part of one basic question: are the high-input (much money spent on equipment, chemicals, building, etc.) high-output systems which involve continued expansion and investment the best way of organizing farming for the future?

Q2
(a) On a copy of Figure 3 complete the blank labels to show both the desired effects and the actual effects (whether intended or not) of agricultural chemicals.
(b) Agricultural chemicals are oil-based. What problems does this pose for the future?
(c) How might the misuse or overuse of chemicals in farming be prevented?
(d) (i) What are the arguments for organic farming?
(ii) Why might farmers be unwilling to move to organic farming?
(iii) What other interests might oppose a change?
(iv) Why do some people buy organically grown produce, even if it is more costly?

● The basis of organic farming is concern about the soil. Bacteria, animal life, plants, minerals, water and gases all interact in the soil ecosystem. The biological energy in the soil can be tapped to fertilize crops and so produce food.

● Plant and animal wastes are returned to the soil. By adding organic matter in the form of compost (plant wastes) and manure, the balance of the soil is not disturbed.

● Chemical fertilizers and pesticides are not used because they disrupt the soil ecosystem.

● Careful cultivation methods, often labour-intensive, are used. Pest control is by natural pesticides and crop rotation.

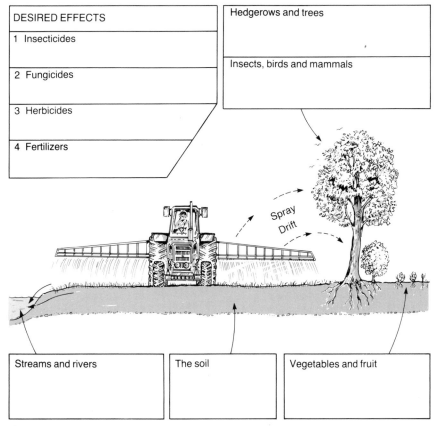

DESIRED EFFECTS		Hedgerows and trees
1 Insecticides		
2 Fungicides		Insects, birds and mammals
3 Herbicides		
4 Fertilizers		

Spray Drift

Streams and rivers	The soil	Vegetables and fruit

Figure 3
Effects of farm chemicals

Figure 4
Organic farming methods

7. Energy

7.1 Energy resources

Sources of energy

Britain is rich in energy resources (Figure 2). For most of its industrial history it has been able to supply its own needs and even export a surplus. About 95 per cent of the energy used is accounted for by three home-produced fuels: coal, oil and natural gas (Figure 3). Oil and, to a lesser extent, coal and gas are also used in the manufacture of chemical products. Known deposits of coal will last 300 years at present rates of use, but Britain's self-sufficiency in oil will soon end.

Manufacturing industry	34%
Lighting and power in houses	28%
Transport	25%
Public services	6%
Other users	7%

Figure 1
How energy is used in Britain

Except for hydro-electricity which accounts for under 2 per cent of production, Britain's electricity is a **secondary** source of energy. It is produced in thermal power stations using coal or oil as a fuel or in nuclear power stations which use uranium. Renewable resources of energy (such as wind power) contribute very little to the country's energy needs; their potential for the future is looked at in Section 7.5.

Changing patterns of energy use

The pattern of energy use in Britain has changed greatly over time, as Figure 3 shows. These

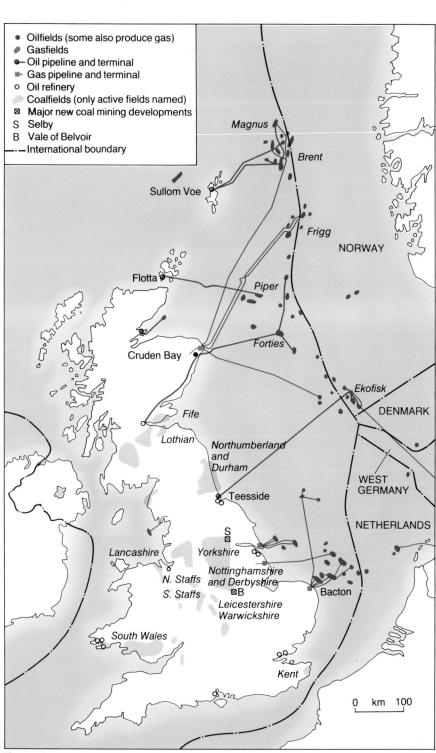

- ● Oilfields (some also produce gas)
- ◗ Gasfields
- ●— Oil pipeline and terminal
- ◗— Gas pipeline and terminal
- ○ Oil refinery
- ◖ Coalfields (only active fields named)
- ⊠ Major new coal mining developments
- S Selby
- B Vale of Belvoir
- —·— International boundary

Magnus
Brent
Sullom Voe
Frigg
NORWAY
Flotta
Piper
Cruden Bay
Forties
Ekofisk
DENMARK
Fife
Lothian
Northumberland and Durham
WEST GERMANY
Teesside
NETHERLANDS
S
⊠
Lancashire
Yorkshire
Nottinghamshire and Derbyshire
Bacton
N. Staffs
S. Staffs
⊠B
Leicestershire Warwickshire
South Wales
Kent

0 km 100

Figure 2
Britain's energy resources

74

changes reflect the development of new sources (such as North Sea gas), changing patterns of demand, technological change and changing price advantages of one fuel over another.

> ## Q1
> **(a)** Using the information in Figure 1, draw a pie graph to show how energy is used in Britain. (3.6° will represent 1%.)
> **(b)** Suggest, giving reasons, how the pattern shown by your graph might differ from the pattern of energy use at the start of the 20th century.

Coal's decline

From about 1950 to the mid 1970s, coal output and consumption declined for the following reasons:

1 Competition came from oil and gas as a fuel for industry and for heating houses and other buildings. Until 1973 oil was a cheaper fuel than coal.
2 From 1967 natural gas replaced gas made from coal.
3 Diesel and electric trains replaced steam trains.
4 Competition came from electricity. Although most electricity is generated in coal-fired power stations, an increasing amount has come from nuclear and oil-fired stations.
5 Oil replaced coal as the major raw material of the chemical industry.

The changing uses of coal are shown in Figure 4. However, a very significant change is the large *increase* in the use of coal for generating electricity. Factories, homes and other users have steadily moved from the direct use of coal to an *indirect* way of using it: electricity.

Oil's rise

Much of the rise in the importance of oil as a source of energy was due to the increasing importance of road transport, which depends on petrol and diesel fuel. This trend, combined with all the reasons for coal's decline listed above, led to oil replacing coal as Britain's main source of energy in 1971.

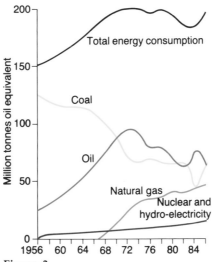

Figure 3
Main fuels' changing shares of the energy consumed in the UK

Figure 4
The changing use of coal

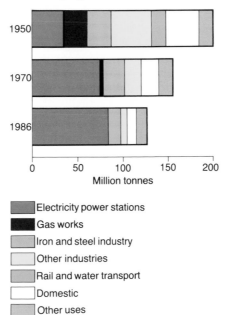

The 1973 and 1979 oil crises

In 1973 the Organization of Petroleum Exporting Countries (OPEC) raised oil prices by about four times. In 1979 the revolution in Iran triggered a second oil supply crisis: oil prices trebled within a year. As a result, the demand for oil fell. Coal became not only cheaper by comparison, but was also seen as a more secure energy source. In Britain the development of North Sea oil after 1975 did not restore oil's competitive edge because it is expensive to produce.

The oil crisis stopped the decline in coal output. However, in the late 1970s the industrial recession began to affect demand for coal. Coal's second largest customer – the steel industry – reduced its use of coal from 25.3 million tonnes in 1970 to 11.6 million tonnes in 1980 because of plant closures and the use of fuel-saving methods. Coal has had to face continued competition from natural gas and nuclear power. Cheap coal imports, the 1984–5 miners' strike and a fall in oil prices in 1986 posed further problems for the coal industry.

> ## Q2
> **(a)** On a large copy of Figure 3, add labels to explain the changing contribution of different fuels to the UK's energy consumption. Some labels will apply to a run of years, for example, 1960–72 – the reasons for coal's declining share; others will apply to one year, for example, the 1973 oil crisis.
> **(b)** Explain how changing oil prices have affected (i) total energy consumption; (ii) oil's share of this total. What major use of oil would it be very difficult for other fuels to replace?

7.2 Coal

Coal was the foundation for Britain's industrial growth. Coal production reached a peak in 1913 when a million miners produced 299 million tonnes. After the First World War the decline in output began, at first because of the loss of export markets and the 1930s industrial depression, later because of competition from other sources of energy.

Figure 1
Coal cutting in the Selby coalfield

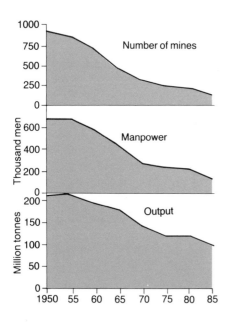

Pit closures and modernization

As coal output declined in the face of competition from other sources of energy in the 1960s and early 1970s, mechanized coal cutting (Figure 1) became widespread and much money was invested in large pits. Also, to make coal competitive, many small mines, where thin and faulted seams made mechanization difficult and costs high, were closed. Figure 2 shows how the number of mines and the size of the labour force were reduced even more quickly than coal output.

Figure 2
Changes in the coal industry

Figure 3
Changing productivity in Britain's mines

OUTPUT PER MANSHIFT, TONNES (UNDERGROUND PRODUCTION)	
1955	1.60
1965	2.35
1975	2.91
1986	4.09

The more hopeful outlook for coal which followed the oil price rise of 1973 slowed down the rate of closures. However, later in the 1970s, the industrial recession and renewed competition from other sources of energy led to a reduced demand for coal. By 1983 huge stocks of coal had built up; production was exceeding demand by about 12 million tonnes a year. The National Coal Board (since renamed British Coal) therefore wished to cut output by closing loss-making pits and concentrate production in large modern mines. These plans involved cutting the workforce from 200 000 to 120 000 over ten years. This crisis in the industry led to the miners' strike of 1984–5. The miners claimed that, besides jobs being lost, the life of old-established communities would be devastated.

Q1
(a) Figure 3 gives figures on productivity in the British coal industry. Give reasons to explain why productivity has risen.
(b) (i) Why is British Coal keen to increase productivity even more?
(ii) Explain how future plans fit in with this aim.
(c) Critics of the government at the time of the miners' strike said that it would cost more money to close some 'uneconomic' pits because of redundancy payments, paying unemployment benefits and other 'social costs', than to keep them open.
(i) What are 'social costs'?
(ii) What are the arguments for the government subsidizing the coal industry? What are the arguments against this?

The changing pattern of coal mining

Figure 4 shows how mining developed in the Northumberland and Durham Coalfield from small surface workings on the exposed coalfield to deep shaft mines on the concealed coalfield. This pattern was also followed in other coalfields. Because of their longer history of mining and more difficult geological conditions, it is the older, exposed coalfields which have been hardest hit by mine closures. On the other hand, the concealed coalfields of Yorkshire and the Midlands with their thick, level seams have seen much new investment. (Figure 2 in Section 7.1 shows the location of coalfields.) The largest new development is the Selby Coalfield (Figure 5) where production began in 1983.

Q2

(a) Look at Figure 4. Study the cross-section and explain the changing pattern of mining on the Northumberland and Durham coalfield.
(b) Describe how the geological conditions and the layout of the Selby mines make for efficient mining and movement of coal.

Have the older coalfields a future?

Although many mines have closed in the older coalfield, some still have a part to play in future plans. This is because:

1 Some areas produce special high-quality coals, for example, smokeless anthracite in South Wales.

2 Coal is expensive to transport and the older coalfields can often supply local markets more cheaply than can distant fields.
3 In places, geological conditions make low-cost production possible, for example, at the proposed Margam pit in South Wales.

Opencast mining

Not all coal is mined underground. Opencast pits produce 14 million tonnes a year (at a profit of £244 million in 1987). Opencast mining takes place down to depths of about 200 metres and although huge amounts of material covering the coal have to be moved, the earth-moving machinery can do the task with only a small labour force. The expansion of opencast mining is restricted because of its major impact on the landscape.

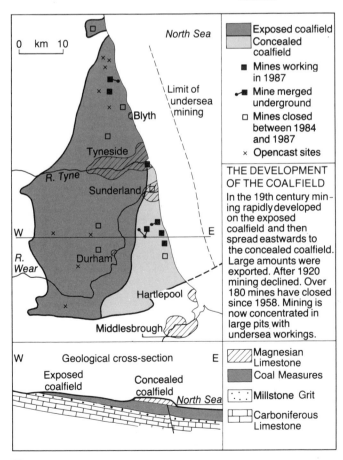

Figure 4
The Northumberland and Durham Coalfield

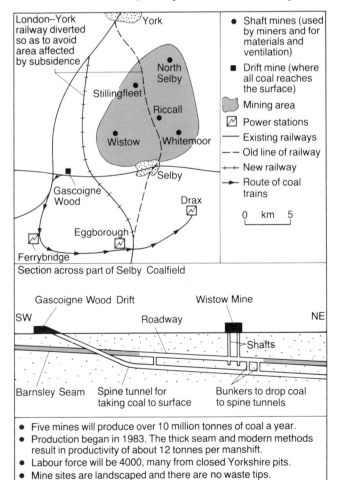

Figure 5
Selby Coalfield

77

7.3 Oil and natural gas

Until the development of North Sea oil, Britain's rapidly rising demand for oil was met almost entirely by imported oil, mainly from the Middle East. In 1975 the first oil from the North Sea was brought ashore and by 1980 production was enough to meet all the country's needs (Figure 1). North Sea gas was first brought ashore in 1967 and over the next few years replaced gas made from coal.

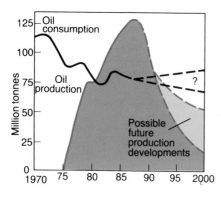

Figure 1
Oil production and consumption in the UK

North Sea oil and gas

Figure 2 shows the geological structures in which oil and gas are trapped. As the map in Section 7.1, Figure 2 shows, the oil fields are found in the central and northern parts of the North Sea. The oil is brought ashore by pipelines or by tanker. The largest of the coastal terminals is at Sullom Voe in the Shetland Islands (Figure 3). Until 1977 all gas production was from the southern part of the North Sea. Since then gas has been extracted from the same areas as the oilfields further north. The gas is piped to coastal terminals where impurities are removed and is then fed into a nationwide grid of pipelines.

Problems of development

The development of the North Sea oil fields is a very expensive operation. Very large sums of money are needed to explore for oil, make test drills and to build production platforms and pipe lines before any oil is extracted. Development is put in the hands of large oil companies who lease areas to explore and develop from the government. The government taxes the oil produced. Other problems of development include:

1 Drilling rigs and production platforms have to operate in water up to 200 metres deep. Severe storms with high winds and 30 metre waves are a major hazard. Bad weather can hold up development and increase costs.
2 As production is often far from land, transport of men and materials is expensive and sometimes hazardous.

Q1
(a) Refer to Figure 1. (i) Describe and suggest reasons for the changes in oil consumption. (ii) Explain why it is difficult to predict the extent to which North Sea oil will meet Britain's future needs.
(b) Explain why the government has put oil development into the hands of large international oil companies.

Effects of development

The main effect of North Sea oil is that Britain no longer has to rely on imported oil. Saving on import spending has helped Britain's **balance of payments** (the balance between the value of exports and the value of imports).

Besides creating jobs on the oil and gas rigs, the development of North Sea oil and gas has created many jobs on land, especially in parts of Scotland and North-East England where unemployment has traditionally been high. The impact has been particularly great at the supply bases and at the oil and gas terminals. Aberdeen is the largest supply base; the harbour has had to be expanded and altered, facilities built for supply and servicing firms and the airport greatly expanded. The Shetland Islands have been particularly affected. Figure 3 gives details of the oil industry's impact on the Islands. The need for oil rigs and production platforms has benefitted some traditional ship building centres such as Clydeside. New construction yards were developed on the coast of northern Scotland (see Section 11.4).

Figure 2
How oil and natural gas occurs in the Magnus Oilfield

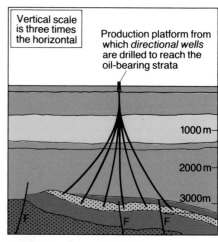

Vertical scale is three times the horizontal

Production platform from which *directional wells* are drilled to reach the oil-bearing strata

1000 m
2000 m
3000 m

Oil — Impermeable rocks
— Magnus Sandstone
— Impermeable clay

/F Geological fault

A combination of faulting and folding forms the geological structure which traps the oil in the porous sandstone. The impermeable rocks above the sandstone act as a caprock, preventing the oil from escaping.

The impact of Sullom Voe Oil Terminal

● The terminal is Europe's largest. In 1980 7 000 people were working on its construction. Over 6 000 of the workforce were from outside the Shetlands – a major upheaval for islands with a population of only about 20 000. The permanent workforce of the terminal is about 650.

● Besides the terminal, shore base facilities supplying the oil rigs provide employment opportunities. Before North Sea oil many people had to leave the islands for work.

● Shetland's airport at Sumburgh was expanded.

● Rates paid by the oil terminal have enabled the Shetland Islands council to invest in new facilities and improved services for the islanders.

● The oil terminal and the oil tankers using it pose a pollution threat to an area with rich bird and marine life. Some damage has occurred despite the many precautions which have been taken.

Figure 3
Sullom Voe Oil Terminal, Shetland Islands

Q2
(a) Suggest why conservationists have opposed many of the oil industry's onshore developments, such as the Sullom Voe terminal.
(b) Explain why oil rig and production platform construction yards provide only short-term employment opportunities.

Britain's oil refineries were built before North Sea oil was developed. They were located by deep water estuaries which could take supertankers. Their distribution in Britain is shown in Figure 2 in Section 7.1.

Q3
(a) Why is Britain both an oil exporter and importer?
(b) Since the development of North Sea oil why does a location by a deep-water estuary remain suitable for an oil refinery?

taken place on land over a wide area of southern England where the Wytch Farm oil field in Dorset already produces one million tonnes a year.

Figure 4
Brent C oil and gas production platform in rough seas

Oil refining and the market for oil

Crude oil needs to be refined into usable products. The production of the oil refineries needs to match as closely as possible the pattern of demand for the different products. North Sea oil is a relatively light crude oil and the refining processes produce more light oil products (such as petrol) than the country needs, but less heavy oil products (such as fuel oil). Because of this, about half the North Sea crude oil is exported and heavy crude oils from the Middle East are imported to meet Britain's demand for heavy oil products.

The future for oil and gas

Oil and gas reserves are much less than those of coal. After 1990 an increasing amount of oil will have to come from areas other than the North Sea. By 2020 North Sea oil and gas may have run out. Further exploration for oil and gas has taken place to the west of the Shetland Islands – where sea and weather conditions are even more difficult – and in the Irish Sea. Exploration has also

7.4 Electricity

Originally, each town in Britain had its own small power station to supply local needs. Large-scale generation of electricity, long-distance transmission and a rising demand for electricity, led to the building of large power stations supplying electricity to a high voltage national supply grid. In England and Wales, two companies, National Power and PowerGen, generate electricity and transmit it to twelve Area Electricity Boards who distribute and sell it to the customers. In Scotland, the North of Scotland Hydro-Electric Board and the South of Scotland Electricity Board both generate and distribute electricity.

Coal-fired power stations

Most of Britain's electricity is generated using coal as a fuel, as Figure 1 shows. The process requires huge quantities of

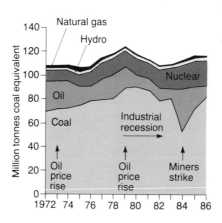

Figure 1
The changing importance of different electricity generation methods

cooling water: 2 000 million litres an hour in the largest power stations. The location of coal-fired power stations (Figure 2) therefore reflects the availability of coal and cooling water, together with the location of the main urban areas

and the availability of large flat sites. The largest group of power stations is in the Trent Valley and West Yorkshire. Low-cost coal is obtained locally and cooling water comes from the rivers Trent, Aire and Calder. The river flood plains provide large flat sites (Figure 3).

Oil-fired power stations

Cheap oil in the 1960s and early 1970s led to the construction of oil-fired power stations, usually close to oil refineries. Most are in the south where transport costs make coal more expensive (Figure 2). By 1972 almost 30 per cent of the fuel used in thermal power stations was oil. Oil price rises led to several stations being converted to coal-firing while others now only generate to meet peak demands.

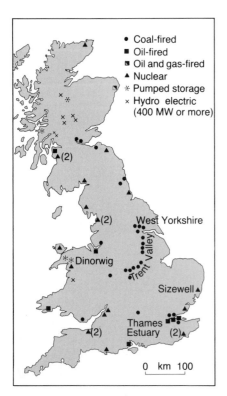

Figure 2
Location of electricity power stations

Figure 3
Drax power station, Yorkshire

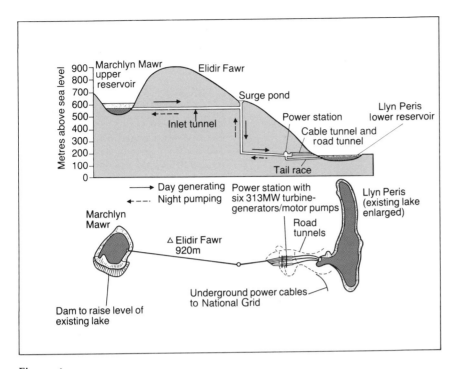

Figure 4
Dinorwig pumped storage scheme, North Wales

Hydro-electricity

Less than 2 per cent of Britain's electricity is produced in hydro-electric power stations. This is because there are few suitable sites for dams and reservoirs and water catchment areas are too small to produce the large flows of water which are needed for large schemes. The Scottish Highlands are the main area of production but all the HEP stations in this area together produce less electricity than Drax coal-fired station.

Four particularly important HEP stations are the pumped-storage schemes. At night these power stations use electricity from the National Grid to pump water to an upper reservoir. During the day this water is used to generate electricity to meet peak periods of demand. Figure 4 gives details of the largest of these schemes: the 1800MW Dinorwig power station.

Nuclear power

Nuclear power accounted for 13 per cent of the electricity generated in Britain in 1985. The principle of nuclear power is the splitting or **fission** of atoms of uranium. The energy produced is used to generate electricity in the same way as in coal or oil-fired stations (Figure 5). The older nuclear power stations built in the 1960s have Magnox reactors which use gas (CO_2) as a coolant. Site requirements were the availability of large amounts of cooling water, stable geological conditions (for firm foundations) and nearness to the already existing National Grid. All were built away from built-up areas because of the dangers of radioactivity in the event of an accident. The second generation nuclear stations have Advanced Gas-Cooled Reactors (AGRs). Considerable delays occurred in completing several of the AGR stations.

In December 1979, the government announced a plan for ten more nuclear power stations. It was decided that these would be Pressurized Water Reactors (PWRs) which would be cheaper to build than AGRs. PWRs use water under pressure as a coolant. Sizewell in Suffolk was selected as the first site for a PWR station. A long public enquiry was held to consider the plans for Sizewell. Although much opposition was voiced, the enquiry's report, issued in early 1987, recommended that the PWR station should be built.

Figure 5
Pressurized Water Reactor

1 Core containing uranium fuel rods
2 Steel pressure vessel
3 Concrete shield
4 Fuel rod handling equipment
5 Boiler producing steam
6 Turbine
7 Generator
8 Condenser cooling water

☐ Steam

☐ Water

☐ Coolant (water under high pressure)

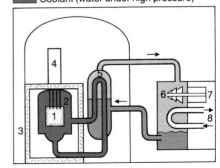

7.5 Energy for the future

To provide for Britain's future energy needs, several important questions need to be considered:

1 What will the future demand for energy be?
2 Should greater emphasis be placed on coal?
3 How should the relatively limited reserves of oil and gas be best used?
4 Does nuclear energy pose an unacceptable risk or is it an important source of cheap energy for the future?
5 Should more money be spent on energy conservation?
6 Should greater efforts be made into researching alternative sources of energy?

We have already looked at the future prospects for coal and oil, so this section will concentrate on the other major energy issues.

Q1

(a) Using examples to illustrate your answer, explain how the answer to any one of the above questions has a bearing on the answers to others.
(b) Figure 1 shows the costs of different types of energy in the late 1980s.

(i) Suggest why the diagram shows costs of each type of energy as broad bands rather than a precise figure.
(ii) Past experience has shown that it is difficult to forecast future energy costs. Explain this statement, quoting examples (see Section 7.1).
(iii) In planning future energy supplies, why is cost not the only factor to consider? What other factors should be considered?

The nuclear debate

When Britain's first experimental nuclear power station was opened at Calder Hall, Cumbria in 1956, nuclear power was seen as being a major source of cheap energy for the future. The government (1989) still claims that nuclear energy is cheap and reliable and is the best way to fill the anticipated 'energy gap' at the end of the century when oil and gas reserves have been reduced.

However, opposition to nuclear power has grown, largely on the grounds that the risks involved, even if slight, are unacceptable. The radiation leak at Three Mile Island PWR in the USA in 1979 which led to thousands of people being evacuated from the surrounding area and the Chernobyl disaster in the USSR in 1986 have led to the growth of opposition. There is also the major problem of how to dispose of radioactive waste. The used fuel rods from the reactors are at first stored in cooling ponds and then taken by rail (Figure 2) to a reprocessing plant at Sellafield in Cumbria. Some uranium remaining in the fuel rods is recovered and the waste is stored. However, no long-term solution to storing this waste has yet been worked out.

Figure 3 shows the arguments for and against nuclear energy. Notice that besides the main issue of safety, there is disagreement over the relative costs of nuclear and coal-generated electricity. Also involved in the debate are the issues of whether there will be an 'energy gap' or not in the 1990s and the future roles of coal, oil and alternative sources of energy.

Two important decisions concerning nuclear energy face the government. The first is whether to complete the plan for ten PWR power stations. The second is whether research into

Figure 1
Energy costs

Figure 2
A nuclear waste train

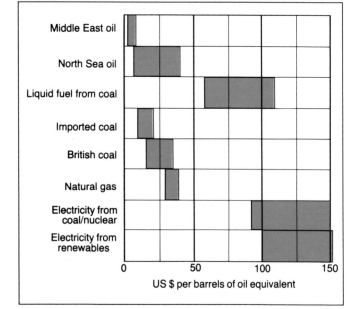

US $ per barrels of oil equivalent

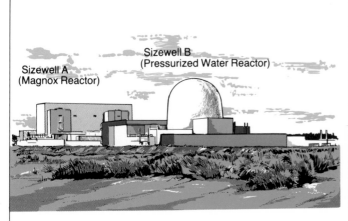

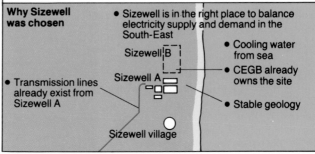

After a public enquiry lasting for almost a year, the government gave consent for the building of Sizewell B, Britain's first Pressurized Water Reactor (PWR) nuclear power station in March 1987. Full output electricity is planned for mid-1994.

Why Sizewell was chosen

- Sizewell is in the right place to balance electricity supply and demand in the South-East
- Cooling water from sea
- CEGB already owns the site
- Transmission lines already exist from Sizewell A
- Stable geology

Sizewell B
Sizewell A
Sizewell village

The case for nuclear energy

1 Increased demand for energy combined with falling oil and gas supplies will lead to an 'energy gap'. Nuclear energy is needed to fill this gap; new alternative sources of energy are too costly.
2 More nuclear power stations will end an overdependence on coal.
3 The PWR power stations produce electricity at a lower cost than coal, oil or other nuclear stations.
4 Many safety features make the risks of accidents minimal.
5 PWR technology developed in the USA is being transferred to the UK and will enable British companies to compete in the world nuclear energy market. Many jobs will be created.
6 One tonne of uranium fuel used in a nuclear reactor can produce as much electricity as 25000 tonnes of coal.
7 Nuclear waste is produced in small amounts and can be stored safely underground.

The case against nuclear energy

1 The 'energy gap' will not occur; future demands for energy have been overestimated. Future energy needs should be met by existing power stations and new alternative sources of energy.
2 Nuclear power stations are very costly to design and build, and to repair. The costs are not worked out correctly: for example, major costs of research and development are not included.
3 The dangers of nuclear power are too great. The nuclear industry has a long record of 'minor' accidents. The effects of small doses of radiation take many years to become evident. Only one major accident would kill many and permanently damage an area.
4 The problems of waste disposal have not been solved.
5 Most proposed nuclear sites are in rural locations; valued natural environments would be damaged.
6 Plutonium, extracted from nuclear fuel waste, is used to make nuclear weapons.

fast-breeder reactors should continue or not. These reactors 'breed' more fuel than they use. However, the fuel produced, plutonium 239, is especially dangerous and is also used in nuclear weapons. Construction costs of such reactors would be very high.

Q2
(a) Study Figure 3. Suppose that a public enquiry over the building of a second PWR power station at Sizewell were to be held. Both National Power and local opposition groups are mounting publicity campaigns in the local area before the enquiry starts. Design leaflets to put forward the cases of both sides.

(b) The plan for ten PWR power stations was announced in 1979. What developments have since taken place concerning (i) Britain's energy demands and (ii) the safety record of nuclear energy?

Conserving energy

The conservation of energy resources is a vital part of planning for future energy needs. It has been estimated that over 30 per cent of heat loss from Britain's homes could be prevented by improved insulation and devices to recover waste heat, such as heat pumps.

In industry, the use of already developed methods could save considerable amounts of energy.

Figure 3
Sizewell B and the nuclear debate

Figure 4
These flats in Sheffield are heated with hot water produced in the refuse incineration plant in the background

These would involve new manufacturing processes, insulation, recovering waste heat and more sensitive control systems. Using by-products of one process for making other products and recycling waste materials also contribute to energy saving in industry.

In electricity power stations, only about one-third of the energy used to raise steam for the turbines is converted into electricity. The remainder is waste heat discharged into the air, rivers and the sea. Hot water from power stations has been used to a very limited extent for heating buildings and greenhouses. Specially designed combined heat and power (CHP) stations can convert as much as

Figure 5
Some ways to save energy

The Association for the Conservation of Energy compared Britain's efforts at energy conservation with that of other EEC countries and recommended the following:

● Building regulations should have higher standards of insulation and other energy-saving measures. To encourage existing houses to be brought up to building regulations standards, an energy certificate scheme should be introduced (as in Denmark).

● A homes insulation campaign, backed by government grants and covering homes with existing, but limited, insulation (as in Holland).

● Allowances against income tax for energy-saving measures (as in France).

● Compulsory labelling of domestic appliances such as washing machines to detail the amount of energy they use (as in Italy and Holland).

● Low interest loans for energy-saving measures made in factories and other business premises (as in France, West Germany and Italy).

Figure 6
This wind generator in the Orkney Islands produces 3 megawatts of electricity. Together with a 250 kilowatt generator it supplies about a seventh of Orkney's electricity

85 per cent of the fuel burnt into usable energy. However, in Britain only a few mini-CHP stations (using natural gas as a fuel) have been built to heat and light large building complexes).

Q3
(a) In Britain, the government has promoted 'Save It' and 'Monergy' campaigns. How might these help to save energy? Is a save energy campaign more effective in the home or in factories, schools and offices? (Consider who uses and who pays for the energy.)
(b) Figure 5 shows some recommendations for energy saving made by the Association for the Conservation of Energy. How might each of these help to save energy?

Alternative sources of energy

There has been research into alternative, renewable sources of energy because of rising energy costs, the limited reserves of some fossil fuels, doubts over the safety of nuclear energy and air pollution caused by the burning of fossil fuels. One renewable source is already well-established: hydro-electricity. Other renewable sources are wave power, wind power, solar energy, tidal energy and geothermal energy.

● **Wave power** appears to be the least promising of the alternatives as expensive installations are needed to produce a limited power output; the installations are also very vulnerable to storm damage.

● **Wind power** (Figure 6) although depending on unreliable weather conditions, can produce electricity as cheaply as conventional methods and the prototype generators in the Orkney Islands already supply consumers. However, there remains the question of whether huge 'wind-farms' of several hundred windmills would be acceptable on scenic coastlines.

● **Solar energy** (Figure 7) is also dependent on the weather, but other countries at a relatively northerly latitude, for example, Sweden and Japan, have

Figure 7
This house in Milton Keynes has been designed to make use of solar energy. Living areas, including a conservatory, face south. Electricity is partly supplied by photovoltaic cells in the conservatory roof

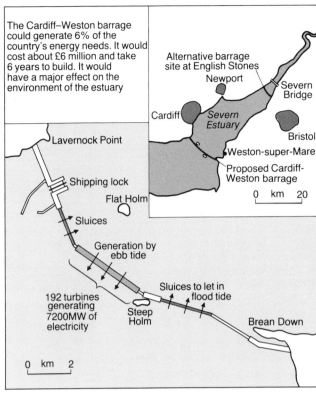

The Cardiff–Weston barrage could generate 6% of the country's energy needs. It would cost about £6 million and take 6 years to build. It would have a major effect on the environment of the estuary

Figure 8
Proposals for a Severn Barrage to generate electricity by tidal power

Figure 9
Geothermal power – from hot rocks beneath Cornwall

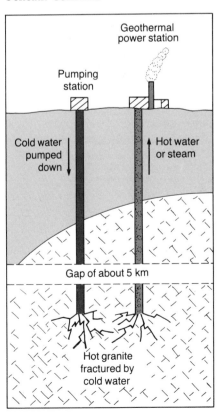

pressed ahead with solar district heating schemes and other installations.

● Generating electricity by harnessing the rise and fall of the **tides** (Figure 8) could make a large contribution to Britain's energy needs. Proposals have been made to build barrages for electricity generation by the tides across the Severn and Mersey estuaries. The Rance scheme in northern France already operates successfully. The main disadvantages are high construction costs and the impact on the estuaries' environment.

● Tapping heat in the lower layers of the earth's crust, **geothermal** heat (Figure 9), is another alternative, with the granite rocks of Cornwall appearing to offer the greatest potential.

The Atomic Energy Authority spends about fifteen times more money on nuclear energy research than the government invests in research and development into all forms of alternative energy. Much more research is needed into the alternatives if they are to make a

large contribution to Britain's energy needs in the 21st century. In the short-term, the greatest use of alternatives such as wind power and solar energy is likely to be on a local scale such as producing electricity on offshore islands or to supplement existing energy sources, for example, in heating homes.

Q4
(a) Why is it important to investigate alternative sources of energy?
(b) Offshore islands usually rely on electricity produced by small diesel generators. Why are wind turbines a good alternative for such places?
(c) Refer to Figure 8. List the gains and losses which would result from building a barrage across the Severn Estuary.
(d) Solar energy can be used to supplement the use of electricity and gas in the home. Explain the meaning of this statement.

8. Manufacturing industry

8.1 Industrial patterns

The distribution of manufacturing industry

Figure 1 shows the main industrial regions of Britain. Some are long-established; others are relatively new. Most of the older industrial regions are on the coalfields. They grew up in the late 18th and 19th centuries when manufacturing depended on coal for steam power. Many of these coalfield-based regions are declining in importance. Several specialize in particular industries, although less so than in the past, as a variety of new industries has developed in the place of old, declining activities. This process is known as **industrial diversification**.

Industry has also concentrated in urban areas away from the coalfields. London is the largest such concentration with its large local market, excellent road and rail links and port facilities. Another reason why industry clusters together is that factories benefit from being near each other – not just to reduce transport costs of items moving from one factory to another – but for reasons such as the ease of making contacts between managers and the need to be near specialist services.

An important feature of the distribution of industry (not shown in Figure 1) is that manufacturing is becoming increasingly important in rural areas and in small towns.

Industrial companies

The patterns of some major British industries – the iron and

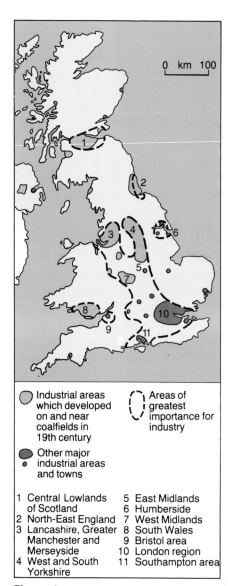

Figure 1
Industrial regions

Legend:
- Industrial areas which developed on and near coalfields in 19th century
- Other major industrial areas and towns
- Areas of greatest importance for industry

1 Central Lowlands of Scotland
2 North-East England
3 Lancashire, Greater Manchester and Merseyside
4 West and South Yorkshire
5 East Midlands
6 Humberside
7 West Midlands
8 South Wales
9 Bristol area
10 London region
11 Southampton area

steel industry, the motor industry and high technology industry – are studied later in this chapter. The country's major industrial companies are also responsible for important industrial patterns which help to shape the national map in Figure 1. Few industrial companies have only one factory; most have several, often making different products. Factories

within a company are often linked: one factory produces parts for another. Some companies are involved in both manufacturing and providing services.

Figure 2 gives details of the geography of two contrasting companies. Premier Brands produces a variety of food products at several different locations. Although linked together for administration, distribution and marketing, the different factories operate as largely separate units. The scattered distribution of factories largely reflects the way the company has grown as a result of mergers and take-overs of smaller firms. The Ford Motor Company's factories are very closely linked together, with complex flows of components and sub-assemblies (large units of vehicles such as engines) between them. There are also links with Ford's factories elsewhere in Europe.

Q1
Explain why the factories of some companies are much more closely linked to each other than those of other companies. (Consider the contrasting examples of Premier Brands and Ford.)

Multinational companies

The Ford Motor Company is a large multinational company. Such a company begins operations in one country (in Ford's case, USA) and then develops factories in other countries. A large and increasing

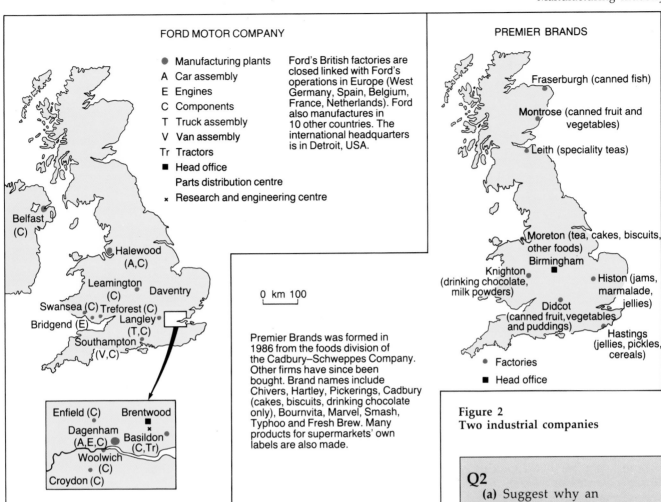

FORD MOTOR COMPANY

- Manufacturing plants
- A Car assembly
- E Engines
- C Components
- T Truck assembly
- V Van assembly
- Tr Tractors
- ■ Head office
- Parts distribution centre
- × Research and engineering centre

Ford's British factories are closed linked with Ford's operations in Europe (West Germany, Spain, Belgium, France, Netherlands). Ford also manufactures in 10 other countries. The international headquarters is in Detroit, USA.

Belfast (C)
Halewood (A,C)
Leamington (C)   Daventry
Swansea (C)   Treforest (C)
Bridgend (E)   Langley (T,C)
Southampton (V,C)

Enfield (C)   Brentwood
Dagenham (A,E,C)   Basildon (C,Tr)
Woolwich (C)
Croydon (C)

0 km 100

Premier Brands was formed in 1986 from the foods division of the Cadbury–Schweppes Company. Other firms have since been bought. Brand names include Chivers, Hartley, Pickerings, Cadbury (cakes, biscuits, drinking chocolate only), Bournvita, Marvel, Smash, Typhoo and Fresh Brew. Many products for supermarkets' own labels are also made.

PREMIER BRANDS

Fraserburgh (canned fish)
Montrose (canned fruit and vegetables)
Leith (speciality teas)
Moreton (tea, cakes, biscuits, other foods)
Birmingham
Knighton (drinking chocolate, milk powders)
Histon (jams, marmalade, jellies)
Didcot (canned fruit, vegetables and puddings)
Hastings (jellies, pickles, cereals)

- Factories
- ■ Head office

Figure 2
Two industrial companies

proportion of Britain's manufacturing is in the hands of these companies; Figure 3 lists some important examples. Decisions are therefore taken abroad about the location of many of Britain's factories, as are decisions on whether to close down or keep open factories.

Figure 3
Some of the largest multinational companies in the UK

There are British multinational companies as well, with manufacturing plants throughout the world (Figure 4). Their decisions can attract just as much controversy, as when, for example, production is moved from a British to a foreign factory.

Figure 4
Lucas; a British company with manufacturing plants abroad

Q2
(a) Suggest why an increasing proportion of manufacturing, both in Britain and other countries, is in the hands of large multinational companies.
(b) Why is Britain keen to attract investment from foreign companies? What are the risks?
(c) Why do large British companies establish factories abroad? What gains are there for Britain? What losses are there?

Company	Country
Ford	USA
Philips	Netherlands
Vauxhall	USA
Michelin	France
IBM	USA
Kodak	USA
CIBA-Geigy	Switzerland
Massey-Ferguson	Canada
Peugeot-Talbot	France
Texaco	USA

Three divisions:
Lucas Aerospace (aerospace systems and components)
Lucas Automotive (vehicle electrical and electronic components)
Lucas Industrial (mainly other electronic systems, for example, ships' navigation systems)

22 subsidiary companies in UK (1986 sales £930 million)
45 subsidiary companies abroad (1986 sales £741 million)

Manufacturing plants in UK, Argentina, Australia, Belgium, Brazil, Canada, France, Greece, India, Italy, Japan, Korea, Malaysia, Mexico, New Zealand, Pakistan, Portugal, South Africa, Spain, USA, West Germany and Zimbabwe

8.2 The location of industry

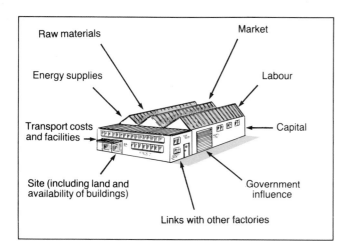

Figure 1
Factors influencing the location of industry

Figure 2
Alcan aluminium smelter with its own power station receiving coal by conveyor belt from Lynemouth colliery

Location factors

Most companies aim to locate their factories where costs of raw materials, labour, energy, land and transport can be kept to a minimum: the **least-cost location**. However, yesterday's least-cost location may not be today's: many locations reflect past conditions. Also, there are factors at work other than economic ones. Figure 1 shows in diagrammatic form the main factors which have influenced the location of Britain's industry. They are not necessarily separate from each other; for example, transport costs are involved in bringing in raw materials and sending out products. Any explanation of the location of a particular factory is likely to be complicated, with several factors exerting a pull or influence.

The Lynemouth aluminium smelter

Figure 2 shows the Alcan aluminium smelter at Lynemouth in Northumberland, opened in 1972. It is a good example of how a number of location factors influence decisions on where to build a factory. Figure 3 explains why Alcan chose Lynemouth for its smelter. Cheap energy supplies was the most important factor, but government influence, transport facilities, and labour all played a part in the final decision. Alcan has over twenty fabricating plants in Britain which manufacture aluminium into sheets, cooking foil, window frames and other products. Their location had no influence on the location of the smelter because the transport of aluminium products is twice as expensive as the transport of aluminium ingots.

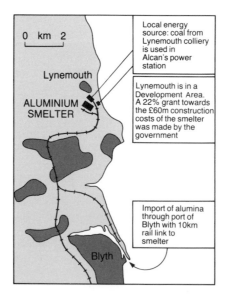

Local energy source: coal from Lynemouth colliery is used in Alcan's power station

Lynemouth is in a Development Area. A 22% grant towards the £60m construction costs of the smelter was made by the government

Import of alumina through port of Blyth with 10km rail link to smelter

Figure 3
Factors influencing the location of Lynemouth aluminium smelter

Q1
(a) Write an explanation of why Lynemouth was chosen as a location for an aluminium smelter.
(b) Suggest what factors might influence the location of aluminium fabricating plants.

Changing locations: Rochdale and Swindon

A comparison of two towns shows how the importance of different location factors changes over time. Rochdale (Figure 4) grew rapidly in the last century as a centre of the cotton industry. Its coalfield location was a major factor in its development as the cotton mills depended on coal for steam power. Mills and other factories were built beside canals, the only means of transporting coal and bulky raw materials cheaply. The cotton industry remains in Rochdale, but on a much smaller scale than in the past. Old industrial buildings by the canals remain although water transport is no longer used. The cost of moving is greater than the inconvenience of an old building on a cramped site. This situation is known as **industrial inertia**.

Rochdale also has modern industries, as Figure 4 shows. Some are located in former mills, but most are in newer buildings or industrial estates with good road access. They tend to produce complex products, using a wide variety of components and materials. Such 'footloose' firms have located in Rochdale for a variety of reasons including the availability of suitable premises at a reasonable cost or rent, personal links that managers have with the town, good road links, the availability of government aid and links with existing industries in the area.

Swindon (Figure 5) also grew up as an industrial town during the last century. In the 1880s the Great Western Railway chose Swindon as the location for its railway workshops as the town occupied a central position within its network. Over recent years, employment in railway engineering declined and in 1986 the workshops were closed. Yet Swindon today is one of Britain's most successful industrial towns, its population doubling since 1945. Early post-war growth was based on industries making car components, electrical goods and other engineering products. More recently, Swindon has attracted much high technology industry, including electronics and pharmaceuticals, and has become a major distribution centre. Several multinational companies, for example, Fuji and Honda, have chosen Swindon as their British base. The following factors have contributed to Swindon's success in attracting modern industry:

- Its excellent position on the M4 motorway and a major inter-city railway line. It is one hour from London airport.

- An attractive environment with modern industrial estates and pleasant surrounding countryside.

- Swindon is an Expanded Town so new industrial estates have been built. Factory rents and rates are lower than in Greater London.

- Former workers in railway engineering provided a pool of skilled labour.

Q2
(a) Explain why Rochdale became an important industrial town in the 19th century.
(b) Describe the types of site on which industry developed in Rochdale in (i) the 19th century; (ii) since 1945.
(c) Why has Swindon been more successful than Rochdale in attracting modern industry?

Figure 4
Industry in Rochdale

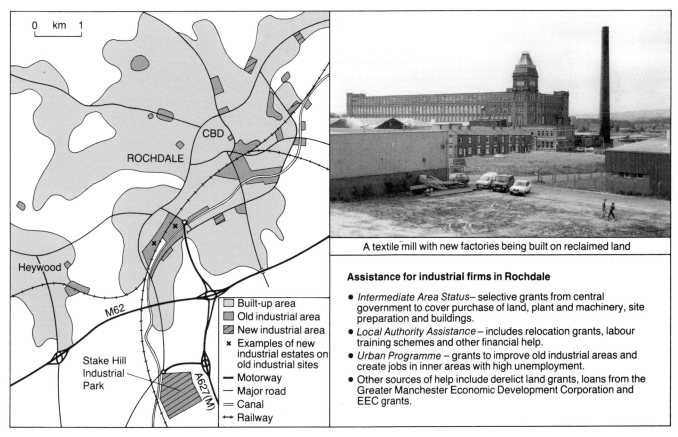

A textile mill with new factories being built on reclaimed land

Assistance for industrial firms in Rochdale

- *Intermediate Area Status* – selective grants from central government to cover purchase of land, plant and machinery, site preparation and buildings.
- *Local Authority Assistance* – includes relocation grants, labour training schemes and other financial help.
- *Urban Programme* – grants to improve old industrial areas and create jobs in inner areas with high unemployment.
- Other sources of help include derelict land grants, loans from the Greater Manchester Economic Development Corporation and EEC grants.

Built-up area
Old industrial area
New industrial area
× Examples of new industrial estates on old industrial sites
━ Motorway
— Major road
= Canal
↔ Railway

Choosing a location for a factory

Making decisions

When a company decides where to locate a new factory, the site where costs are least and profits greatest may not necessarily be the one chosen. Managers may have incomplete or inaccurate information about the sites they are considering, especially in areas of which they have little personal knowledge. Places may develop bad or good reputations, only partly based on fact, which will colour people's views of them.

Q3

(a) Comment on the cartoon in Figure 6 which shows an American industrialist considering locating in Scotland.
(b) Draw a similar cartoon to show the thoughts of a London-based manager with mixed feelings about locating a new factory in the north of England.

New companies

When a new company, entering manufacturing for the first time, starts up, its activities are usually on a very small scale. Many new small companies are started by people who have been working in the same or a related industry. They will tend to look for a site in the area in which they already live and possibly have business contacts. Small 'starter factories' have been built in many areas to attract new companies (Figure 7).

A few of these small firms may grow into the large companies of the future. Many explanations of why a factory is to be found in an unexpected location involve the initiative of an individual who started up a business on a small scale many years ago.

Moving factories

Sometimes a factory is closed down and production moved to a

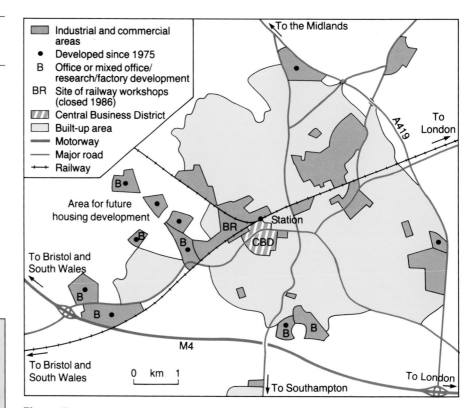

Figure 5
Industrial areas in Swindon

new site elsewhere. The old site may have no room for expansion and buildings may be outdated. Most moves are over short distances, for example, from inner city areas to new industrial estates on the edge of cities, because small companies in particular wish to maintain existing links, contacts and workforce. Some moves may be to a different region, usually where government financial help is available. Section 8.4 takes a closer look at such moves.

Decisions by multiplant companies

Most new factories are built by large companies, who already have a number of manufacturing centres. If a new factory makes components for an existing factory, transport links with the existing plant are an important consideration. The location of the Ford factories in Britain (Section 8.1) is an example of such thinking. Some branch factories are set up to supply a particular region with the same product already being made in existing

Figure 6
An industrial location decision

Figure 7
'Starter' factories

factories. For example, the large bread-making companies aim to have a bakery supplying each major urban area.

Figure 8 is a 'model' of where large multiplant companies are likely to locate their different operations. Notice how these different activities are located in quite different areas. The facts support this model: over 90 per cent of Britain's large companies (those employing over 30 000) have their headquarters in London.

Decisions by multinational companies

In Section 8.1 we saw that multinational companies own a large and increasing part of British industry. When a foreign company locates a new factory in Britain, several important factors are at work:

● The choice of location may be between Britain and another country. If a company wishes to build a large plant employing many people it is in a very strong bargaining position in obtaining special financial help from the government.

● American companies, in particular, look for attractive surroundings in which to locate (and in which their American managers will have to live). Southern England and central Scotland have proved very attractive to such companies.

● Nearness to an international airport is considered to be important by many American managers.

● If the first foreign companies to locate in a particular region are successful, others from the same country may follow. This has been the case with Japanese companies in Wales.

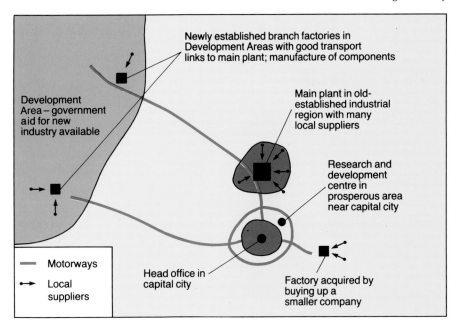

Figure 8
The location of a multiplant company's factories

Figure 9
Factors to be considered when location decisions are made

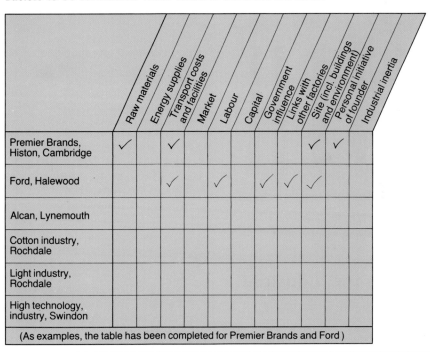

(As examples, the table has been completed for Premier Brands and Ford)

Q4

(a) Figure 9 lists several industrial location decisions which have been referred to between pages 86 and 91. On a copy of the table, for each decision, put ticks against the location factors which apply.
(b) What advantages has South-East England when decisions are taken by (i) the London-based directors of multiplant companies; (ii) the directors of American companies?
(c) If a multiplant company has to cut back production, which locations are most at risk? Explain your answer.

8.3 Industrial decline and change

In the late 1970s British manufacturing industry was hit by recession. Many companies were forced to cut production, shed labour and make major changes. Some were forced to close down. Industrial decline continued into the early 1980s and unemployment rose rapidly. The graphs in Figure 2 show how employment in both the **Primary** and **Secondary** (manufacturing) sectors of the economy have declined in recent years while employment in the **Tertiary** sector (services) has risen.

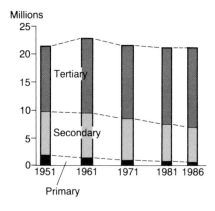

Figure 2
Britain's changing employment structure

Reasons for industrial decline

The reasons for the decline of Britain's manufacturing industry are complex. Those which apply to one industry may not apply to another. Some of the major factors which have been suggested are as follows:

● Competition from countries which were able to produce goods that were cheaper, more reliable or technically more advanced than British products.

Figure 1
Press headlines from the late 1970s and early 1980s

● Production costs have been high in many industries because of overmanning and the use of outdated and inefficient equipment.

● Poor industrial relations between management and labour, leading to wage disputes, arguments over working practices and a general failure to work together.

● The worldwide industrial recession of the late 1970s and early 1980s led to a reduced demand for industrial products throughout the world.

Q1
Figure 3 shows how a number of these factors combined together in the decline of the ship building industry in North-East England.
(a) Give reasons for the decline of the ship building industry.
(b) Suggest why the shipyards on Wearside survived longer than most of those on Tyneside.
(c) Why does the ship building industry still face a very uncertain future?

Figure 3
The decline of the ship building industry

	Percentage of world's ships built in Uk	UK employment in shipbuilding and marine engineering
1955	27	300 000
1985	3	90 000

REASONS FOR DECLINE
1 Severe competition from overseas especially Japan and, more recently South Korea
2 Failure to invest in modern methods such as undercover yards and automatic welding machinery
3 Many labour disputes
4 Slowness to adapt to changing demands
5 Since the mid-1970s world seaborne trade has declined, resulting in a fall in orders for new ships

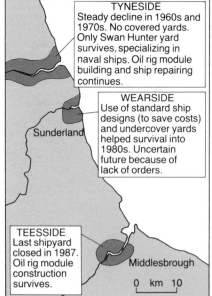

TYNESIDE
Steady decline in 1960s and 1970s. No covered yards. Only Swan Hunter yard survives, specializing in naval ships. Oil rig module building and ship repairing continues.

WEARSIDE
Use of standard ship designs (to save costs) and undercover yards helped survival into 1980s. Uncertain future because of lack of orders.

TEESSIDE
Last shipyard closed in 1987. Oil rig module construction survives.

| | 1960 | 1985 | PER CENT |
	(THOUSANDS)		CHANGE
Food, drink, tobacco	704	631	−10
Chemicals	499	326	−35
Metal manufacture	626	285	−54
Engineering & electrical goods	2031	1540	−24
Shipbuilding & marine eng.	237	90	−62
Vehicles	838	514	−39
Other metal goods	525	381	−27
Textiles	790	242	−69
Clothing & footwear	546	270	−51
Bricks, pottery, glass	321	180	−44
Timber, furniture	304	206	−32
Paper, printing, publishing	605	487	−20
Other manufacturing	355	240	−22

Figure 4
Employment changes in main industrial groups

A changing industrial structure

Figure 4 shows how employment in different industries has changed between 1960 and 1985. Many heavy and old-established industries show a steady decline during the 1960s and early 1970s which then accelerated with the industrial recession. Others such as the motor industry and engineering, which were growth industries of the 1960s, suffered a rapid fall in employment in the late 1980s. The industries which have shown the smallest decreases in recent years are the lighter industries.

The decline in employment in many traditional industries and the rise of lighter, footloose industry has resulted in a changed **industrial structure** in Britain. Britain's industry is now more varied than in the past. The regional picture has also changed. Figure 5 gives employment statistics for North-West England. Traditional industries no longer dominate and employment in services has grown more important. Diversification has gone hand-in-hand with industrial decline.

Q2
(a) Using the statistics in Figure 5, draw pie graphs to show the changing employment structure in North-West England.
(b) Describe the changes shown by your graphs.
(c) Refer back to the study of Rochdale in Section 8.2. What evidence is there that Rochdale has followed the general trends of industrial change in North-West England?

Where have the jobs been lost?

The conurbations and cities have lost jobs more quickly than the towns while manufacturing employment in rural areas has actually increased. It is not just the northern industrial cities with old-established industries which have lost many jobs. The greatest decline, whether measured in total numbers of jobs lost or in percentage terms, has been in Greater London. This reflects both the decline of some traditional industries and the movement out of London by expanding firms. In fact, the congestion of urban areas, lack of room to expand and higher costs (such as factory rents, rates and wages) have been major factors behind job losses in the conurbations and cities.
Employment in services has

| | PERCENTAGE OF LABOUR FORCE | | |
	1951	1961	1981
PRIMARY	5	4	3
SECONDARY			
Textiles	12	7	2
Clothing and footwear	4	4	2
Metal manufacture	3	2	1
Mechanical engineering	11	12	5
Vehicles	1	1	3
Electrical engineering	2	3	3
Food, drink, tobacco	1	2	4
Other manufacturing	10	10	12
TERTIARY	51	55	66

Figure 5
Employment changes in North-West England

grown especially quickly in London and so has helped to offset the decline.

In the old-established industrial areas of northern England, central Scotland and South Wales, industrial decline has been at a faster rate than the national average because:

● These regions have a relatively large share of traditional 19th century industries.

● Some of the newer industries attracted to these areas by the government's regional aid policies (see Section 8.4) have closed down or cut production.

● Some of these areas have had difficulties in attracting new high technology industries. Central Scotland is an important exception, however.

Industrial decline in the West Midlands

In contrast to other old-established industrial regions, the decline of manufacturing in the West Midlands has *not* been the worsening of a long-term trend.

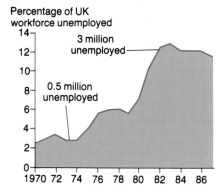

Percentage of UK
workforce unemployed

Figure 6
The changing unemployment rate in the UK

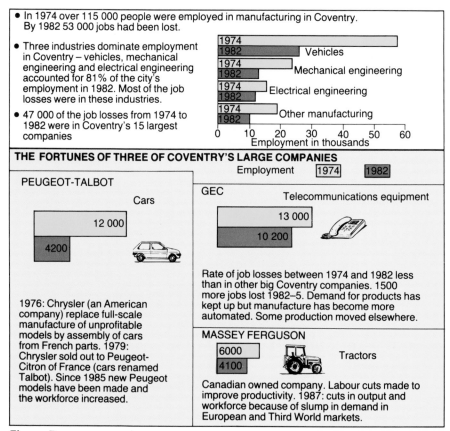

- In 1974 over 115 000 people were employed in manufacturing in Coventry. By 1982 53 000 jobs had been lost.

- Three industries dominate employment in Coventry – vehicles, mechanical engineering and electrical engineering accounted for 81% of the city's employment in 1982. Most of the job losses were in these industries.

- 47 000 of the job losses from 1974 to 1982 were in Coventry's 15 largest companies

THE FORTUNES OF THREE OF COVENTRY'S LARGE COMPANIES

Employment [1974] [1982]

PEUGEOT-TALBOT Cars

12 000
4200

1976: Chrysler (an American company) replace full-scale manufacture of unprofitable models by assembly of cars from French parts. 1979: Chrysler sold out to Peugeot-Citron of France (cars renamed Talbot). Since 1985 new Peugeot models have been made and the workforce increased.

GEC Telecommunications equipment

13 000
10 200

Rate of job losses between 1974 and 1982 less than in other big Coventry companies. 1500 more jobs lost 1982–5. Demand for products has kept up but manufacture has become more automated. Some production moved elsewhere.

MASSEY FERGUSON Tractors

6000
4100

Canadian owned company. Labour cuts made to improve productivity. 1987: cuts in output and workforce because of slump in demand in European and Third World markets.

Figure 7
Industrial decline in Coventry

Here the loss of manufacturing jobs followed years of expansion and prosperity in the 1950s and the 1960s. The government had prevented industry growing too rapidly by controlling the location of new factories. Many new developments were diverted to the north of England, Scotland and Wales and jobs which might have come to the West Midlands went elsewhere.

When the motor and engineering industries of the West Midlands were hit by the industrial recession in the late 1970s, there was a huge knock-on effect through the interlinked chain of assembly, component-making, metal-shaping and metal-making industries. Coventry lost 53 000 manufacturing jobs in the eight years between 1974 and 1982 – almost half of its manufacturing jobs. Unemployment rose from 3 per cent to 17 per cent over the same period. Figure 7 looks at the pattern of job losses in Coventry. The city suffered greatly from the recession for two main reasons:

1 There was an overdependence on the motor industry and mechanical engineering, industries which were hit particularly hard by the recession throughout Britain. Seventy-seven per cent of the jobs lost in Coventry were in these two industries.

2 The companies involved in these two industries in Coventry were less successful than their rivals elsewhere in Britain, for example, the car makers Peugeot-Talbot (formerly Chrysler) and Austin Rover (formerly British Leyland).

Q3
Refer to the information table in Figure 7.
(a) List the reasons for the decline of Coventry's major industrial companies.
(b) Describe the ways in which companies have managed to survive the recession.
(c) (i) What evidence is there of a brighter future for some of Coventry's companies?
(ii) Is employment likely to expand as fast as production? Give a reason for your answer.

Unemployment

In 1973 500 000 people were unemployed in Britain. By 1982 the figure had risen to over 3 million (Figure 8). This dramatic rise in unemployment reflects:
1 The decline in manufacturing output.
2 Automation and increased productivity in manufacturing.

Figure 8
Industrial change in Liverpool; a new electronics factory contrasts with old factory buildings behind

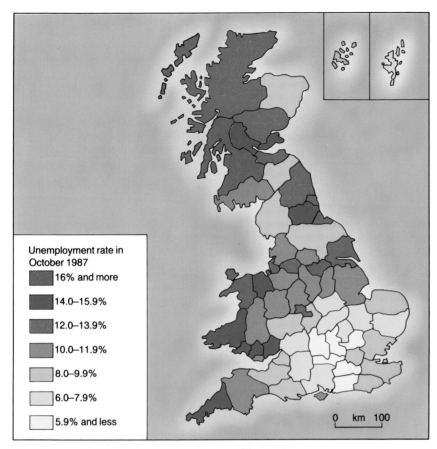

Figure 9
Unemployment rates in Great Britain 1987

3 Job losses in primary industries such as coal mining and fishing.
4 Many transport jobs on the railways, in the ports and in shipping have been lost because of the industrial recession and the introduction of new methods and equipment.
5 The building and construction industry has declined and shed labour.
6 The labour force has grown in size, largely because of the relatively high population growth rate of the 1950s and 1960s. Also increasing numbers of women have sought full-time employment.

Unemployment would have been even greater if the expansion of service industries such as retailing, financial services and the tourist and leisure industry had not taken place. The map in Figure 9 shows the pattern of unemployment in Britain. It was only in the recession of the 1970s that large parts of the Midlands joined most of the North and West as areas of higher than average unemployment.

Q4
(a) Describe and attempt to explain the pattern of unemployment as shown in Figure 9.
(b) Figure 10 lists Britain's unemployment blackspots.
(i) Mark them on an outline map of the country.
(ii) Describe their distribution.
(iii) Does your map reveal any facts about unemployment patterns not shown on the map in Figure 9?
(c) Figure 11 shows that some groups of people are affected by unemployment more than others. Describe and attempt to explain what the diagrams show.

Figure 11
Unemployment: by age and sex and by occupation

Figure 10
Unemployment blackspots, 1987

	PERCENTAGE UNEMPLOYED
ENGLAND	
Hartlepool	21.0
Liverpool	19.0
Middlesbrough	19.2
Newquay	21.1
Reduth & Camborne	18.8
Rotherham & Mexborough	19.3
Skegness	21.0
South Tyneside	22.5
Sunderland	18.6
WALES	
Aberdare	19.9
Cardigan	24.0
Fishguard	20.9
Holyhead	20.7
Pwllheli	23.9
South Pembrokeshire	21.9
SCOTLAND	
Alloa	19.3
Arbroath	19.0
Campbeltown	19.5
Cumnock & Sanquhar	27.5
Dumbarton	19.4
Forres	20.0
Girvan	24.0
Greenock	19.0
Invergordon & Dingwall	19.7
Irvine	21.7
Lanarkshire	18.3
Newton Stewart	18.5
Skye & Wester Ross	18.8
Western Isles	20.8

All NORTHERN IRELAND except Belfast and Ballymena has an unemployment rate of over 18%.

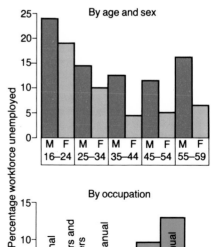

8.4 Government aid to industry

For over 50 years the government has given help to areas where unemployment is relatively high, to encourage new industery. This help is known as **regional aid**. Until the 1970s regional aid was accompanied by a policy of restricting new industrial development in the more prosperous and congested regions.

Regional aid

Figure 1 shows the present pattern of the assisted areas which are called **Development Areas** and **Intermediate Areas**. They are much smaller in extent than in the 1970s, but include areas of the West Midlands where industry had been refused permission to develop in the past. Figure 2 shows the types of financial help which are available to industry in the assisted areas. In Scotland and Wales, Development Agencies provide additional aid for industry. Northern Ireland has its own schemes to attract industry.

The government has also spent money on improving the **infrastructure** of the less prosperous areas, for example, on road building and the reclamation of derelict land. In addition, the EEC has provided money for new industrial and other developments.

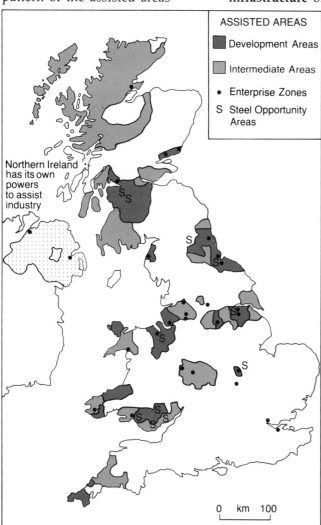

**Figure 1
Assisted areas**

**Figure 2
Aid for industry**

ASSISTED AREAS

- ■ Development Areas
- □ Intermediate Areas
- • Enterprise Zones
- S Steel Opportunity Areas

Northern Ireland has its own powers to assist industry

0   km   100

Q1
(a) Describe the pattern of assisted areas shown in Figure 1. (You will find it useful to refer to the map of industrial areas on page 86 and the unemployment map on page 95.)
(b) Why would the boundaries of these assisted areas be modified regularly?

Development Areas
Grants and loans towards cost of new buildings and machinery. Until 1988 grants were given automatically. Also, other types of aid such as grants for training workers and innovation grants for small firms.

Intermediate Areas
As Development Areas but lower grants.

Enterprise Zones
No rates to pay for ten years, relaxed planning controls, tax reductions.

Steel Opportunity Areas
(Areas affected by the decline of the steel industry) Loans, factories rent-free for two years, workforce training.

Freeports
No customs duties on goods imported for processing and re-export. There are six Freeports: Birmingham Airport, Liverpool, Southampton, Cardiff, Prestwick Airport and Belfast Airport.

Urban Development Corporations
Provide land for development, build factories and improve infrastructure. (See Section 5.3.)

Assistance for industry is also available from New Town Development Corporations, the Welsh and Scottish Development Agencies, the Northern Ireland Office, the European Regional Development Fund (EEC aid), the Highland and Islands Development Board, the Development Board for Rural Wales, the government's Urban Programme (mainly for inner city areas) and local authorities.

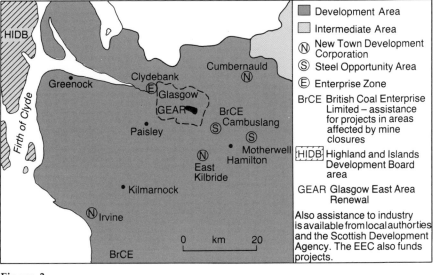

Figure 3
Aid to industry in western central Scotland

In the 1960s four car assembly plants were built in the assisted areas, with government financial aid: three in Merseyside, (Halewood, Speke and Ellesmere Port) and one in Scotland (Linwood near Glasgow). In 1978 British Leyland closed its Speke plant with the loss of over 3 000 jobs and in 1981 Peugeot-Talbot closed its Linwood plant which employed 8 000. Both plants produced unprofitable models and had problems of bad labour relations and poor quality cars. Ford continue to produce successfully at Halewood as do Vauxhall at Ellesmere Port, although labour forces were severely cut back in the early 1980s.

Figure 4
The fate of car assembly plants built in the assisted areas in the 1960s.

Aid for unemployment blackspots

Economic decline in inner city areas, the closure of major steel works and development of other unemployment 'blackspots' has, in recent years, led to the introduction of other schemes to help industrial development: Enterprise Zones, Steel Opportunity Areas, Freeports and Urban Development Corporations. Figure 2 gives details of these schemes, many of which are also concerned with other ways of regenerating declining areas. As Figure 3 shows in the case of western central Scotland, some regions have a large number of different schemes and bodies at work.

The effects of government aid

Only a little over one-third of the new industrial developments in Britain since 1945 have been in the assisted areas. Since 1960 between 250 000 and 400 000 manufacturing jobs have been created in the assisted areas by government policies. However,

the industrial recession hit these areas badly, because of the continued decline of traditional industries and the closure of relatively new factories, in many cases set up with government aid (Figure 4). Criticisms of government aid to the assisted areas have been made on several grounds:

- Many firms which were diverted away from the South and the Midlands have been faced with extra transport costs.

- Pockets of high employment in the South and the Midlands are partly due to government restrictions on industrial development in the 1960s and early 1970s.

- Many of the new factories are branch factories, which are the first to close when companies have to cut production.

- Jobs have been created at too great a cost, possibly as much as £40 000 per job.

- Too much money has gone into large capital-intensive industries such as steel and chemicals. In Teesside (Cleveland), £400 million was invested in the 1970s yet the area is now an unemployment blackspot.

- Policies have concentrated too much on manufacturing jobs at

a time when the service sector was expanding.

In recent years, despite the rise in unemployment, the amount of money spent on industrial regional aid has been cut. There are different views as to what is the best course for the future. Some people want a policy which involves large Development Areas with grants tied to the number of jobs created. Others say help should be concentrated more locally in the unemployment blackspots and that greater attention should be given to improving the environment of areas scarred by industrial decline and dereliction.

Q2
(a) Consider the factors which influence the decisions of multiplant and multinational companies (see Section 8.2). What factors will persuade them to locate new factories in the assisted areas?
(b) Why are publicity campaigns, including advertising, important in attracting new industry? Design a poster to promote the advantages for industry of either your local area or western central Scotland (see Figure 3).

8.5 The iron and steel industry

In recent years the British iron and steel industry has undergone an upheaval. The problems it has faced and the changes which have taken place are typical of many of Britain's traditional industries which grew up in the 19th century. Figure 1 shows how a steady decline in steel production in the 1970s turned into a drastic fall after 1979.

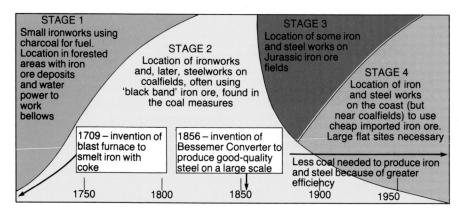

STAGE 1
Small ironworks using charcoal for fuel. Location in forested areas with iron ore deposits and water power to work bellows

STAGE 2
Location of ironworks and, later, steelworks on coalfields, often using 'black band' iron ore, found in the coal measures

STAGE 3
Location of some iron and steel works on Jurassic iron ore fields

STAGE 4
Location of iron and steel works on the coast (but near coalfields) to use cheap imported iron ore. Large flat sites necessary

1709 – invention of blast furnace to smelt iron with coke

1856 – invention of Bessemer Converter to produce good-quality steel on a large scale

Less coal needed to produce iron and steel because of greater efficiency

1750   1800   1850   1900   1950

Figure 2
Stages in the location of the iron and steel industry

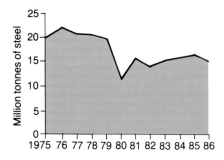

Figure 1
UK steel production, 1975–1986

Figure 3 (below)
Charging a 300 tonne steel furnace at Scunthorpe

The location of iron and steel making

Iron and steel works require a location where the transport costs of bulky raw materials and products can be kept low. Over time, locations have changed as new technological developments were introduced and new sources of raw materials developed (Figure 2). In the past, iron making and steel making were often carried on at separate sites; now large **integrated works** with blast furnaces, steel furnaces and rolling mills on the same site (Figure 3) dominate production.

Cutback and closures

In 1972 the British Steel Corporation announced a £3 000 million scheme to modernize the steel industry and raise production by expanding the large integrated works on or near the coast, for example, at

Redcar-Lackenby on Teesside (Figure 4). But by the late 1970s BSC was producing more steel than it could sell and was losing over one million pounds a day. Therefore from 1979 production was cut, mainly by closing down the older works. Most of these were inland on coalfields (Figure 5), but they also included the orefield works at Corby and some coastal works. In some cases, the whole works was demolished, in others some finishing processes (for example, tube making at Corby) survived.

> ## Q1
> Draw simple inputs/outputs diagrams to represent each of the stages in the location of the iron and steel industry as shown in Figure 2. State the type of location for each diagram.

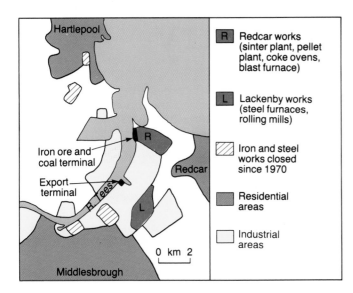

Figure 4
Changes in the iron and steel industry, Teesside
Derelict blast furnaces at Middlesbrough

Major reasons for the cutbacks were:

- Falling demand for steel from industries such as the motor industry.

- The use of materials such as plastics and aluminium instead of steel.

- Competition from Third World steel producers (Brazil, Mexico, South Korea, India and Taiwan) who have increased production and have undercut the prices of European producers.

Figure 5
Location of the iron and steel industry

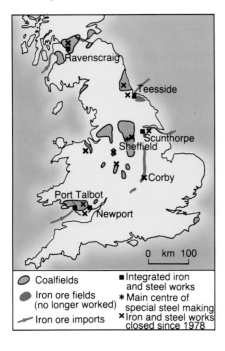

The five integrated works

Iron and steel production is now concentrated in five large integrated works (Figure 5). Two (Redcar-Lackenby and Port Talbot) have their own deepwater terminals for importing iron ore and some coal. Ore for Llanwern (Newport) is brought by rail from

Figure 6
Changes in Corby following the closure of the steel works in 1980

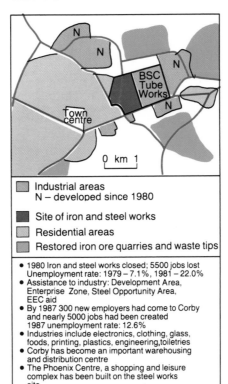

Industrial areas
N – developed since 1980

Site of iron and steel works

Residential areas

Restored iron ore quarries and waste tips

- 1980 Iron and steel works closed; 5500 jobs lost
  Unemployment rate: 1979 – 7.1%, 1981 – 22.0%
- Assistance to industry: Development Area, Enterprise Zone, Steel Opportunity Area, EEC aid
- By 1987 300 new employers had come to Corby and nearly 5000 jobs had been created
  1987 unemployment rate: 12.6%
- Industries include electronics, clothing, glass, foods, printing, plastics, engineering, toiletries
- Corby has become an important warehousing and distribution centre
- The Phoenix Centre, a shopping and leisure complex has been built on the steel works site

Port Talbot. Scunthorpe, originally based on local ore, and Ravenscraig also have to bring in iron ore by rail from coastal terminals. These works have not escaped the cutbacks. For example, to lower production costs and reduce output, the labour force at Port Talbot was cut from 20 000 to 6 000.

In addition to the 'big five' works, there are a number of separate steelworks and rolling mills, both BSC and privately-owned. Most concentrate on making special high-quality steels. Sheffield is the main centre of special steel making, but has suffered cutbacks just like other steel making centres.

Q2
(a) Refer to Figure 5. In what types of location were most of the works which were closed after 1978? What disadvantages do such locations have for modern steel making?
(b) Figure 6 shows the changes which have taken place at Corby since the closure of the iron and steel works in 1980.
(i) What were the effects of the closure of the works?
(ii) What has been done to encourage new industry to locate in Corby? How successful has job creation been?

8.6 The motor industry

About one million people in Britain have jobs connected with the making of cars and other vehicles. They are employed both by the motor companies and by a large number of firms which make components. Many other industries, such as steel and plastics, rely heavily on the custom of the motor industry. Figure 1 shows the complex way in which the different parts of the motor industry are linked to each other and to other industries.

The motor industry is dominated by four large companies: Ford, Vauxhall, the Rover Group (formerly British Leyland) and Peugeot-Talbot (formerly Chrysler). Figure 2 shows the location of vehicle assembly plants. Many component factories are found in the same areas as the assembly plants, with the largest concentration being in the West Midlands.

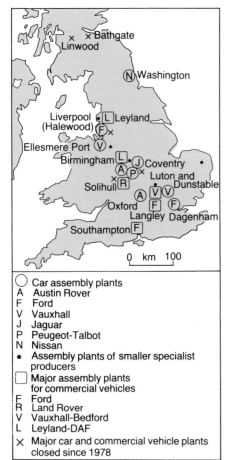

Figure 2
Location of vehicle assembly plants

○ Car assembly plants
A Austin Rover
F Ford
V Vauxhall
J Jaguar
P Peugeot-Talbot
N Nissan
• Assembly plants of smaller specialist producers
☐ Major assembly plants for commercial vehicles
F Ford
R Land Rover
V Vauxhall-Bedford
L Leyland-DAF
✗ Major car and commercial vehicle plants closed since 1978

The development of the motor industry

Many of the early motor companies developed in the West Midlands where engineering and metal-working skills were already concentrated. The London area was another early centre of production because of local engineering traditions and the large market, and in 1931 attracted Ford's main factory to Dagenham. In the 1950s and 1960s the government diverted much new industrial development to the Development Areas. The motor companies built assembly plants on Merseyside and in Central Scotland and component factories in South Wales and Northern Ireland.

Crisis in the '70s, restructuring in the '80s

In 1972 British car production reached a peak of 1 921 000 cars Ten years later only 880 000 cars were made. Why did such a decline occur? The graphs in Figure 3 show three important trends: (a) after 1972 demand for new cars in Britain stopped rising; (b) car imports rose by 133 per cent between 1972 and 1982 and (c) car exports fell by 63 per

cent between the same years. Imports rose and exports fell because British car makers were unable to compete successfully with foreign producers. Reasons for this included:

1 There were too many relatively small factories making too many models. The economies which come from large-scale production could not be made.

Figure 1
The motor industry's links

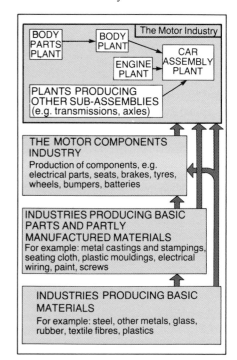

Figure 3
The motor industry; production, exports and imports

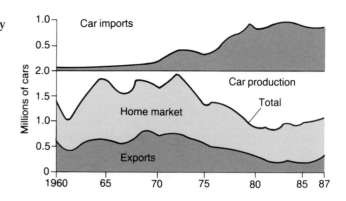

Figure 4
Using a talking computer to check quality at the end of the Rover 800 assembly line, Cowley, Oxford

Car makers switch back to Britain

American controlled car makers Ford and Vauxhall are switching production back to Britain from the continent.

Improved quality and productivity matching that of German factories are the reasons. Ford has announced plans to raise output by 200,000 jobs over the next four years and recruit 1,000 workers. Vauxhall plan to raise output by 20 per cent over the next three years, but will continue to shed labour.

RECORD YEAR FOR JAGUAR

Booming sales in U.S.A. have helped Jaguar to achieve a record level of output. The company is building up its workforce as demand continues to outstrip supply for its luxury models.

Jobs boost at Ryton

After years of cutting jobs, Peugeot-Talbot is to recruit more labour for its Ryton, Coventry plant. This follows the announcement to assemble the medium size 405 at Ryton.

Nissan to expand at Washington

Nissan has announced the go-ahead for an expansion of its new Washington factory

Exports up at Austin-Rover

An increase in sales to Europe

Figure 5
A brighter outlook for the motor industry?

2 Low labour productivity, lack of investment in new technology and poor labour relations led to high costs and poor quality cars.
3 As the multinational motor companies integrated their British operations with their continental plants, they imported more cars than they exported.

British Leyland was especially hard hit by the falling demand and large losses led to the company being rescued by a government takeover in 1975. The company had to cut production, close factories, reorganize and invest in a new range of models. The labour force was cut from 170 000 in 1978 to under 100 000 in 1982. The Jaguar factories were sold off and have since made rapid progress. Huge sums of government money were needed for the recovery programme. In 1986 the company was renamed the Rover Group. Its car making division now assembles cars at only two locations and has signed agreements with the Japanese Honda company to develop jointly new models such as the Rover 800 series (Figure 4).

Q1
(a) (i) Why has the motor industry become dominated by large multinational companies?
(ii) How do small producers such as Rolls-Royce, Jaguar and Lotus manage to succeed?
(b) (i) Why would the government have considered it worthwhile to spend large sums of money in rescuing British Leyland from collapse? (Consider the links in Figure 1).
(ii). Suggest why the Rover Group has co-operated with Honda of Japan.

The other large motor companies also had to reduce their labour forces and reorganize. The American Chrysler Corporation sold off its British operations to the French Peugeot-Talbot company which closed the Linwood assembly plant in Scotland in 1981 with the loss of 8 000 jobs. Vauxhall cut its labour force by 11 000, while Ford, the

most successful company, made smaller cutbacks. By 1986 there were some more hopeful signs for the future of the motor industry, as the press headlines in Figure 5 show. However, commercial vehicle manufacturing was hit by a major slump in demand in the early 1980s. The effects of this slump included the closure of Leyland Trucks' Bathgate plant and the ending of Bedford truck production by General Motors at Dunstable.

Q2
(a) One of the headlines in Figure 5 states that productivity in British car plants matches that in European factories. Why is this important? What bearing has it on some of the other headlines?
(b) In 1986 the Japanese Nissan Company began car assembly at Washington in North-East England. Who might welcome this development? Who might have doubts?
(c) The assembly plants built in the 1960s at Linwood and Bathgate in Scotland lasted only about twenty years. What disadvantages did these locations have for assembly?

8.7 High technology industry

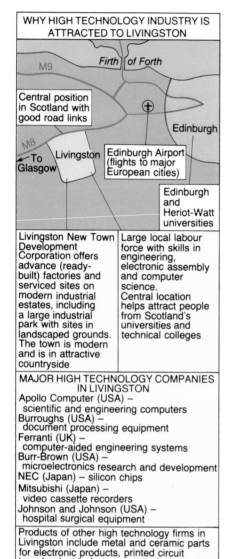

WHY HIGH TECHNOLOGY INDUSTRY IS ATTRACTED TO LIVINGSTON

Central position in Scotland with good road links

Edinburgh Airport (flights to major European cities)

Edinburgh and Heriot-Watt universities

Livingston New Town Development Corporation offers advance (ready-built) factories and serviced sites on modern industrial estates, including a large industrial park with sites in landscaped grounds. The town is modern and is in attractive countryside	Large local labour force with skills in engineering, electronic assembly and computer science. Central location helps attract people from Scotland's universities and technical colleges

MAJOR HIGH TECHNOLOGY COMPANIES IN LIVINGSTON

Apollo Computer (USA) – scientific and engineering computers
Burroughs (USA) – document processing equipment
Ferranti (UK) – computer-aided engineering systems
Burr-Brown (USA) – microelectronics research and development
NEC (Japan) – silicon chips
Mitsubishi (Japan) – video cassette recorders
Johnson and Johnson (USA) – hospital surgical equipment

Products of other high technology firms in Livingston include metal and ceramic parts for electronic products, printed circuit boards, electrical components, lenses, power control systems, specialised textile fibres, medical equipment (ranging from ultrascan machines to fibre optic probes)

Electronics, information technology and biotechnology are all examples of **high technology** industry. The range of products is extremely wide: they include computer hardware and software, telecommunications equipment, scientific instruments, and many electronic components used in the products of other industries. Very important in the growth of high technology industry has been the development of **micro-electronics**, the making of electronic components on silicon chips.

Electronics and other high technology firms have factories and research centres in many parts of Britain, but there are particular concentrations in parts of southern England and central Scotland.

'Silicon Glen'

In central Scotland the electronics industry employs over 40 000 people, more than the traditional industries of coal, steel and ship building put together. Some of the major companies are long-established British firms, for example, Ferranti at Edinburgh, but most of the factories are branch plants of American and other multinational companies.

Figure 1
High technology industry in Livingston New Town, Scotland

The foreign companies have been attracted by relatively cheap labour for assembly work, an attractive environment, the Scottish universities, government grants and promotion efforts by the Scottish Development Agency. New towns have proved to be particularly successful in attracting these companies (Figure 1).

'Sunrise Strip'

A major concentration of electronics and other high technology industry is found along a corridor of land following the M4 westwards from London – the 'Sunrise Strip' (Figure 2). As in Scotland, there are many American companies, but more are involved in research and development. High technology industry has also spread further west along the M4 to Bristol and over the Severn Bridge into Gwent.

The 'Cambridge Phenomenon'

In 1974 there were about a hundred high technology firms, mostly very small, in and around the university city of Cambridge. By 1987 the number was approaching four hundred. Here the industry is dominated by small, locally-founded firms involved in developing new products and applications in fields such as computer-aided design and scientific instrumentation. Figure 3 shows how much of this rapid development – referred to as the 'Cambridge Phenomenon' – was linked to the University.

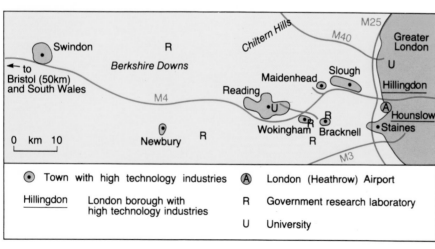

Symbol	Description	Symbol	Description
⊙	Town with high technology industries	Ⓐ	London (Heathrow) Airport
Hillingdon	London borough with high technology industries	R	Government research laboratory
		U	University

Figure 2
The M4 corridor: 'Sunrise Strip'

Q1

(a) Refer to Figure 2. Considering the factors that influence the location of modern industry, why do you think the M4 corridor has been an attractive location for high technology industry?
(b) Suggest why specializations, such as computer software for industry at Cambridge, may develop in one centre.
(c) Refer to Figures 1 and 3. Compare high technology industry in Livingston and Cambridge. Refer to location factors, products and types of company. Which centre appears to have the brightest future? Give reasons for your answer.

Future prospects

Although a new industry of growing importance, high technology industry has its share of uncertainties for the future:

- The industry is a 'high risk' activity. Large investments have to be made for products with short lives and research time and money does not always result in a successful product.

- Much of the industry is owned by foreign companies.

- Assembly work is likely to be more automated in the future and so demand for semi-skilled labour will fail.

Such problems have resulted in some factories closing after only a short period of operation. The expansion of high technology industry depends on huge amounts of money being made available for research. Government investment has been very much less in Britain than in countries such as Japan.

Q2

Write an account of the factors which influence the location of high technology industry in Britain, using the following headings: Links between firms, Links with universities, Labour, The environment, Other influences.

Figure 3
High technology industry in the Cambridge area

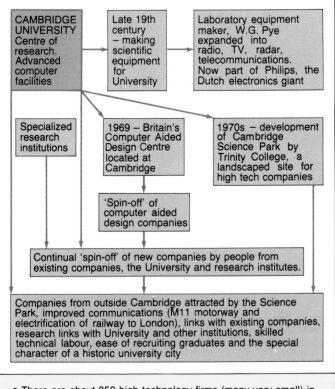

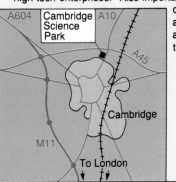

THE NAPP LABORATORIES BUILDING ON CAMBRIDGE SCIENCE PARK

Napp produces pharmaceuticals (drugs) for treating pain and asthma. Workforce: 300 (one-third involved in research.) Napp moved to Cambridge in 1983: 'We chose the Cambridge Science Park because it is a prestigious location. We wanted to be associated with other successful high tech enterprises.' Also important were the good communications to London and links with the University and Cambridge's large teaching hospital

9. Service industries

9.1 Shops

People's shopping habits have changed greatly over the past 30 years or so. The changes have been especially great in recent years. Rising incomes have led to people spending more and buying a greater variety of goods. Increased car ownership has meant that people are willing to travel further to shop, are more likely to buy in bulk and so shop less frequently. People increasingly buy from supermarkets, superstores, warehouse-type establishments, from stores owned by large companies (the 'multiples') and by mail order rather than from independent shops.

Shopping centres vary in size from those in large city centres down to individual shops. Besides shops, there are offices and services which rely on good access to customers.

Figure 2 shows the location of different types of shopping centre within a city. Notice how a **hierarchy** of centres exists. At the top of the hierarchy is the CBD with the largest number and

- Freeman Hardy Willis
- Manfield
- Trueform
- Saxone
- Lilley and Skinner
- Dolcis
- Shoe City
- Roland Cartier
- Curtess
- Miss Selfridge
- Wallis
- Olympus Sport
- Mappin and Webb
- Fosters
- Dormie
- Esquires
- Millets
- Adams

Figure 1
Shops belonging to Sears Holdings

variety of shops; it serves all the city and a large surrounding area. The individual shop or small community shopping centre is at the bottom of the hierarchy, serving the needs of people living nearby for goods which are bought frequently and have a small range (see Section 4.5.).

Some shopping centres within the city are difficult to fit precisely into the hierarchy. The inner city shopping ribbons have shops serving local needs together with discount warehouses serving much wider areas. Out-of-town superstores may have catchment areas as large as that of a CBD but do not provide many of the CBD's shopping facilities and services.

The Central Business District

We have already looked at some features of the Central Business District in Section 5.1. As far as shopping is concerned, many CBDs have faced problems in recent years, losing some of their trade to shopping centres in the suburbs, to discount warehouses and to out-of-town superstores

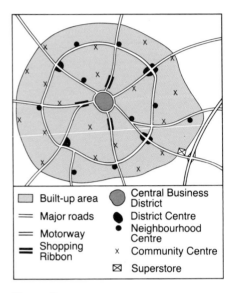

☐ Built-up area	⬤ Central Business District
═ Major roads	● District Centre
═ Motorway	• Neighbourhood Centre
═ Shopping Ribbon	x Community Centre
	⊠ Superstore

Figure 2
The pattern of shopping centres in a city

- Closure of Woolworth's two stores
- Closure of Debenham's department store
- Closure of Co-operative department store. The site is now occupied by 'The Pavilions', a multi-level complex of shops
- Refurbishment of the indoor Birmingham Shopping Centre, now renamed 'The Pallasades'
- Closure of two large furniture stores
- Major refurbishment of Lewis's department store
- It is proposed to rebuild the Bull Ring Shopping Centre, a two-level indoor shopping and markets complex built in the 1960s

---

Figure 3
Changes in shopping in Birmingham's CBD since 1980

Q1

(a) How are the shopping habits of a car-owning family likely to differ from those of a family who have to rely on public transport?
(b) Why have many independent shops not been able to compete with the multiples?
(c) Figure 1 lists the names of shops which belong to Sears Holdings, a company which owns many multiple chains. What products are sold by these shops? Why would one company sell the same products, say shoes, under a number of names?

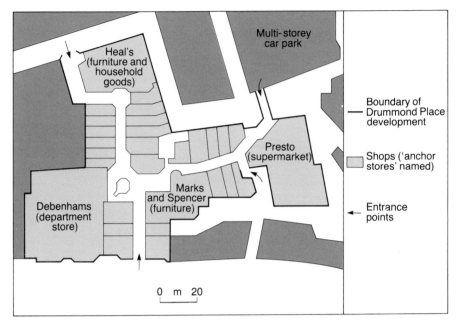

Figure 4
Drummond Place shopping centre, Croydon

and hypermarkets. A major factor in this loss of trade is the problem of car parking and traffic congestion in central areas of cities although the CBD remains very convenient for shoppers travelling by bus. High CBD rents and rates have led to some shops closing. The shops which remain most successful are likely to specialize in high-order goods with high profit margins, have a high turnover of goods, be multiples rather than independent shops and have good locations within the CBD. Figure 3 lists some of the major changes in shopping in Birmingham's CBD since 1980.

Not all CBDs are losing trade. In a smaller town, the CBD is the only centre where many goods can be bought. Here the CBD is more important for food shops, whether supermarkets or smaller shops such as butchers and greengrocers. In most cities, large enclosed centres have been built to attract more shoppers to the CBD. Figure 4 shows the Drummond Place development in Croydon, south London. A key feature of this and many similar schemes is the inclusion of **anchor stores** such as department stores and large supermarkets.

Suburban shopping

Outside the CBD, as Figure 2 shows, there is a variety of types of shopping centre. Plans of three contrasting centres are shown in Figure 5. In big cities, large **district centres** have many features in common with the CBDs of smaller towns, with large supermarkets, branches of multiple stores, banks and offices. The **inner city ribbon** in Figure 5 has a similar number of shops as the district centre, but with a different mix of shop types. The **neighbourhood centre** has a smaller number of shops serving a smaller catchment area and sells lower order goods.

Superstores and hypermarkets

The high costs of land and rates in CBDs, together with lack of space and the difficulties of car parking, have led to the development of superstores and hypermarkets, usually at the edge of cities. A superstore has at least 2 500 square metres of selling area. Hypermarkets are larger, usually with a selling area of over 5 000 square metres.

Asda developed Britain's first superstores in northern England and was soon followed by the major supermarket chains, sometimes in combination with other retail firms (for example, Savacentre stores are joint

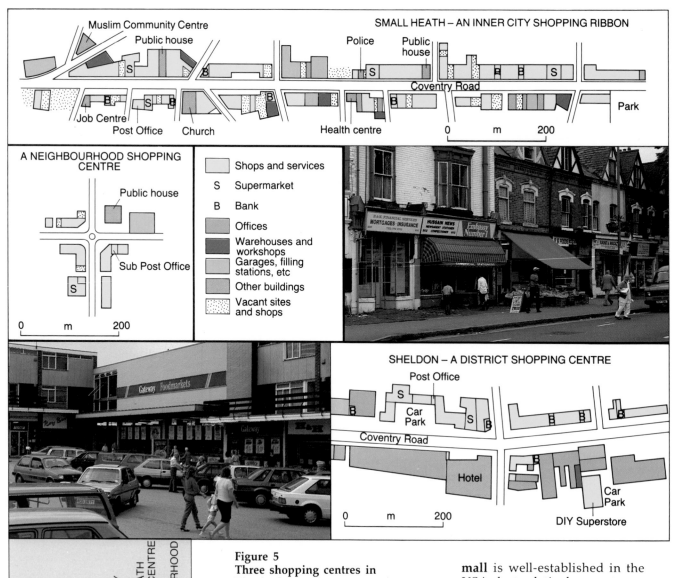

Figure 5
Three shopping centres in Birmingham

	INNER CITY RIBBON SMALL HEATH	DISTRICT CENTRE SHELDON	NEIGHBOURHOOD CENTRE
Supermarket	4	2	1
Other food shops	15	9	10
Clothes, shoes, drapery	26	8	4
Newsagent/tobacconist/ confectioner	3	3	2
Hardware/DIY supplies	5	2	3
Electrical goods/TV	6	5	
Furniture, carpets	8	2	
Other shops	18	17	4
Banks	7	6	
Building societies	6	6	
Estate agents, insurance, travel agents	21	10	3
Post offices	1	1	1
Other services	17	10	2
Restaurants, cafés, take-away food	13	7	4
Vacant premises	28		4
Number of shops belonging to national multiple chains	**1**	**10**	**1**

developments by Sainsbury's and British Home Stores). Besides food a wide variety of other goods are sold. Figure 6 shows the advantages of an out-of-town location for a superstore.

Out-of-town shopping centres

The Metrocentre in Tyne and Wear, opened in 1986, (Figure 7) is a purpose-built shopping centre with a range of shops typical of a CBD but sited away from established business districts. This type of centre with large areas of surface car parking and an enclosed, air-conditioned

mall is well-established in the USA, but relatively new to Britain. Developers of these centres prefer truly out-of-town greenfield locations close to major road and motorway junctions. Both the Metrocentre and Britain's first out-of-town centre – Brent Cross in north London – are located at very accessible points within existing built-up areas. The Metrocentre is the pioneer for the latest trend in shopping developments, combining a major shopping centre with large-scale leisure developments.

Another type of out-of-town development is the **retail warehouse park**. Here a small number of stores sell goods such as do-it-yourself products, motor accessories, carpets, furniture and electrical goods in warehouse-type buildings with plentiful car parking space.

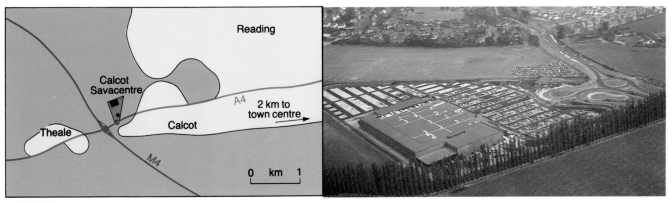

Figure 6
The site of this Savacentre superstore at Calcot near Reading has the advantage of a large greenfield site on the edge of an urban area near a motorway junction

Figure 7
The Metrocentre, Gateshead, Tyne and Wear

Q4

(a) Use the information in Figure 6 to draw a labelled sketch map showing the advantages of Savacentre's site near Reading.

(b) Planning consent for superstores and out-of-town shopping centres on sites at the edge of cities has often been refused. What groups of people are likely to object to these new developments?

(c) Refer to Figure 7.

(i) Explain why Gateshead was an attractive site for the developers of the Metrocentre.

(ii) Briefly describe the main features of the Metrocentre, explaining why they should be attractive to customers.

(iii) Why are developers keen to build combined shopping and leisure centres such as the Metrocentre that provide 'day out' destinations?

(d) (i) Explain why stores such as B and Q and Allied Carpets usually occupy warehouse-type buildings.

(ii) Suggest what factors influence the choice of locations for such stores. (Consider the locations of any similar stores that you know.) Why may retail warehouses be keen to group together?

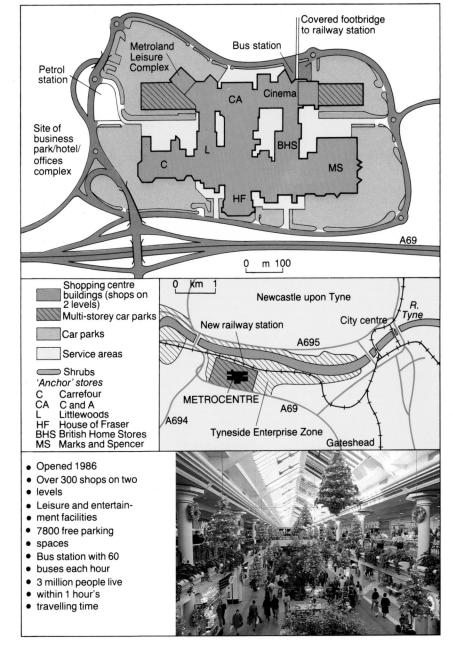

- Opened 1986
- Over 300 shops on two
- levels
- Leisure and entertain-
- ment facilities
- 7800 free parking
- spaces
- Bus station with 60
- buses each hour
- 3 million people live
- within 1 hour's
- travelling time

107

9.2 Offices

As Figure 1 shows, offices vary greatly from accommodation in converted houses to towering blocks. Office buildings are occupied by a wide variety of organizations: industrial companies, government, insurance companies, banks and many others.

Offices in London

Central London has the greatest concentration of offices and office jobs in Britain. The main reason for this is London's status as a capital city. London is the location for the headquarters offices of most large British companies and the main British office for many foreign companies. It is one of the world's major financial centres. In addition, government departments employ many office workers.

The City
Banking and other financial services (activities such as insurance and dealing in companies' shares) are concentrated in the City of London (Figure 2). Here, over 225 000 people work in offices and 68 per cent of all floor space is

Figure 2
The City of London

Figure 1
Contrasting offices

given over to office use. During the 1980s three major trends have led to a greatly increased demand for office space:

1 The adoption of modern information technology has led to the need for new office designs.
2 International links in banking have expanded and foreign financial firms have been allowed to take part in the City's activities.
3 There has been a general expansion of financial services.

Pressure for more office development in the City is being resisted by the planners. As a result, new development has been pushed towards the fringes of the City and the Docklands (Figure 2). These sites have the

advantages of lower costs for developers and lower rents for users.

Q1
What are the advantages of banks and other financial firms concentrating together in the City of London? What problems are caused by such a concentration?

The suburbs
The outer suburbs of London have attracted much office development. Many of these offices are occupied by firms who have moved out of central London, seeking new offices with lower rents and rates. As Figure 3 shows, most of the recent development has been towards the west and south. Croydon has become the largest office centre, employing over 30 000 office workers.

Office development in South-East England

Many towns in the South-East outside London have attracted new office development. In the 1980s development has been greatest along the M4 and M3

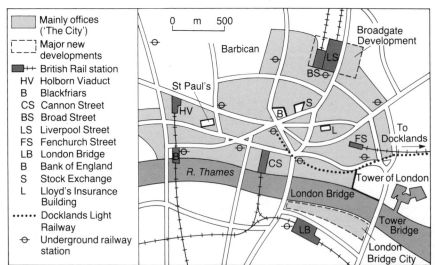

▭	Mainly offices ('The City')
⌐ ┐	Major new developments
■+++	British Rail station
HV	Holborn Viaduct
B	Blackfriars
CS	Cannon Street
BS	Broad Street
LS	Liverpool Street
FS	Fenchurch Street
LB	London Bridge
B	Bank of England
S	Stock Exchange
L	Lloyd's Insurance Building
·····	Docklands Light Railway
⊖	Underground railway station

108

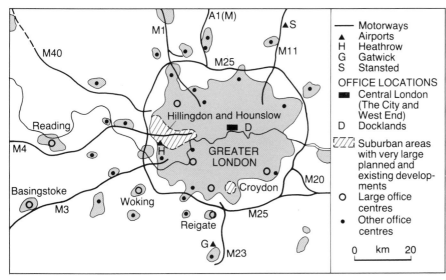

Figure 3
Office development in the London region

Hierarchies of offices

Organizations such as major insurance companies have a hierarchy of offices, as Figure 4 shows. When such a pattern is multiplied by the offices of many other companies, a hierarchy of office centres over the country results.

FIRE OFFICES (handling house insurance, motor insurance, etc.)

Head office: Norwich

Branches: Aberdeen, Belfast, Birmingham, Brighton, Bristol, Cambridge, Cardiff, Chelmsford, Croydon, Edinburgh, Glasgow, Hull, Ipswich, Leeds, Leicester, Liverpool, London (City), London (West End), Manchester, Newcastle-upon-Tyne, Norwich, Nottingham, Plymouth, Preston, Reading, Sheffield, Southampton, Stoke-on-Trent, Watford

Local Branches and Local Offices: 73 locations

(Norwich Union also has a parallel structure of life insurance offices. There are also specialist finance and investment offices and marine insurance offices.)

---

corridors. In addition to lower costs, there are plenty of modern offices on attractive sites, yet firms are still within easy access of London. When a move is made out of London, key staff will not have to move far, if at all, while a plentiful supply of clerical and secretarial staff exist throughout the region. There are good road and rail links and international airports are nearby. Many newer developments are on landscaped business parks, rather than in town centres.

and government. Some are locations of the head offices of major insurance companies (for example, Norwich and Edinburgh) and building societies (for example, Leeds).

In the late 1960s and the 1970s the government encouraged the movement of offices out of London. Many major government offices were moved to regional centres, for example the Driver and Vehicle Licensing Centre to Swansea. However, most companies stayed within the South-East.

Figure 4
Norwich Union offices

Q2
Refer to Figure 3. Describe and explain the pattern of recent office development as shown on the map. What are the particular advantages of the M4 and M3 corridors?

Office location outside the South-East

Outside South-East England it is the regional capitals such as Birmingham, Manchester, Bristol and Edinburgh which have the greatest number of offices. They are the natural locations for regional offices of both companies

Q3
(a) Why would the government wish to encourage offices to move from London to regional centres?
(b) Suggest why the policy has not been as successful as was hoped. (Besides considering the wishes of office users, bear in mind that most offices are built by property development companies who make their profits both out of rising property values and the rents they charge.)

Q4
(a) On a map of the UK, plot the locations of the Norwich Union's head office and branch offices.
(b) Compare your finished map with an atlas map which shows population distribution and the sizes of cities and towns. Why does the spacing of branches and thus the size of the areas they serve vary over the country?

109

9.3 Leisure activities and facilities

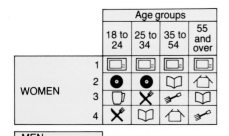

		Age groups			
		18 to 24	25 to 34	35 to 54	55 and over
WOMEN	1	Watching television	Watching television	Watching television	Watching television
	2	Listening to music	Listening to music	Reading books	Knitting & sewing
	3	Drinking out	Eating out	Gardening	Reading books
	4	Eating out	Reading books	Knitting & sewing	Gardening

MEN					
Professional and Managerial	1	Drinking out	Listening to music	Watching television	Watching television
	2	Listening to music	Watching television	Reading books	Gardening
	3	Watching television	Drinking out	Household DIY	Reading books
	4	Sport	Eating out	Gardening	Listening to music
Skilled manual	1	Drinking out	Drinking out	Watching television	Watching television
	2	Watching television	Watching television	Household DIY	Household DIY
	3	Sport	Listening to music	Drinking out	Gardening
	4	Listening to music	Household DIY	Gardening	Reading books
Unskilled manual	1	Drinking out	Watching television	Watching television	Watching television
	2	Watching television	Drinking out	Drinking out	Gardening
	3	Listening to music	Listening to music	Gardening	Household DIY
	4	Sport	Household DIY	Household DIY	Drinking out

People were asked which leisure activities they took part in regularly. The four most frequently mentioned activities for each group are listed in the table. (Total sample size 550)

- ▭ Watching television
- ● Listening to music
- ▯ Drinking out
- ✗ Eating out
- ▱ Reading books
- ⌂ Knitting & sewing
- ⚘ Gardening
- ⌐ Household DIY
- ⌚ Sport

Figure 1
Results of a leisure time survey

Figure 2
Different sports need different specialist facilities

Leisure activities have increased greatly in importance in recent years. The reasons for this are connected with the greater amount of time that people have available for such activities: shorter working hours, longer holidays, earlier retirement and less time being needed to do routine household tasks. Other reasons for the leisure boom include rising incomes, increasing car ownership and faster road and rail travel. To provide for people's leisure time the variety and number of leisure amenities have grown and so help to fuel the leisure boom further. The tourist industry which caters for people's holiday needs has had its growth boosted by an increased number of overseas visitors to Britain. Figure 1 shows the results of a survey on the use of leisure time.

Q1

(a) Refer to Figure 1. Describe the main contrasts in leisure activities between: (i) men and women; (ii) the 18 to 24 age group and the over 55 age group: (iii) the profession/managerial and the unskilled occupational groups. Suggest reasons for the contrasts.
(b) What important leisure activities have declined in popularity over the past 30 years or so? What important activities have increased in popularity? Name some activities which did not exist 30 years ago.

Leisure facilities in towns and cities

Many leisure activities rely on special facilities. Different leisure facilities show contrasting patterns of location within towns and cities. Frequently used facilities to which people only travel a short distance will be found throughout the urban area, for example, public houses and children's play areas.

The Central Business District will be the main location of cinemas, theatres, restaurants and clubs which serve the whole town or city and the surrounding area. In some large cities an 'entertainment district' may well develop in one part of the central area. Space-consuming amenities which serve all the urban area

may be located in accessible inner city areas (for example, professional football and other major sports grounds) or in suburban locations with good road access and space for car parking (for example, sports/ leisure centres).

Q2

(a) Why is the CBD an attractive location for some leisure facilities? Why can only high-earning, small space-consuming activities profitably locate in the CBD? What non-commercial 'cultural' facilities run by the local authority are often found in central locations?
(b) Why are professional football grounds usually located in inner city areas? (Accessibility is only one factor to consider.)
(c) What sporting facilities (for both participating and spectating) are more frequently found on the edge of urban areas? Give reasons for your answer.

Open space

In most cities the amount of open space increases with greater distance from the city centre. The small areas of open space in the inner city areas reflect both high land values and the lack of planning when these areas were developed in the past. In the suburbs, however, land is cheaper and planning has taken greater care to provide housing areas with the open space they need. Occasionally, however, major parks and other areas of open space are found close to central areas of cities for historical reasons (for example, the Royal Parks of London) or because land was unsuitable for building (for example, a river flood plain).

Areas of countryside at the edge of cities – the urban fringe – also provide space and amenities for the use of people in

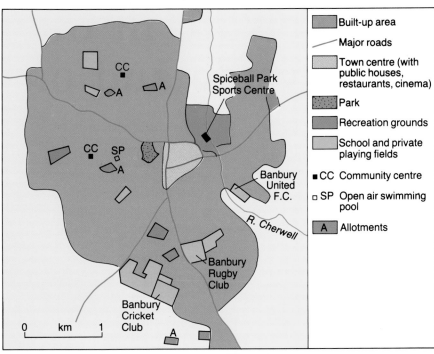

Figure 3
Leisure facilities in Banbury, Oxfordshire

neighbouring urban areas. Playing fields, golf courses, horse- riding stables and country parks (see Section 9.4) are examples of such urban fringe leisure provision.

Q3

Figure 3 shows some of the leisure facilities in the town of Banbury, Oxfordshire. Some of these also serve the surrounding rural area. (About 90 000 people live in Banbury and the area it serves.)
(a) Describe the pattern of open space in Banbury.
(b) The Spiceball Park Sports Centre is a recent development. What advantages has its site for such a facility?
(c) What facilities on the map would serve only parts of Banbury? What facilities would serve Banbury and the surrounding area?
(d) What facilities found in larger towns are not present in Banbury? Why are they absent?

Figure 4
Spiceball Park Sports Centre, Banbury

9.4 Leisure in the countryside and on the coast

An important part of many people's leisure time is spent visiting places away from the immediate home area, either for a day trip or for a holiday. Their destination may be somewhere in the countryside or on the coast, a town or city of special interest or, in the case of many holidays, another country. This section looks at destinations in the countryside and on the coast, while Section 9.5 considers tourist towns and cities.

Leisure provision in the countryside

Areas of attractive or dramatic scenery are visited by many thousands of people each year. Some people enjoy driving around or resting in such areas while others take part in more energetic activities, such as hill-walking, climbing, caving, sailing and skiing. Many areas of land and smaller sites have been specially set aside or developed for visitors. These include:

- Country parks (Figure 1) developed by either local authorities or private landowners.

- Country houses and historic sites owned and managed by the National Trust or the government.

- Privately-owned historic houses and estates which have been opened to visitors, often with added attractions such as safari parks, theme parks and specialist museums.

- Scenic sites, either privately owned or owned by the National Trust and National Park authorities.

- Sites developed by organizations such as the Forestry Commission (see Section 3.3) and the water authorities.

- Major leisure attractions such as Alton Towers and holiday villages (Figure 2).

- Other specialist attractions ranging from steam railways to zoos.

Figure 3 shows the variety of attractions which may be found within the Severn Valley of Shropshire and Worcestershire. Such attractions for visitors in a scenic area are accompanied by the development of all types of facility and service for the visitors: camping and caravan sites, bed and breakfast establishments, cafés, tourist shops and so on. In an area such as the Severn Valley, which caters mainly for day visitors, many of these facilities may be thinly spread over a wide area. However, in areas visited by many holidaymakers besides day visitors, the tourist industry becomes a key element in the local economy and the main activity of some settlements.

Figure 2
Center Parcs' holiday village, Nottinghamshire

Figure 1
Hollingworth Lake Country Park, Rochdale

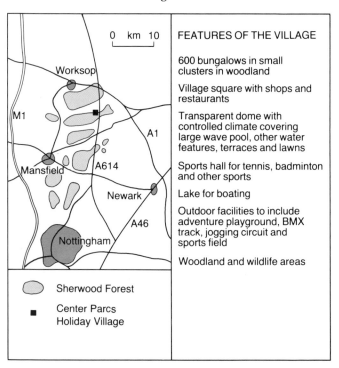

	Country Park
=	Roads
P	Car park
⊼	Picnic area
▲	Camp site
	Fishing area
I	Information
T	Toilets
C	Café
B	Boating, sailing and board sailing

⌃⌃ Boom to keep boats out of nature reserve
-- Footpaths (a footpath also follows the lake shore)

Visitor Centre (I,T,C)

Hotel
Rochdale 6 km
Lakebank (T,C, ⊼ ,B)
Harbour
HOLLINGWORTH LAKE
Pavilion (T,C)
Ferry
Nature Reserve

The lake is a reservoir built in 1804 to supply water to the Rochdale Canal

0 m 200

0 km 10

FEATURES OF THE VILLAGE

Worksop
M1
A1
Mansfield
A614
Newark
A46
Nottingham

Sherwood Forest
■ Center Parcs Holiday Village

600 bungalows in small clusters in woodland

Village square with shops and restaurants

Transparent dome with controlled climate covering large wave pool, other water features, terraces and lawns

Sports hall for tennis, badminton and other sports

Lake for boating

Outdoor facilities to include adventure playground, BMX track, jogging circuit and sports field

Woodland and wildlife areas

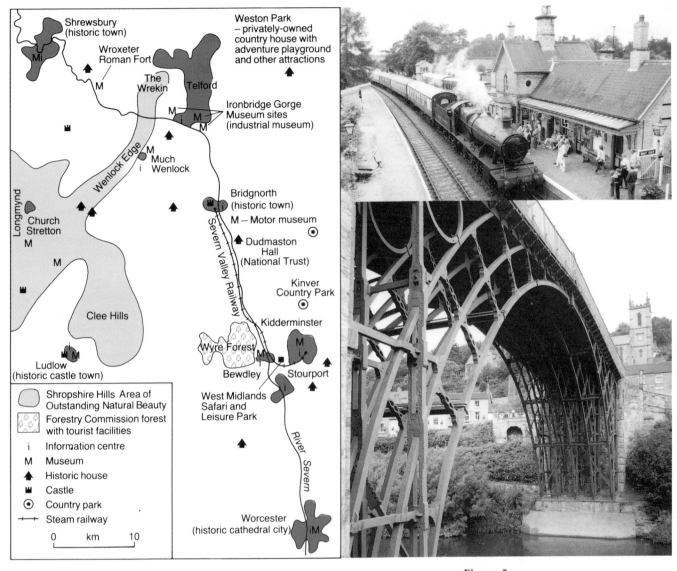

Figure 3
Tourist attractions in the Severn Valley

Q1
(a) For each of the types of tourist site listed above, name examples from Figure 3.
(b) Suppose you were responsible for planning the itinerary of a four day coach tour for foreign visitors to the Severn Valley. Draw a labelled diagrammatic map to show a suitable itinerary, beginning at Worcester and finishing at Shrewsbury.
(c) Describe how the economy of an area may benefit from the development of a tourist industry.

Planning for leisure

Careful, detailed land use planning is needed to cater for visitors and, at the same time, protect the environment and the interests of other people such as farmers. At Hollingworth Lake (Figure 1), several of the leisure uses to which people wished to put this lake and its surrounds were **incompatible** with each other. The solution has been to zone the area for different uses. Such **parallel use** of an area for two or more purposes is the usual solution to such problems. At a larger scale, the same issues have to be dealt with in National Parks (Section 12.1).

Q2
(a) Refer to Figure 1. Describe the way in which the zoning of Hollingworth Lake for different purposes has reduced potential conflicts.
(b) Suggest why waterskiing and fast power boats are banned from the lake.
(c) Suggest why (i) car parking is restricted to only three locations and (ii) there is no car access to the lake's southern shore.

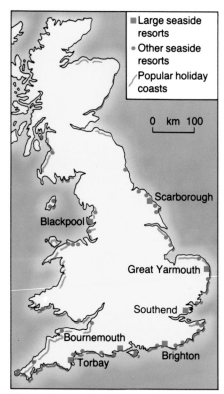

Figure 4
Britain's coastal resorts

Figure 5
Land use in Llandudno

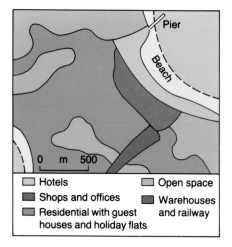

The coast

The long coastline of Britain is a very important destination for holidays and day visits (Figure 4). Beaches, attractive scenery, picturesque fishing villages, sheltered water for boating and the leisure and entertainment facilities of seaside resorts attract millions of people, mostly during a relatively short summer season.

Seaside resorts

Seaside resorts first developed in the late 18th and early 19th centuries as places which the rich would visit for health reasons. The development of cheap rail transport later in the 19th century led to the rapid growth of seaside resorts to cater for people from the industrial towns. During the early 20th century, holidays with pay together with people's greater spending power and the development of road transport led to the further growth of resorts. Boarding houses which offered cheaper accommodation than the hotels grew up in the streets behind the sea front. Llandudno's development (Figure 5) is typical of most resorts. In the 1950s two important trends enabled an even greater number of people to be able to afford a seaside holiday: the opening of holiday camps and the development of caravan sites for self-catering holidays.

However, the 1950s also marked the turning point in the fortunes of many resorts. Seaside holidays

Figure 6
The attractions of Blackpool

in Britain became less popular with the development of cheap 'package' holidays abroad and the widening of people's leisure interests. Smaller resorts with poorer road access from major cities or with less scenic surroundings have suffered most from the decline in seaside holidays. The very large resorts have been more successful in attracting visitors. They have a wider range of entertainment and leisure facilities, in the case of Blackpool (Figure 6) on a particularly large scale. They have been able to afford major new developments such as Rhyl's Suncentre (Figure 7) and Brighton's boat marina. Conference facilities have been developed so as to spread business throughout the year. The large resorts also have the advantage of good road access, particularly important for attracting day visitors.

Q3

(a) Refer to an atlas map. Suggest why Hunstanton in Norfolk and Aberystwyth in Dyfed have declined as resorts. Why has Blackpool, Britain's largest resort, continued to prosper?
(b) What natural advantage have resorts on the south coast of England over those elsewhere in Britain? (See Section 2.3.)
(c) How have the former holiday camps responded to competition from foreign package holidays?

Seaside resorts have an important additional function in providing housing for many retired people who wish to live near the sea. Retirement, nursing and convalescent homes have been developed in many resorts. Some resorts in South-East England, for example, Brighton and Worthing, are important residential centres for people who commute by train to London.

Business and employment prospects in seaside resorts have always had to face two major problems. Firstly, catering for holidaymakers and day visitors is seasonal; in summer casual labour has to be taken on in the peak weeks, while in winter many people are unemployed. Secondly, resorts have to face the uncertainties of the British climate; a bad summer will keep away day visitors and businesses will lose income.

Figure 7
Suncentre, Rhyl

Q4
(a) How do holiday resorts attempt to attract out-of-season business and so reduce seasonal unemployment?
(b) What developments in resorts attempt to overcome the problem of unreliable weather?

Figure 8
Polperro, a Cornish fishing village and the resort of Torquay

Tourism in Devon and Cornwall

The holiday industry on the coast is not confined to seaside resorts, with their highly developed entertainment facilities. Coastlines with attractive scenery and small fishing villages attract many visitors, as do areas with sheltered inlets suitable for boating. The coast of Devon and Cornwall (Figure 8) has such attractions combined with the climatic advantages of early springs, warm summers and high average sunshine totals. However, the region's tourist industry has had to face several difficulties:

- Competition from foreign 'package' holidays.

- Remoteness from major cities, so discouraging day visitors.

- The seasonal nature of the holiday trade.

- A number of summers with poor weather (1985 and 1986).

- Congestion of visitors and their cars in July and August at the small resorts.

Q5
(a) Describe the attractions of Devon and Cornwall for holidaymakers.
(b) What are the gains and losses resulting from the tourist industry for the region?
(c) Suggest why Devon and Cornwall has proved to be a popular retirement area. What problems might this popularity cause?

9.5 Tourist towns and cities

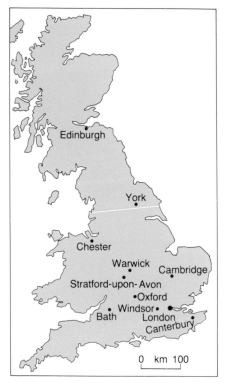

Figure 1
Major tourist towns and cities

Many of Britain's historic towns and cities are important tourist centres. They are very important in attracting large numbers of foreign visitors to Britain. Figure 1 shows the location of Britain's most important tourist towns and cities. London is Britain's most important tourist centre. Day visitors and British and foreign holidaymakers are attracted to London by its historic buildings, ceremonial events, museums, art galleries, theatres, shops and special tourist attractions.

Two tourist cities

York is one of Britain's most important tourist cities. It has a long history and many buildings survive from the Middle Ages when it was one of Britain's largest cities. Figure 2 gives details of its major attractions to visitors. It has major museums besides many historic buildings.

In addition to the traditional tourist centres shown on the map in Figure 1, many other towns and cities have attempted to attract visitors and take a share of the expanding tourist industry. Bradford is a city which has made great efforts to develop tourism. Some people might consider a northern industrial city an unlikely tourist centre, but Bradford has capitalized on its industrial past and promotes itself as a centre for touring the surrounding area (Figure 3).

Q1
(a) Describe the attractions of Bradford for the visitor. How do they differ from those of York?
(b) What aspects of the surrounding area does Bradford promote in its publicity material?

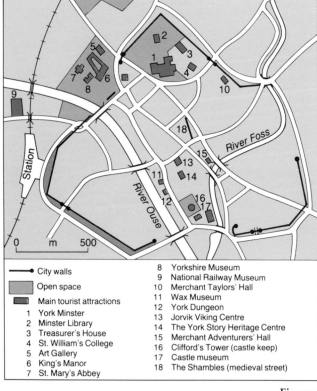

- City walls
- Open space
- Main tourist attractions
  1 York Minster
  2 Minster Library
  3 Treasurer's House
  4 St. William's College
  5 Art Gallery
  6 King's Manor
  7 St. Mary's Abbey
  8 Yorkshire Museum
  9 National Railway Museum
  10 Merchant Taylors' Hall
  11 Wax Museum
  12 York Dungeon
  13 Jorvik Viking Centre
  14 The York Story Heritage Centre
  15 Merchant Adventurers' Hall
  16 Clifford's Tower (castle keep)
  17 Castle museum
  18 The Shambles (medieval street)

Figure 2
York

Bradford
– a surprising place

For the visitor, Bradford has much on offer. Discover its history and industrial heritage. Spend time in the city's museums and galleries which include the National Museum of Photography, Film and Television – Britain's newest national museum with its giant IMAX cinema. Hunt for textile bargains in the millshops.

Beyond the city centre, Bradford encompasses open moors and valleys. The villages have their own attractions: Haworth, the Worth Valley steam railway; Saltaire, the Victorian 'model' village; Ilkley, a perfect base for touring the Yorkshire Dales National Park.

Figure 3
Bradford – an unlikely tourist centre?

Planning problems in tourist towns and cities

Historic towns which attract many visitors face difficult decisions when planning for the future. Their residents expect services and amenities to be developed just as with other towns. This needs to be done while still conserving the historic buildings and other features which attract the visitors. Old town centres with narrow streets are unsuitable for the smooth flow of traffic, especially when visitors' cars add to the congestion. New road schemes to relieve such congestion have often been very controversial. The pressure of visitors may lead to other problems such as litter, inadequate car parking, accommodation shortages and the development of some tourist attractions and shops which do not fit in with the character of old towns. Figure 4 shows how some of these problems have affected Stratford-upon-Avon.

> **Q2**
> **(a)** Why has Stratford-upon-Avon developed as a major tourist centre?
> **(b)** What businesses have capitalized on its attraction to visitors?

Figure 4
Tourism in Stratford-upon-Avon

The tourist industry

The tourist industry is one of the most rapidly growing service industries. Figure 5 shows how employment and earnings from tourism have grown in recent years. It is a labour-intensive industry. Without it the unemployment situation would be very much worse in many parts of the country. The influx of foreign visitors brings in much foreign currency and makes a vital contribution to Britain's balance of trade.

However, as we saw in the case of some seaside resorts, tourism is not a growth industry everywhere and future planning needs to take account of changing holiday patterns and use of leisure time.

> **Q3**
> **(a)** Explain how spending by foreign tourists might help sectors of the economy other than the tourist industry itself.
> **(b)** Explain how the package tour industry for British people holidaying abroad provides business and employment in the UK.

Figure 5
Tourism is one of Britain's growth industries

STRATFORD'S ATTRACTIONS

- Royal Shakespeare Theatre
- Shakespeare Birthplace Trust (Shakespeare museum & records)
- Old houses and other buildings
- River Avon

THE IMPACT OF TOURISM

1 Severe traffic congestion
2 Car parking problems
3 Congestion of people
4 Litter, especially on open spaces
5 Development of many souvenir and craft shops, tea rooms and restaurants
6 Expansion of old hotels and building of 250 room Moat House International Hotel
7 Development of additional tourist attractions such as a motor museum and waxworks

EMPLOYMENT IN TOURISM AND LEISURE
About 1 million people work in jobs connected with tourism. Between 1971 and 1983 employment in entertainment and recreation increased by 58000 and employment in hotels and catering increased by 225000.

EARNINGS FROM TOURISM
- In 1983 overseas visitors spent £3655 million(compared with £726 million in 1973).

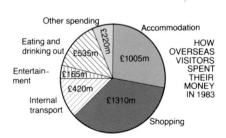

HOW OVERSEAS VISITORS SPENT THEIR MONEY IN 1983

Other spending £220m
Accommodation £1005m
Eating and drinking out £535m
Entertainment £165m
Internal transport £420m
Shopping £1310m

- In 1983 British people on holiday spent £3625 million within the UK and £2750 on foreign holidays.

10.1 Road and rail transport

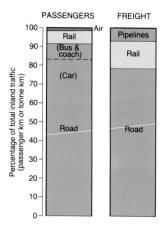

Figure 1
The shares of different modes of transport in the carriage of passengers and freight

Figure 2
A comparison of rail, road and air transport between London and Manchester 1987

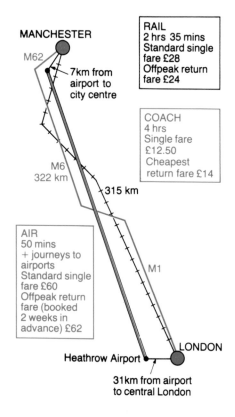

RAIL
2 hrs 35 mins
Standard single fare £28
Offpeak return fare £24

COACH
4 hrs
Single fare £12.50
Cheapest return fare £14

AIR
50 mins
+ journeys to airports
Standard single fare £60
Offpeak return fare (booked 2 weeks in advance) £62

Road and rail transport dominate the movement of passengers and freight within Britain, as Figure 1 shows. Of these two, road transport is by far the more important. When comparing different methods of transport, distance along the various routes, time taken and cost have to be considered. As an example, Figure 2 compares the different modes of transport available for passenger traffic between London and Manchester.

Q1
(a) Look at Figure 2. What are the advantages and disadvantages of the different methods of transport for passenger travel between London and Manchester?
(b) Would the comparison between the methods be different for a cross-country journey over a similar distance, say, from Norwich to Shrewsbury? Explain your answer.

Road transport for passengers

The graphs in Figure 1 are a result of a steady increase in both passenger and freight traffic on the roads over the past 30 years or so. The growth of passenger traffic reflects a large increase in travel by private car, a trend linked to the growth of car ownership. Although the costs of car ownership are great, cars have the advantages of convenience and, over many journeys, speed.

The growth of passenger traffic by road is entirely due to transport by car; travel by bus has declined. The move away from public transport, whether bus, coach or rail, has led to poorer services in rural areas and on some urban and cross-country routes. Yet the large section of the population who do not have cars still need public transport; they include many old people, children, many housewives and all those who cannot afford to own and run a car. Figure 3 looks at the particular problem of providing public transport in rural areas.

Road transport for freight

The growth of freight traffic on the road reflects the fact that over most distances and for most types of goods, road transport is cheaper than rail. The major exception is the transport of bulk goods over longer distances. Rail transport lacks a time advantage in most cases as well, because it cannot usually provide door-to-door transport. Transfer of loads from wagons to lorries for delivery costs money besides time. Other changes have helped to give road transport the competitive edge over railways: the development of larger lorries (Figure 4) and the growth of the motorway network (Figure 5).

The expansion of freight traffic on the roads has led to problems however:

● The heavy weight of lorries and the vibration they cause damages roads, bridges and buildings. Noise and exhaust fumes cause further nuisance.

● Lorries create much traffic congestion, especially in towns with narrow roads.

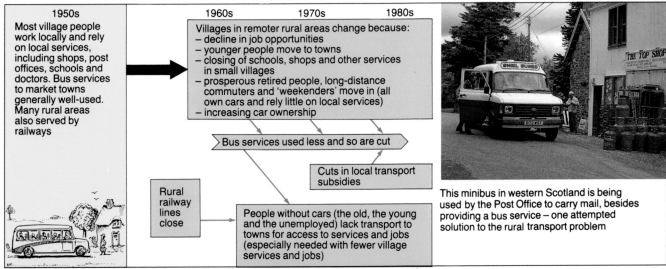

| 1950s | 1960s | 1970s | 1980s |

Most village people work locally and rely on local services, including shops, post offices, schools and doctors. Bus services to market towns generally well-used. Many rural areas also served by railways

Villages in remoter rural areas change because:
– decline in job opportunities
– younger people move to towns
– closing of schools, shops and other services in small villages
– prosperous retired people, long-distance commuters and 'weekenders' move in (all own cars and rely little on local services)
– increasing car ownership

Bus services used less and so are cut

Cuts in local transport subsidies

Rural railway lines close

People without cars (the old, the young and the unemployed) lack transport to towns for access to services and jobs (especially needed with fewer village services and jobs)

This minibus in western Scotland is being used by the Post Office to carry mail, besides providing a bus service – one attempted solution to the rural transport problem

Figure 3
The rural transport problem

Figure 4
Larger lorries have lowered transport costs

- Transport by road uses energy much less efficiently than rail or water transport, as Figure 6 shows.

- Motorways and other major roads take up large areas of land and have a major impact on the environment.

Q2

(a) Why has the road transport industry pressed for the limits on lorry size and weight to be raised? Why is such a trend frequently opposed?

(b) Refer to Figure 6. What changes in transport would produce important energy savings? Describe the problems of bringing about the changes you mention.

Rail transport

During the late 1950s and 1960s Britain's railway systems underwent major changes: diesel and electric trains replaced steam trains, many other aspects of railway operation were modernized and large numbers of loss-making lines and stations were closed. During the 1970s and early 1980s, however, investment in the railways has been at a relatively low level. Some important changes took place, such as the completion of electrification of the London to Glasgow route in 1974 and the introduction of the diesel High Speed Train (HST125) in 1976. Investment was concentrated on the more profitable Inter-City routes, while other lines suffered from problems of track being overdue for renewal and equipment being obsolete and worn-out. Progress with

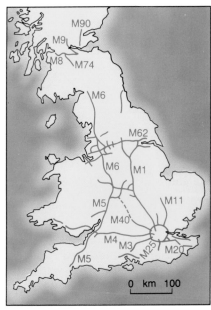

Figure 5
The motorway network

Figure 6
Energy use by different transport modes

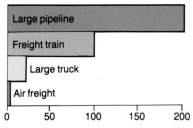

Tonne km/litre (i.e. the number of tonnes which can be carried over 1km using 1 litre of fuel)

119

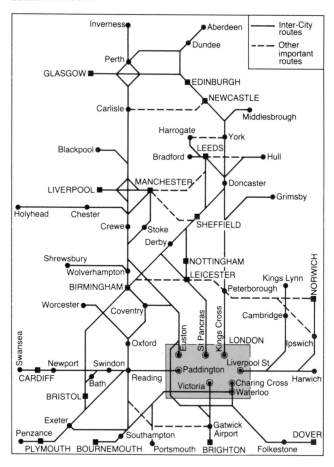

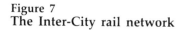
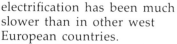

Figure 7
The Inter-City rail network

Figure 8
A unit freight train of oil tank wagons

Figure 9
British Rail's new Class 91 locomotive, designed to provide high speed services on the West Coast Main Line (Euston to Glasgow) and the newly electrified East Coast Main Line (Kings Cross to Edinburgh)

electrification has been much slower than in other west European countries.

British Rail runs at a loss and has to be subsidized by the government. However, this subsidy is at a lower level than in other European countries. Government help is needed to keep open 'socially valuable' lines in relatively remote areas, and to invest in new track, trains and other equipment needed for the future. Some of the commuter services in the London region are not particularly profitable, but require continuing investment. If these services were allowed to run down, traffic would be diverted to already overcrowded roads.

The main Inter-City services operated by British Rail (Figure 7) are profitable and competitive. The speed of the services makes them very popular with business travellers, but complicated

systems of special fares and railcards are necessary to attract the custom of other people.

The mainstay of freight traffic on the railways is the carrying of coal from the mines to power stations and major industrial users and other bulky cargoes such as minerals, steel, grain, cement, oil products and chemicals over longer distances. Where 'unit trains' (Figure 8) can run directly between one industrial plant and another on a regular basis, rail transport is particularly competitive. The railways have lost most of their general freight traffic to roads. Freightliner trains which take standard size containers are important over long distances, for example, from ports in South-East England to northern England and Scotland. Over shorter distances though, road transport has the advantages of speed, flexibility

and lower cost. British Rail is trying to capture a larger share of freight traffic by, for example the promotion of private factory sidings (with firms being helped in development costs).

Q3

(a) Why are commuter services to London and other major cities difficult and expensive to operate?
(b) Explain why unit trains can operate very economically.
(c) Suggest why rail container traffic is less competitive with road transport over shorter distances.

Q4

Figure 10 shows the rail network of North-East England.
(a) Which passenger services in the North-East would seem to face the brightest future? Which ones are likely to be less profitable? Give reasons for your answers.
(b) Describe the nature of the goods carried by Railfreight services in the North-East. Why is rail transport particularly suitable for these goods?
(c) Suggest reasons for the changes in Railfreight services listed in the diagram.

Q5

(a) Draw a 'cause and effect' diagram (High subsidies → Hold down fares – and so on) to summarize the argument in the previous paragraph. Draw a second diagram to show the effect of no subsidies or government investment in the railways.
(b) Do you agree with one of these two approaches or should some middle course be followed? Give full reasons for your views.

The future for British Rail

In 1983 British Rail put forward a modernization plan involving the investment of £5700 million to electrify main lines, introduce new rolling stock and make other improvements. The government gave the go-ahead for the electrification of the East Coast route to Scotland (London–York–Edinburgh) but did not provide all the money asked for.

Some people claim that more investment than British Rail asked for in 1983 is needed and that subsidies should hold down fares. Thus more people would be encouraged to use trains. High subsidies and positive moves to divert freight traffic back to the railways would, it is argued, lead to less money being needed for new roads. This would reduce the environmental problems resulting from expanding road transport. Recently the government has suggested that investment by private business in the rail network is the way forward, following the example of financing the Channel Tunnel.

PASSENGER SERVICES
1 *Inter-City Services*
East Coast Main Line servies to London, Scotland and other destinations. Also Middlesbrough to London
2 *Local Services*
On other passenger lines

EXAMPLES OF FREIGHT SERVICES
Starting or ending in the North-East
1 Coal to Blyth Power Station, power stations in West Yorkshire, Tyne Dock and Blyth (for export)
2 Alumina from Blyth import terminal to Lynemouth and Fort William, Scotland
3 Aluminium from Lynemouth to Teesside and South Wales
4 Steel from Lackenby and Tees Yard to Corby (BSC pipes) and Sunderland (shipyards)
5 Nuclear waste from Hartlepool to Sellafield, Cumbria
6 Potash from Boulby to Teesport
7 Chemicals from Billingham (ICI) to Grangemouth, Scotland (BP chemicals)

Passing through the North-East
1 New cars from Dagenham and Oxford to Scotland
2 Freightliner containers from Felixstowe to Coatbridge, near Glasgow
3 Grain from Lincolnshire to whisky distilleries in Scotland

Speedlink services
Wagonload traffic between the North-East and the rest of Britain

Services withdrawn between 1980 and 1988
1 Iron ore from Teesside to Consett and steel from Consett
2 Coal from closed colleries
3 Freightliner container service to and from Newcastle (where Freightliner terminal has closed)

Figure 10
Rail services in North-East England

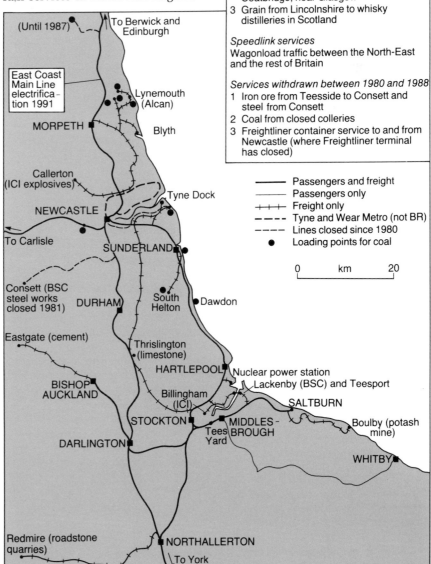

10.2 Transport in urban areas

Figure 1
Traffic congestion

Figure 2
An urban motorway: the Aston Expressway, Birmingham

Most urban areas are severely affected by problems of traffic congestion. There are many factors which combine together to cause traffic congestion. Some of the most important ones are:

- A mixture of many types of traffic occupying the roads, with delivery vehicles and frequently-stopping buses slowing traffic flow.

- Complex patterns of relatively narrow streets in central areas which cannot efficiently handle large traffic flows.

- Major roads leading to city centres (radial roads) with too few traffic lanes and many junctions.

- Inadequate car parking space in city centres, resulting in street parking restricting traffic flow.

- Through traffic using a town's roads when travelling between other towns.

- Heavy traffic flows during twice-daily rush hours.

The delays which result from traffic congestion are not just inconvenient and annoying; they make the commercial activities of urban areas less efficient. Noise and pollution reduce the quality of life of people living near major roads. At major road junctions pollution may be at dangerous levels, while vibration from heavy traffic can damage buildings.

Solutions

Many ways of dealing with the problem of traffic congestion have been attempted. The city of Cambridge has introduced a number of 'solutions' as Figure 3 shows. Cambridge has a number of special problems: the central shopping area is hemmed in by historic colleges and other buildings and so has little room to expand, cycle traffic is unusually heavy, and it is a major tourist city. In addition, the Cambridge area is an expanding centre of high technology industry. Despite the schemes which have been introduced, car parking remains a particular problem for the city.

In larger cities, the construction of urban motorways (Figure 2) may speed traffic flows, but large areas of land are used up and people living nearby are seriously affected by noise and fumes.

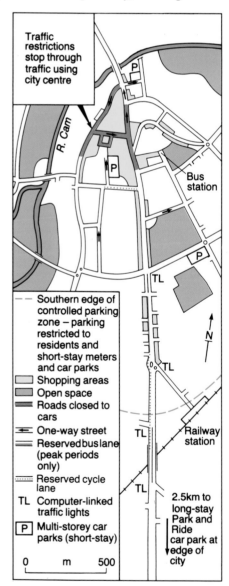

Figure 3
Traffic planning in Cambridge

122

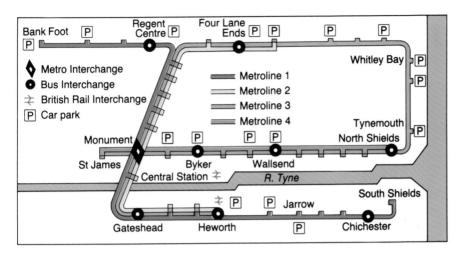

Figure 4
The Tyne and Wear Metro

Q1
(a) Refer to Figure 3. Describe and explain the purpose of the various 'solutions' to traffic congestion which have been attempted in Cambridge.
(b) What are the gains and losses which result from the building of urban motorways?

Public transport in urban areas

Most bus and many local train passengers have no choice in the transport they use as they do not have the use of a car. Car users usually prefer the convenience of their own vehicles and are reluctant to use public transport. In London underground and suburban railway networks are used by many car owners for commuting because of their speed and the difficulty of parking in the central area. However, many car owners will only be attracted to public transport by low fares in addition to frequent, efficient services.

In 1986 public transport was **deregulated** to allow greater competition between transport concerns. It was hoped that competition would give the public more services and increase

efficiency. Critics of deregulation maintain that it is a recipe for muddle, with people away from main routes being inadequately served.

Q2
(a) List the arguments for and against subsidizing public transport in urban areas.
(b) If fares rise beyond a critical point, many people will not use services and income for the operator falls. What might then happen? Which groups of people will suffer most?

Many transport planners believe that future investment in urban transport should be in efficient public transport systems with 'rapid-transit' light railways integrated with bus services, rather than complex road schemes. The first stage of such a scheme was opened in Tyne and Wear in 1980. The light railway, known as the Metro, mostly follows existing railway lines but also passes through new underground tunnels (Figure 4). Because of the huge investment needed for systems like the Metro, some cities have more limited schemes of improving existing suburban railways and developing bus/rail interchange points.

In smaller urban areas with

shorter travelling distances the best approach for the future may well be road improvements to speed traffic flow, combined with improved bus services involving reserved bus lanes or roads on main routes. Frequencies of services in many residential areas can be improved with the use of minibuses (Figure 5).

Q3
(a) What problems are involved in the building of light railways in urban areas?
(b) What are the advantages of an integrated public transport system?

Figure 5
The use of public minibuses has increased greatly in recent years

10.3 Air transport and airports

Air transport is of very great importance for the carriage of passengers, high-value cargo and mail between Britain and other countries. However, only 3 per cent of the passengers travelling by public transport between British cities use air transport.

Air transport within Britain

The three major air routes within Britain are between London (Heathrow) and Glasgow, Edinburgh and Belfast. Although flight times are much less than by rail, extra time is spent travelling between city centres and airports and the fares are more expensive. Over a shorter distance, for example, between London and Birmingham, air transport has little time advantage over rail for city centre to city centre travel. However, short distance services are important as 'feeders' for international flights from Heathrow and Gatwick.

Air transport within Britain is of little importance for the movement of cargo. However, an important exception is the handling of much first class mail by overnight services.

International air transport

Air transport between Britain and other countries has grown rapidly since 1945. By the mid 1960s air transport had become a cheaper besides a quicker method of long-distance travel. This followed the introduction of jet aircraft on the major intercontinental routes. In the 1970s long-haul air travel expanded with the widespread use of the Boeing 747 'Jumbo' jet and other wide-bodied aircraft. The growth of the package holiday industry in the 1950s and 1960s led to development of charter air services to the holiday areas, mainly in southern Europe.

Scheduled air services to the major cities of western Europe have grown less rapidly than the other two types of service, partly because of relatively high fares. They are particularly important for business travel. For such short distances travel to the continent almost eight times as many people use either road and sea or rail and sea transport.

International air freight traffic has also expanded greatly. In terms of value of goods handled, London's Heathrow airport is Britain's leading 'port', handling over 12 per cent of Britain's international trade (compared with 1 per cent in 1960). Mechanized handling methods and the use of special containers (Figure 1) speeds loading and unloading.

Figure 1
Loading containers on a jumbo jet

Q1

(a) Explain why (i) intercontinental services and (ii) holiday charter services have expanded more rapidly than scheduled services between London and the major cities of western Europe. (You will need to consider factors such as fares, distances, alternative types of transport available and developments in aviation.)
(b) Name examples of goods for which air transport is important.

London's airports

Heathrow Airport is the world's leading international airport. It is only twenty kilometres from central London with which it is linked by motorway (M4) and underground railway (journey time 45 minutes). The opening of a fourth passenger terminal in 1986 expanded Heathrow's capacity from about 26 million passengers a year to 38 million.

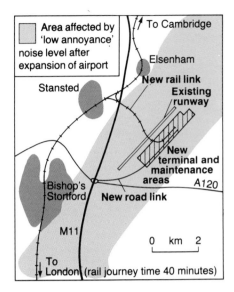

Figure 2
The development of Stansted as London's third airport

Heathrow has suffered from congestion and it is government policy for further growth to take place at other airports. Gatwick's capacity has also been expanded by building a second terminal to raise capacity from 11 to 25 million passengers a year.

Proposals have been made for a third London airport ever since the early 1960s. Three times decisions on a site were made and then overturned. The rejection of such decisions led to the development of the new Heathrow and Gatwick terminals. Eventually, a study in 1978, followed by a public enquiry in 1981–3 led to the choice falling on Stansted in Essex (Figure 2). Stansted already has a long runway and, with the construction of a new terminal, can be developed to handle 15 million passengers a year relatively cheaply. Although much employment will be created, there has been considerable local opposition to the development of Stansted. Luton is an additional airport for London, handling about two million holiday charter flight passengers each year.

Figure 4
Birmingham Airport's new terminal. It is linked by the 'Maglev' monorail to Birmingham International railway station and the National Exhibition Centre

Q2
(a) What developments in aviation enable Heathrow and Gatwick to expand passenger handling capacity without building new runways?
(b) Refer to Figure 2. What advantages has Stansted for the location of London's third airport? What are the gains and losses for people who live in this area?

Regional airports

In the 1930s most of Britain's cities developed their own airports at locations with a 20 to 40 minute bus journey to city centres. As a result many airports grew up close together. For example, Liverpool and Manchester airports are only 50 kilometres apart. The development of modern roads and widespread car ownership should enable traffic to be handled at a smaller number of regional, rather than city airports, each large enough to attract a wide variety of services. The existence of so many airports led the government to classify those in England and Wales into the four categories shown in Figure 3, with the policy being to concentrate services at category A and category B airports. By controlling the issue of permits to use airports, the government can

prevent services operating from unsuitable airports.

Q3
(a) Why is it important to concentrate services into a few regional airports?
(b) Suggest why Birmingham (Figure 4) has proved to be a successful regional airport. (Consider both its location and its facilities.)

Figure 3
Britain's airports

125

10.4 Seaports

With its long coastline, Britain has many ports and harbours. Many are only of local importance but, as Figure 1 shows, there are large numbers of major ports handling international trade. Britain's ports also handle a large coastal trade in bulk products such as oil and coal. In the 19th and early 20th centuries, ports on estuaries such as the Thames, Clyde, Mersey, Severn and Humber grew rapidly to handle Britain's expanding world trade. Docks were cut out of riverside land to provide berths unaffected by tides. During the 1960s and early 1970s great changes in sea transport took place, having a marked effect on Britain's ports.

Changing methods of cargo handling

The development of container transport and **roll on/roll off ships** (lorries drive on and off) for general cargo, together with other new handling methods (Figure 2) have speeded the movement of goods through the ports. The introduction of these capital-intensive methods led to the dock labour force falling from 64 000 in 1965 to 27 000 in 1979. Many old docks were unsuitable for the new methods and could not accommodate large container ships. Therefore new facilities had to be built. Containerization has had to be accompanied by changes in rail and road transport and the development of inland container depots. These depots are points for packing and unpacking containers and centres for the collection and distribution of goods. All these developments enable each container load to be kept together for as far as possible on its journey.

Q1
(a) What are the advantages of transporting goods by container?
(b) Why are roll on/roll off services best suited to shorter sea journeys?
(c) Look at the photographs in Figures 2 and 4 and then explain why new facilities are needed for container traffic.
(d) Explain why containerization has led to the numbers of the dock labour force falling.

Other changes in sea transport

Other major changes in sea transport have also affected Britain's ports:

- The introduction of supertankers and large bulk cargo ships carrying goods such as coal, iron ore and grain has led to the development of specialized **deep-water terminals**.

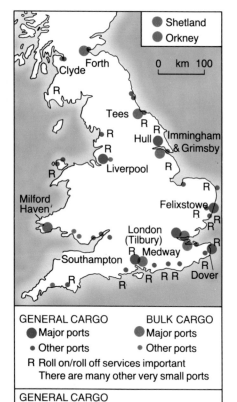

GENERAL CARGO
- ● Major ports
- • Other ports

BULK CARGO
- ● Major ports
- • Other ports

R Roll on/roll off services important
There are many other very small ports

GENERAL CARGO
Most general cargo is handled by *container* (*lift on/lift off*) services and *roll on/roll off* services (lorries drive on and off ships)
BULK CARGO
Oil accounts for most of the bulk cargo handled

**Figure 1
Britain's ports**

**Figure 2
A container berth at Felixstowe**

126

- The decline in long-distance passenger liner services hit Liverpool and Southampton in particular. However, the growth of cross-channel passenger and car traffic has led to expansion at the channel ports, especially Dover.

- Changing patterns of international trade have affected the fortunes of British ports. The value of trade with European countries rose from 36 per cent of the total in 1963 to 58 per cent in 1979. Ports in the East and South have therefore benefitted from this change.

- The development of **feeder-relay services**, consisting of smaller ships ferrying containers to a larger pivot port which serves long-distance shipping lines, has resulted in some British ports losing their transit trade to continental rivals, but has boosted the trade of some smaller east coast ports.

Q2

(a) Refer back to Sections 7.1, 7.3 and 8.5 to explain the distribution of deep-water oil and ore terminals as shown in Figure 1.

(b) Explain how the system of feeder-relay services allows shipping lines to easily transfer their centre of operations from one European port to another.

(c) Explain why most of Britain's east coast ports have increased their share of the country's sea trade since about 1970.

Adapting to change

The old-established ports faced difficulties in adapting to the changes in sea transport, especially to containerization. In the 1960s new container ports were built at Tilbury (by the Port of London Authority) and at Seaforth, Liverpool, but prolonged labour disputes over the loss of jobs elsewhere in the ports of London and Liverpool led to custom from the shipping lines being lost. Much international transit trade went to continental ports such as Rotterdam and Antwerp. Because of these difficulties and the problems of old dock facilities, London's docks upstream from Tilbury and many of Liverpool's docks (Figure 3) have been closed.

An established port which has had greater success is Southampton. Much investment in new facilities combined with commercial initiative led to the port attracting major shipping lines.

Felixstowe, a growth port

Felixstowe (Figure 4) has grown rapidly in importance as a container and roll on/roll off port since it was opened in the early 1950s. A new container terminal was opened in 1981 to expand its capacity even more and further developments are in hand. Although much of its success has been due to its position, it also had the advantages of being able to develop on a greenfield site and, unlike the older ports, did not have the problem of labour redundancies and related disputes.

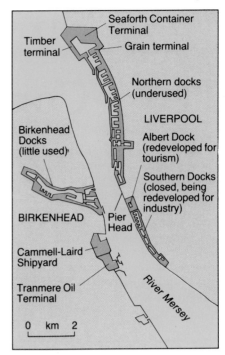

Figure 3
Liverpool Docks

Q3

What advantages of position (within Britain and in relation to other countries) has Felixstowe over Liverpool? What are the advantages of developing new port facilities on a 'greenfield' site as at Felixstowe compared with at an existing port?

Figure 4
The port of Felixstowe

11.1 Contrasts in Britain

Britain is a country of contrasts. These contrasts involve aspects of human and economic geography as well as differences in the natural landscape. This chapter looks firstly at the contrasts in prosperity to be found in Britain and then looks at three contrasting regions: South Wales, East Anglia and the Highlands of Scotland.

Wealth and poverty

Wealth is very unevenly distributed among Britain's people. One per cent of the population owns 23 per cent of all wealth while the bottom 50 per cent own only 6 per cent of all wealth. Fourteen per cent of the population live below the poverty line – the level at which people qualify for Supplementary Benefit.

In recent years the distribution of wealth and income has become more unequal. This is mainly because the level of unemployment rose rapidly in the late 1970s and early 1980s. There are also other reasons such as the increasing number of pensioners, the reduction of rates of taxation on high incomes and the relatively high pay rises of many people in managerial and professional occupations. The unemployed and unskilled are most likely to live in inner city areas and regions with declining industry, so the gap between different places is also increasing. This has led to some people talking of a 'divided nation'.

Measuring contrasts in Britain

Several indicators can be used to show contrasts in prosperity between different parts of Britain. Figure 1 lists several of these for the UK's Standard Regions. Notice that these indicators allow regions to be compared in *relative* terms, by using per capita figures or percentages. Contrasts stand out especially clearly when statistics are mapped (Figure 2).

Figure 1
Regional contrasts

	GDP per head (UK av. = 100)	% workforce unemployed	Annual spending on Supplementary Benefit (£ per head)	Average gross weekly earnings, men (£)	Car and van licences per 1 000 people	% households with central heating
Scotland	96.0	14.0	110.6	189.7	209	56.2
North	90.0	15.2	123.5	179.3	217	68.9
Yorks & Humberside	87.8	12.3	102.1	180.7	232	59.5
North-West	96.0	13.9	126.3	185.2	240	63.8
Wales	86.1	13.5	118.9	179.1	262	58.3
W. Midlands	90.4	12.4	113.1	180.2	279	60.2
E. Midlands	98.5	10.0	88.9	175.5	259	69.0
East Anglia	97.7	8.3	64.1	182.7	306	68.7
South-East	117.0	8.0	92.9	213.8	300	70.9
South-West	95.2	9.2	81.3	179.0	313	67.9
N. Ireland	78.3	18.5	181.0	172.3	219	56.4

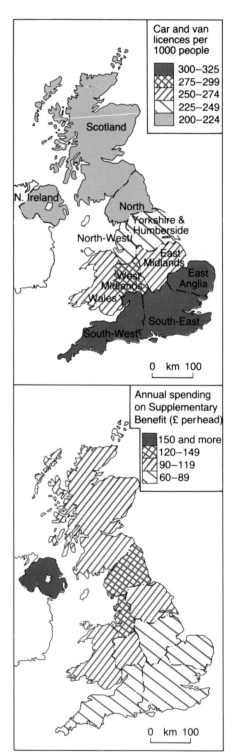

Figure 2
Car ownership; spending on supplementary benefit 1986

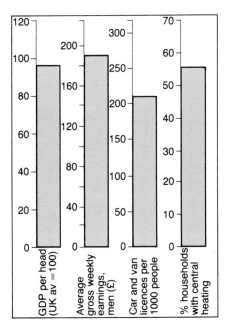

Figure 3
Standard of living profile for Scotland

Q1

(a) Figure 3 shows a standard of living profile for Scotland, made using the figures in Figure 1. Draw Figure 3 and then construct profiles for the other regions of the UK. (This task could be divided between two or three people, but make sure that the profiles are drawn to the same scales.)
(b) Describe carefully the patterns shown by the profiles and the patterns shown on the maps in Figure 2. What parts of the country stand out as being particularly prosperous? What parts stand out as being less prosperous?

The North–South divide

The information in Figures 1 and 2 shows that a line running from the Severn Estuary to the Wash roughly separates the more prosperous parts of the country from the less prosperous parts. The idea of a divided nation has

therefore been linked to the 'North–South divide'. North of the Severn–Wash line there are areas of prosperity, mainly suburban areas of large cities, which do not stand out on maps such as those in Figure 2. South of the line there are pockets of poverty, mainly in inner city areas.

The main reasons for the contrasts in prosperity between the North and South are as follows:

● The decline of manufacturing industry has been greatest in the older industrial regions of the North.

● The South has a relatively large share of high technology industries and industries which have lost relatively few jobs in recent years.

● The expansion of the service sector has benefitted the South most.

● The most important decisions about the future of the country are taken in London and the surrounding area. This is not just because London is the political capital. Of the UK's thousand largest business companies, 458 have their headquarters in London while a further 165 have their headquarters in other parts of the South-East.

Core and periphery

Figure 4 shows a geographical 'model' which attempts to describe contrasts in prosperity within a country. A prosperous **core** area stands in contrast to a fringe of poorer areas known as the **periphery**.

Q2

What part of Britain is the core? Give evidence for the region you name being the core. Name examples of the different types of area to be found in the periphery.

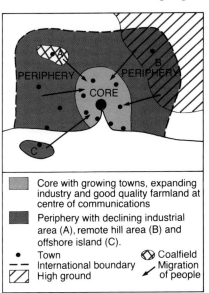

Figure 4
Core and periphery model

The model in Figure 4 shows the migration of people to the core in search of better employment prospects. While this movement has occurred in Britain (see Section 4.2) the higher cost of houses in the South-East and the shortage of housing to rent has restricted movement. Some employers in the South-East cannot find workers with the skills they need.

Q3

(a) Suggest why house prices have risen more rapidly in the South-East than elsewhere. (Consider both factors which boost demand and factors which restrict supply.)
(b) Why are the contrasts in house prices a problem for the country? What restricts the movement of people who rely on housing for rent (either council or privately owned)?
(c) If people do move in large numbers between less prosperous and more prosperous regions, what are the problems for (i) the core region; (ii) the periphery?

11.2   South Wales

South Wales is one of Britain's older industrial regions. Its industrial growth took place in the late 18th and early 19th centuries and was based on coal mining and metal manufacture. Most of the 20th century has been a period of handling the decline of traditional industries and dealing with the problem of how to attract new employment to the area.

been felt most in the valleys where many settlements have lost population.

Q1
Refer back to Section 7.2 to explain why South Wales is a declining coal mining area. Why would the proposed development of a large new pit at Margam near Port Talbot be of such importance to the area?

Figure 1
Sirhowy Valley; the traditional landscape of South Wales

Coal and the metal industries

After the First World War, coal production began to decline and the 1930s were a period of severe unemployment in the mining valleys. Since 1950 employment in coal mining has continued to fall, rapidly in recent years. Over 120 mines have closed since 1960. Employment in the steel industry and other metal industries has also declined. The decline has

Figure 2
South Wales

Industrial change

Since the Second World War, government policies have aimed to attract new industry to South Wales. All the region now has assisted area status. The locations of the major post-war industrial developments are shown in Figure 2. Employment in coal mining and the metal industries is now much less than in the other industries (Figure 3). The

newer industries make a wide range of products, including motor components, electrical goods and clothing. An important feature of the new industrial pattern is that South Wales has Britain's largest concentration of Japanese-owned factories (Figure 4).

In 1976 the Welsh Development Agency (WDA) was set up. It has wide powers to build, rent and sell new factories, to manage industrial estates (including those already established), to reclaim derelict land and to publicize industrial opportunities in Wales.

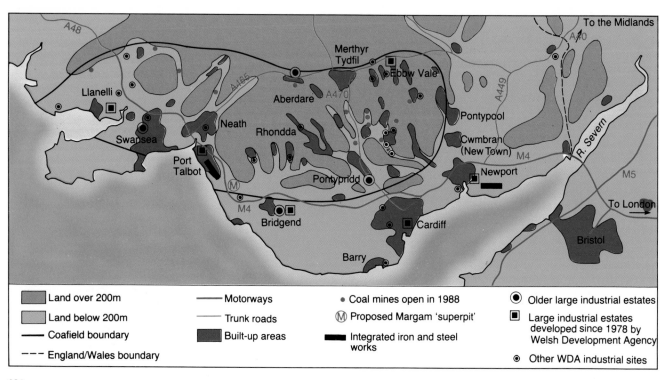

Land over 200m

Land below 200m

Coalfield boundary

– – – England/Wales boundary

Motorways

Trunk roads

Built-up areas

● Coal mines open in 1988

Ⓜ Proposed Margam 'superpit'

Integrated iron and steel works

◉ Older large industrial estates

■ Large industrial estates developed since 1978 by Welsh Development Agency

⊙ Other WDA industrial sites

Most of the newer industries have been developed on the coastal lowlands where there are large flat sites and good communications, including the M4. The valleys have proved to be less attractive for modern industry. New industries have not made up for the continuing decline of coal mining and metal processing. Many valley communities continue to lose population.

Q2
(a) Why has most newer industrial development been on the coastal lowlands of South Wales?
(b) Why are the South Wales valleys relatively unattractive to modern industry?
(c) What are the arguments for and against the government and the WDA encouraging future industrial development on the coastal lowlands rather than in the coalfield valleys?

A changing landscape

The decline of traditional industries, the reclamation of derelict land and the development of new industries has led to great changes in the appearance of the landscape in South Wales. Figure 5 shows how the landscape of the valleys has changed. Similar changes have taken place in industrial areas on the coast.

Q3
Refer to Figure 5. Make a copy of the map showing Cwmfelinfach in 1956, drawing it lightly in pencil. Then using information from the photograph draw in and label the changes which have been made. (There is no need to draw in the individual buildings and roads of the industrial estate; just outline and label this area.)

Figure 5
A new industrial estate built on the site of a coal mine at Cwmfelinfach, Sirhowy Valley

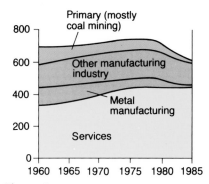

Figure 3
The changing pattern of employment in South Wales

Figure 4
Sony television factory, Bridgend. Other Japanese factories in South Wales include Hitachi (televisions), Aiwa (hi-fi equipment), Yuasa (batteries), Panasonic (televisions, telephones) and Orion Electric (VCRs)

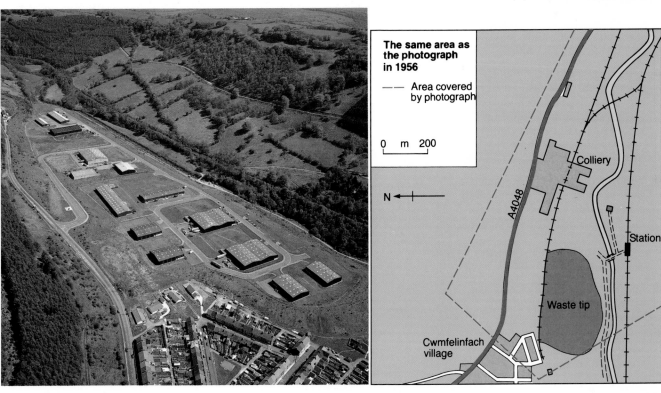

11.3   East Anglia

Since 1960 the population of East Anglia has grown at a faster rate than any other Standard Region of Britain. It is Britain's most productive farming region and manufacturing industry is growing more quickly than in the other regions. Within this 'growth region', however, there are unemployment blackspots and declining villages. Much of the region suffers from poor road communications while average incomes are relatively low.

Growth in East Anglia

Figure 1 shows the pattern of population change in East Anglia. The populations of Norwich, Ipswich and Cambridge are not growing, largely because almost all the land suitable for building within their boundaries has already been developed. The relatively high rates of population growth over most of East Anglia reflects the following factors:

● Several East Anglian towns have become Expanded Towns, taking overspill population from Greater London (Figure 2).

● Much light industry has moved into East Anglia from the Greater London area, while traditional food processing industries have expanded, developing many new products.

● Peterborough was designated a new town in 1967 when it had a population of 81 000. It now has a population of 120 000 and has attracted much new manufacturing and service employment.

● High technology industry has rapidly grown in the Cambridge area.

● Pressures for growth within South-East England have spread into the southern fringe of East Anglia. The M11

motorway and improved rail services have strengthened links with London and have made long-distance commuting easier.

There are several other aspects of economic growth in East Anglia which are less tied up with population growth:

● During the 1970s and early 1980s arable farming became increasingly productive and profitable.

● East Anglia's ports have expanded their trade, Felixstowe becoming one of Britain's largest ports (see Section 10.4).

● The tourist industry has steadily grown in the historic towns and villages and in the Norfolk Broads area.

● The North Sea gas industry has led to the development of a gas terminal and supply bases on the coast.

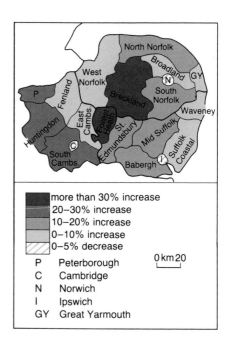

Figure 1
Population change in East Anglia, 1971–1986

Figure 2
East Anglia

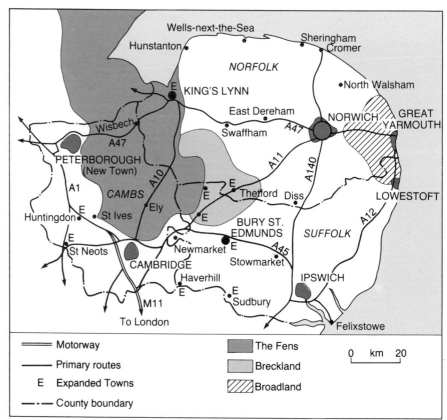

Figure 3
Contrasts in East Anglia: (top) old buildings in Lavenham, Suffolk, (bottom) a high technology factory on the edge of Cambridge

and post offices have also declined. Bus services have proved increasingly uneconomic and have been cut.

Old people have been hit most by the decline in services because they are less likely to have cars and many have low incomes. Some villages in East Anglia have become popular for second home owners from the London area. However, this trend means that many houses will be empty for much of the week, local services will be used to only a limited extent and house prices may be pushed up beyond the reach of local people.

Some of the coastal towns in East Anglia are unemployment blackspots (for example, Hunstanton with a rate of 22 per cent). The seaside resorts have lost much of their trade to larger centres and the Mediterranean, and suffer from both permanent and seasonal unemployment. Great Yarmouth and Lowestoft have also been hit by a decline in the fishing industry and the closure of some old-established factories. Unlike many areas of northern England with similar problems, they have never qualified for government aid to industry.

Q1

(a) Compare the map in Figure 1 with that in Figure 2 and explain the rapid population growth of the following districts: (i) Peterborough; (ii) Huntingdon; (iii) South Cambridgeshire; (iv) Breckland; (v) Forest Heath.
(b) Describe the distribution of districts showing no or relatively small population growth.
(c) Suggest why much footloose industry has been attracted to East Anglia.

Decline in East Anglia

The remoter rural areas of East Anglia and some of the coastal towns have not shared in the expansion. With a continued decline in the farming workforce, few employment opportunities exist in remoter villages so younger people have to move away for work or commute long distances. Village schools have closed because of the decline in numbers of children while many village shops have closed because they cannot compete with larger stores in the towns. Other services such as doctors' surgeries

Q2

(a) Explain carefully why many services in rural areas are in a state of decline.
(b) Describe how the following people might react to the changes which have taken place in East Anglian villages:
(i) A young married couple with a low income and one child. They own an old car and live with the wife's parents.
(ii) A 65-year-old widow who owns her house but has no car. The old age pension is her only income.
(c) Suggest why the coastal towns of Norfolk find it difficult to attract new industry and other forms of employment.

11.4 The Highlands of Scotland

In the Highlands of Scotland, a harsh environment, remoteness and difficult communications combine together to pose major problems for economic development. Only 350 000 people live in the large areas covered by the Highlands and Islands Development Board (Figure 1). Until quite recently the area has lost population, as people moved away to find work elsewhere.

The traditional economy

For most of the 20th century the economy of the Highlands was based on the land and the sea. On the west coast and in the islands **crofting** has been the traditional way of life (Figure 3). This involves cultivating small patches of land to produce oats, hay, potatoes and root vegetables and the use of rough pasture for grazing sheep and cattle. Most crofters combine farming with fishing, forestry or jobs in the service sector. Wide areas of the

Figure 2
Investments by the Highlands and Islands Development Board

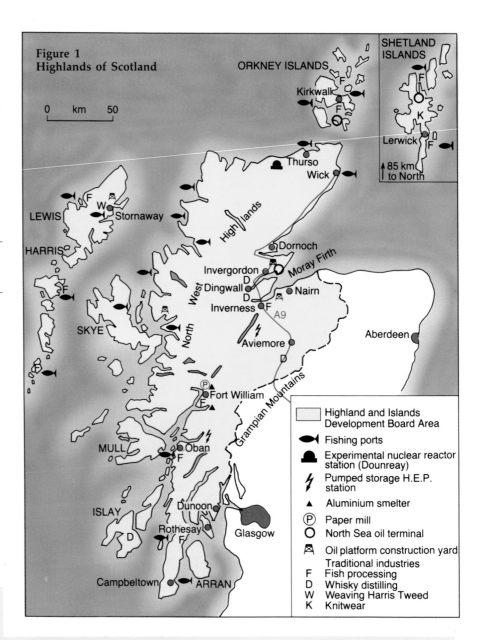

Figure 1
Highlands of Scotland

	Highland and Islands Development Board Area
🐟	Fishing ports
	Experimental nuclear reactor station (Dounreay)
	Pumped storage H.E.P. station
▲	Aluminium smelter
Ⓟ	Paper mill
O	North Sea oil terminal
	Oil platform construction yard
	Traditional industries
F	Fish processing
D	Whisky distilling
W	Weaving Harris Tweed
K	Knitwear

Between 1977 and 1986 the HIDB invested £213 million (grants or loans) to create 19 175 jobs and protect 6 011 existing jobs.

Fishing
Investment in fishing boats, boat building yards, fish farming and processing plants.

Farming and crofting
Assistance to new enterprises ranging from deer farming to farm forestry. Other projects include setting up co-operatives, slaughter houses and new marketing facilities.

Industry
Building factories and workshops. Promotion campaigns to attract industry. Help in marketing goods and in developing new products.

Tourism
Advertising the attractions of the Highlands. Develop skiing, watersports and other leisure facilities and accommodation for visitors. Tourist information offices.

Social development
Setting up community co-operatives. They are particularly important in the islands and are involved in farming, fishing, crafts, building, tourism, shops and other services. Grants to organizations involved in activities ranging from Gaelic language teaching to helping handicapped people.

Figure 3
A croft on the north-west coast of Scotland

Figure 4
Salmon farming has developed rapidly in the Highlands in recent years

western Highlands are occupied by large estates where the land is maintained for shooting and deer stalking or extensive sheep rearing.

Most of the Highlands' farm output comes from the mixed and livestock farms of the Moray Firth lowlands, Caithness and the Orkney Islands, rather than from crofts. Besides crofting and farming, the other traditional mainstays of the Highland economy are fishing, forestry and industries such as whisky distilling. Until the 1960s the only other major industrial developments in the Highlands were the aluminium smelters at Fort William and Kinlochleven.

The Highlands and Islands Development Board

In 1965 the Highlands and Islands Development Board (HIDB) was set up to improve economic and social conditions in the western Highlands and in the islands. Figure 2 shows some of the results of the Board's investment in fishing, farming, tourism, industry and other projects. Much of the future prosperity of the west coast and islands will depend on keeping the crofting communities (townships) going. The HIDB has aimed to improve the efficiency of farming on the crofts and to develop employment opportunities that the crofters can combine with farming.

> **Q1**
> Refer to Figure 2. Describe how the work and investments of the HIDB has (i) developed traditional Highlands activities; (ii) promoted the tourist industry; (iii) developed new forms of employment; (iv) improved social conditions.

Large-scale projects

Since 1960 there have been a number of large-scale projects in the Highlands and Islands, including several related to the North Sea oil industry.
They have created many new jobs and, together with the smaller HIDB projects have served to stop the population decline of the region. However, the development of large projects has not been without setbacks. The Invergordon aluminium smelter which employed 800 closed down after only eleven years of operations. Corpach pulp mill near Fort William closed in 1980, although paper making remains. The closure of large factories in small communities has a major effect on local unemployment rates and has a knock-on effect on local services.

At its peak, the North Sea oil industry directly employed almost 10 000 people in the HIDB region. By the mid-1980s the oil platform construction yards faced a bleak future as the construction and development phase of the North Sea oil industry passed.

> **Q2**
> **(a)** Who benefits from the big projects in the Highlands and Islands? What problems may these projects cause? (Consider, for example, the temporary nature of some jobs and the impact on the environment.)
> **(b)** Suggest why the Moray Firth/Cromarty Firth area has been the location for several major projects.
> **(c)** (i) By referring to an atlas map, explain why communications are difficult in the Highlands.
> (ii) Why is it important for the government to subsidize rail links to the north and west coasts and ferry and air services to the islands?
> (iii) Suggest why particular emphasis has been placed on improving the A9 road between central Scotland and the Inverness area.

12. Environmental issues

12.1 Conserving the landscape

Land is one of Britain's most important resources. Pressure to use the land in many different, often conflicting ways is very great in such a densely populated country. The desire to protect Britain's most scenic landscapes from pressures of development led to the establishment of ten National Parks in England and Wales between 1951 and 1957.

Since then many other areas with attractive landscapes have been set aside as Areas of Outstanding Natural Beauty (AONB) (Figure 1). Scotland has no National Parks, although a number of areas have been identified as National Scenic Areas; planning controls here are much less than in the National Parks of England and Wales.

Figure 2
Why conserve?

1 For **amenity** reasons – protecting the countryside so that it might be enjoyed by people living in towns and cities.
2 For **scientific** reasons – to protect plants and animals because of their special interest and to provide 'outdoor laboratories' for research.
3 For reasons of **usefulness** – the rationing of living resources so that they will not become extinct and will continue to be available in the future.

Figure 1
National Parks, Areas of Outstanding Natural Beauty and Scotland's National Scenic Areas

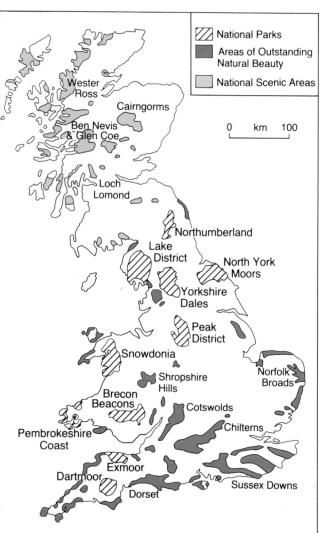

Figure 3
Pressures on the uplands

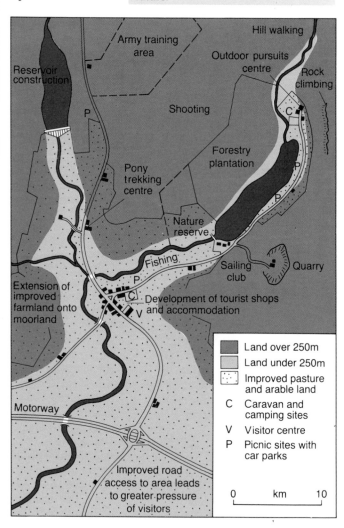

136

Many smaller areas have been protected because of their special interest.

Thus sites of particular importance for wildlife are designated as National Nature Reserves (NNR) and Sites of Special Scientific Interest (SSSI) by the Nature Conservancy Council. Also the National Trust, a charity, buys up wide areas of land (for example 20 per cent of the Lake District National Park) and many smaller sites to safeguard them from development and make them available for the public to enjoy.

Q1

Figure 2 lists and explains three reasons for conserving the countryside. Name the main reasons for conservation involved in each of the following: (i) National Nature Reserves; (ii) conserving and managing a forest of deciduous trees; (iii) National Trust owned land in a National Park; (iv) laws regulating fishing and shooting.

The Countryside Commission

In 1968 the Countryside Commission was set up by the government to watch over and manage many aspects of the countryside. It has the following functions:

● Responsibility for the National Parks.

● Designating Areas of Outstanding Natural Beauty.

● Establishing long-distance footpaths (for example, the Pennine Way).

● Helping local authorities to purchase land for country parks near towns and cities.

● Defining Heritage Coasts and giving grants to local authorities and other organizations for their management.

● Aiding projects which involve conservation and improving the landscape.

● Carrying out conservation research projects.

Pressures on the National Parks

The upland areas of Britain face many pressures for change. Many of the possible uses of these areas conflict with each other. Figure 3 shows the wide variety of competing demands for the use of the uplands. It is because of these pressures and conflicts that the National Parks were established. Conflicts between conservation and development are often very complex, with many government bodies and pressure groups involved.

Q2

Refer to Figure 3. Take each land use in turn and state: (i) what resource is being exploited; (ii) what conflict with the environment may occur; (iii) what conflicts with other uses may occur.

Managing the National Parks

Each National Park is managed by a Park Board or Committee. The local authorities and various other groups who are represented on the Park Boards may well have conflicting interests. Many people argue that the Park Boards do not have enough power or money to do their job well, their main tasks being to preserve the beauty of the parks and to provide opportunities for visitors to enjoy them. The Boards have to protect wildlife, buildings and other places of special interest and, at the same time, protect the interests of people who live and work in their areas. As Figure 4 shows, the National Parks own very little of the land for which they are responsible. They have to rely on the co-operation of other landowners and the local authorities besides the laws which prevent and control developments. If a development is held to be in the national interest, then the views of a National Park Board may well be overruled. Examples of such developments include reservoirs and forestry schemes.

The Peak District National Park

The Peak District National Park (Figure 5), established in 1951, is the oldest of Britain's Parks. Most of the southern part of the Park is a grassy limestone plateau into which rivers such as the Dove have cut deep valleys; this area is the Low or White Peak. To the north is the wilder High or Dark Peak, underlain by Millstone Grit. The Millstone Grit extends southwards to form 'edges' either side of the Low Peak. In addition to the natural scenery, picturesque villages and country houses such as Chatsworth attract visitors.

The pressures on this Park are particularly great because although only 38 000 people live within it, about seventeen million people – nearly one-third the population of the UK – live within 130 kilometres of its boundaries. Most of the visitors wish to travel to the Park at the same time, in the summer, especially at weekends and on fine days. Certain locations in the

Figure 4
Ownership of the National Parks

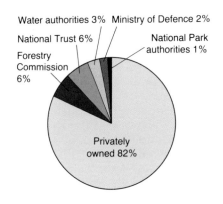

Water authorities 3%   Ministry of Defence 2%

National Trust 6%   National Park authorities 1%

Forestry Commission 6%

Privately owned 82%

Figure 5
Peak District National Park

Figure 6
The impact of visitors on Dovedale, Peak District National Park

An attractive wooded valley with dramatic limestone rock formations, Dovedale attracts large numbers of visitors.

Reynard's Cave

Park – the 'honeypots' – attract very large numbers of visitors. Figure 6 shows the effects that such numbers have had on one of these honeypots, Dovedale, and the measures which have been taken to deal with the problems. It is not just locations easily reached by car which suffer from too many visitors. The boots of thousands of walkers along the Pennine Way have widened the path and have severely damaged the vegetation and peat blanket.

Figure 5 shows that the Park's roughly oval outline has been broken around Buxton. This was done to exclude areas marred by industry, especially limestone quarrying. Proposals to extend

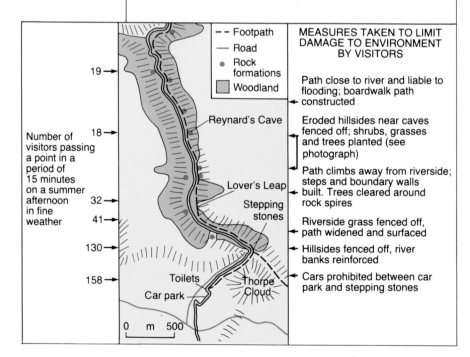

Number of visitors passing a point in a period of 15 minutes on a summer afternoon in fine weather

19
18
32
41
130
158

Footpath
Road
Rock formations
Woodland

Reynard's Cave
Lover's Leap
Stepping stones
Toilets
Car park
Thorpe Cloud

MEASURES TAKEN TO LIMIT DAMAGE TO ENVIRONMENT BY VISITORS

Path close to river and liable to flooding; boardwalk path constructed

Eroded hillsides near caves fenced off; shrubs, grasses and trees planted (see photograph)

Path climbs away from riverside; steps and boundary walls built. Trees cleared around rock spires

Riverside grass fenced off, path widened and surfaced

Hillsides fenced off, river banks reinforced

Cars prohibited between car park and stepping stones

0   m   500

limestone quarrying to areas inside the Park are a major conservation issue.

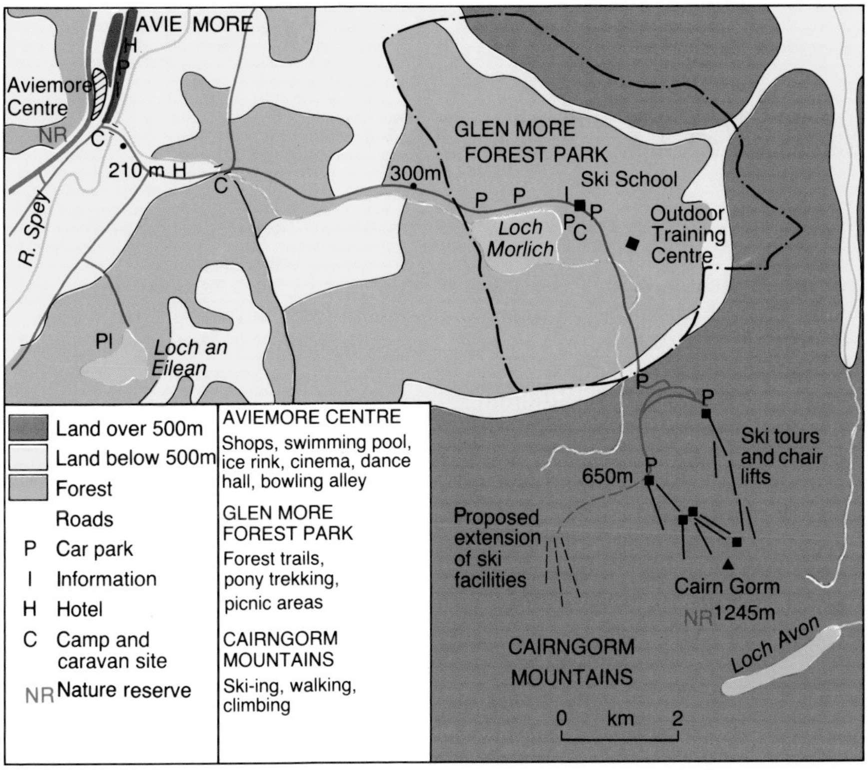

Figure 7
Tourist developments in the Aviemore area of the Cairngorm National Scenic Area

Key (from map):
- Land over 500m
- Land below 500m
- Forest
- Roads
- P Car park
- I Information
- H Hotel
- C Camp and caravan site
- NR Nature reserve

AVIEMORE CENTRE
Shops, swimming pool, ice rink, cinema, dance hall, bowling alley

GLEN MORE FOREST PARK
Forest trails, pony trekking, picnic areas

CAIRNGORM MOUNTAINS
Ski-ing, walking, climbing

Cairngorm National Scenic Area

The Cairngorm Mountains are Scotland's prime candidate for the creation of a National Park. Much of the area is a high, bare plateau rising to over 1200 metres with a sub-arctic climate and vegetation.

Figure 8
A ski tow on the slopes of the Cairngorms

There are also dramatic corries and glacial valleys. The mountain mass is skirted by forests, much of it Scots Pine forest which once covered wide areas of the Highlands. Although the Cairngorm plateau is one of Britain's largest nature reserves and much of the area is remote from roads, the area faces considerable pressures. There has been considerable tourist development around Loch Morlich (Figure 7) and Aviemore has become a major all year resort. But it is the development of ski-runs on the slopes of Cairn Gorm which has had the greatest impact on the environment (Figure 8). Because existing facilities do not meet the demand at peak periods, there are plans to develop new ski-runs and ski-lifts. Naturalists point out that much damage has already been done to the delicate sub-arctic environment and strongly oppose more developments. Well away from these developments, the Cairngorm hillsides have been scarred by high-altitude Land Rover tracks, built for sportsmen to gain access to the moors for grouse shooting and deer stalking.

12.2 Pressures on the urban fringe

Pressures on land at the edge of urban areas – the **urban fringe** – are particularly severe. As a result, careful planning of land use and restrictions on development are needed. In Section 4.2 we saw that although the population of Britain's major cities is decreasing, the population of the surrounding areas is increasing. Towns and villages near the major urban areas have attracted both people and businesses from the cities. Many people who live in such urban fringe areas commute to work in the cities.

Land use in the urban fringe

Farming is the main land use in urban fringe areas. However, farming next to urban areas has its problems: trespassing, damage to farm property, rubbish dumping and the worrying of livestock. Some farmers find the letting of land for horse grazing a profitable business. Others may sell their land to property companies who hope to make profits from future urban development. Such land is sometimes allowed to fall into neglect.

Much land in the urban fringe is used for purposes linked with the cities (Figure 1). Examples include reservoirs, sewage farms, waste disposal sites, airports and golf courses. They take up too much space or cause too much of a nuisance to be located within urban areas.

Green Belts

Much urban fringe land is protected by Green Belt policies which tightly restrict development. The first Green Belt was established in 1947 to restrict the outward growth of London.

Since then other Green Belts have been established to limit the growth of other conurbations and cities (Figure 2). Green Belts have the additional aims of providing recreational areas for city dwellers and protecting farmland from urban development. Although Green Belts have severely restricted urban sprawl, much housing development has simply 'leap-frogged' them.

London's Green Belt

The Green Belt around London has had to face considerable pressures for development. In the 1950s and 1960s a large 'overspill' population from inner areas of London undergoing redevelopment needed housing. Most of this demand for houses was met by the New Towns just beyond the Green Belt (see Section 4.7). The rapid growth of population in the South-East in the post-war period led to much

**Figure 1
Sewage farm and gravel pits in the London Green Belt**

**Figure 2
Green Belts in England and Wales**

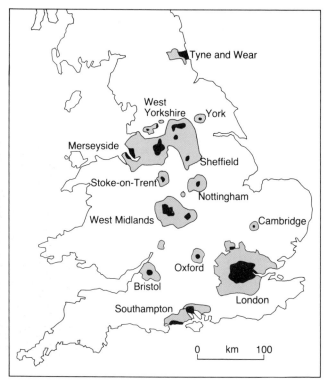

housing being built in other towns beyond the Green Belt as well, especially those with good road and rail links to London. To slow down the growth of these towns, the Green Belt was extended outwards in several areas (Figure 3). Yet demand for new housing remains very high and there is relatively little land available. House-building firms and developers wishing to build industrial estates, offices, warehouses, shopping centres and leisure facilities have demanded that Green Belt land should be released for building.

The completion of the M25 Motorway (through the Green Belt) around London has led to more pressure for development. As Figure 3 shows, the pressures for development are particularly great to the west of London near Heathrow Airport. Locations where the M25 crosses motorways and 'A' roads radiating from London are very attractive to developers, who buy up land in the hope that planning controls will be lifted.

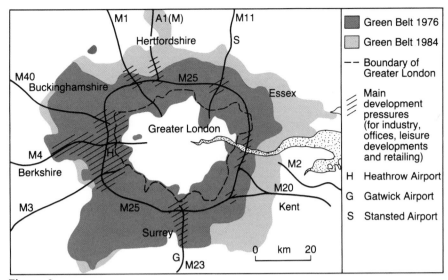

Figure 3
London's Green Belt

extending the National Exhibition Centre and building a high technology industrial estate nearby. British Coal has announced the development of a new mine on the edge of Coventry. The central question is should the Green Belt be preserved at all costs, even if some of the land is partly urbanized, or should the national interest and the need to put new life into a declining region be the priority?

Q1

(a) Why was the London Green Belt first established? Why has it been extended?
(b) Suggest why development pressures in the London Green Belt are greater to the west of London than to the east. Why are locations near junctions on the M25 particularly attractive to developers?

Q2

(a) Suggest why the eastern edge of Birmingham was an attractive site for the National Exhibition Centre.
(b) What are the arguments for and against each of the major new developments shown in Figure 4?
(c) Should development be allowed in those parts of the Meriden Gap already partly urbanized or made unattractive by, for example, gravel pits and neglected farmland? Justify your views.

The Meriden Gap

Figure 4 shows part of the West Midlands Green Belt between Birmingham and Coventry – the Meriden Gap. Major developments, including the National Exhibition Centre, have been allowed in this area. Many people fear that the gap between the two cities is being filled up and that any future development should be prohibited. Yet developments have continued. In 1987 a start was made on

Figure 4
Developments in the Meriden Gap, West Midlands Green Belt

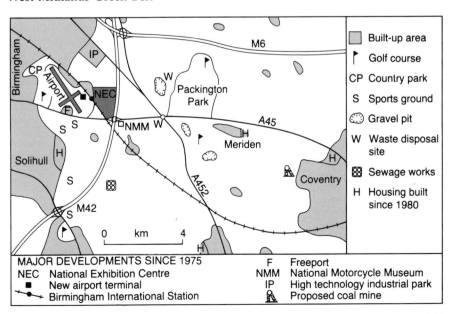

12.3 Farming and the changing countryside

Britain's farming landscapes have been changing over many hundreds of years. Since about 1950, however, farming methods have changed greatly and rapidly. The more intensive methods, combined with the expansion of the area under crops, have had serious effects on wild plants and animals and have changed the appearance of many areas. Conservation and wildlife interests have opposed such drastic change. During the 1970s and 1980s the debate over the changing countryside has grown more and more intense.

Changes in the countryside

The major changes which have taken place in the countryside are:

- The increased use of intensive farming methods, including chemical sprays.

- The widespread loss of hedgerows.

- The reclamation of moorland for improved grazing or arable land.

- The drainage of low-lying wetlands for arable farming.

- The ploughing up of chalk grasslands and lowland heaths.

- The loss of wide areas of ancient deciduous woods.

These changes especially the widespread use of chemicals (see Section 6.4) have had a major impact on wildlife. Figure 1 lists some of the losses among plants and animals which have been caused largely by changes in farming.

Figure 2
Norfolk Broads Environmentally Sensitive Area

Q1
(a) Explain why farmers have removed many hedges. What are the arguments for keeping plenty of hedges in the countryside?
(b) Why are many changes in the countryside difficult to reverse?

Farming and conservation

Since 1981, landowners and farmers who wish to carry out work (such as draining a wetland area) in a National Park or on a Site of Special Scientific Interest (SSSI) have had to consult the Park authorities or the Nature Conservancy. Government farm grants for such works may be refused on conservation grounds. However, the farmers must be compensated for the value of production lost by not going ahead with the work.

In 1986 the government named Britain's first Environmentally Sensitive Areas (ESAs). In these

- Since 1930, out of 1423 native flowering plants and ferns, ten species have been lost completely and 149 have declined by at least 20%.

- Thirty-six species of birds have declined because of lost or damaged habitats.

- Of 55 breeding species of butterfly, one has become extinct, ten are endangered and thirteen others are in decline.

- Bats and some other small mammals are also declining in number.

Figure 1
The effects on wildlife of changes in farming

areas farmers qualify for payments (from EEC funds) if they continue or adopt farming practices which safeguard the special environment (Figure 2).

Outside SSSIs and National Parks conservation is by persuasion only. Even in the ESAs farmers are not forced to take conservation measures. Some farmers are more willing to be involved in conservation than are others. An interest in protecting the environment and wildlife has to be considered against the need to make a profit and the availability of grants and subsidies which encourage greater

AIMS IN MANAGING THE NORFOLK BROADS ENVIRONMENTALLY SENSITIVE AREA (ESA)

- Conserve the landscape, plant and animal life of the grazing marshes

- Prevent more grazing land being deep-drained and converted to arable farming

- Extend the area of grazing marshes by adopting traditional farming methods on land with more intensive farming output. As Figure 3 shows, some farmers have made positive efforts at conservation.

Planning for the future

Deciding on how the countryside should be managed and what conservation measures should be taken is a difficult task. At the same time, over-production of many farm products is a major problem (see Chapter 6). Already the levels of grants for expanding production have been reduced and payments are made to farmers to take land out of crop production (the 'set aside' policy). It is planned that more areas should become ESAs with less intensive farming methods. Farmers are being encouraged to develop alternative activities (Figure 4). Many conservationists believe that new developments should be carefully controlled, for example, restricting tree-planting grants to deciduous species and introducing planning controls on farmers' activities. Figure 5 shows what the countryside might be like in the near future, if current trends in farming and conservation continue.

Figure 3
On this Shropshire dairy farm the farmer has developed wildlife habitats and a waterfowl sanctuary

Figure 4
Current developments in planning for the countryside's future

- Reducing EEC subsidies and intervention prices (see Section 6.2).
- Increasing grants to farmers for conservation projects.
- Setting up Environmentally Sensitive Areas (ESAs), in which farmers qualify for payments if they continue with or adopt less intensive farming practices which safeguard the environment.
- Encouraging (and paying) farmers to set aside arable land so as not to produce surplus crops.
- Increasing grants for planting trees, especially broad-leaved species.
- Encouraging farmers to develop leisure and tourist facilities such as self-catering accommodation, camp sites and nature trails.
- Developing small-scale manufacturing and craft industries, sometimes using old farm buildings.

Q2
(a) Which of the planning approaches in Figure 4 aim to (i) grow less food on existing land; (ii) use land in alternative ways; (iii) provide alternative employment in the countryside?
(b) Refer to Figure 5. Consider: (i) the uplands; (ii) the lowlands. For each, list the possible gains and the possible losses for the countryside in the near future.

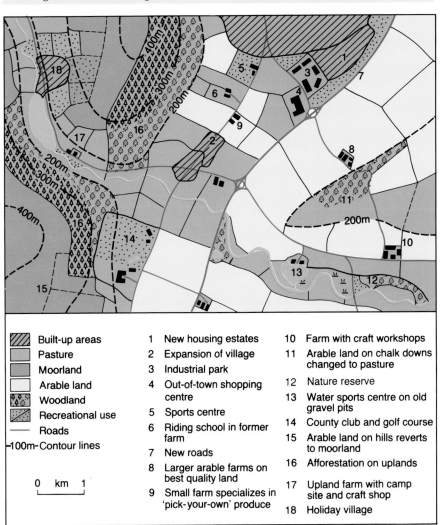

Built-up areas	1 New housing estates	10 Farm with craft workshops
Pasture	2 Expansion of village	11 Arable land on chalk downs changed to pasture
Moorland	3 Industrial park	
Arable land	4 Out-of-town shopping centre	12 Nature reserve
Woodland	5 Sports centre	13 Water sports centre on old gravel pits
Recreational use	6 Riding school in former farm	14 County club and golf course
Roads	7 New roads	15 Arable land on hills reverts to moorland
100m Contour lines	8 Larger arable farms on best quality land	16 Afforestation on uplands
	9 Small farm specializes in 'pick-your-own' produce	17 Upland farm with camp site and craft shop
0 km 1		18 Holiday village

Figure 5
The future countryside

12.4 Pollution and waste

Air pollution

Urban areas are particularly affected by air pollution because of their large concentrations of factories and vehicles. Air pollution affects people's health, damages buildings and reduces the amount of sunlight reaching cities. The cost to Britain in terms of health and repairing damage to buildings amounts to about £5 000 million a year. As polluted air drifts away from the cities, rain falling through it will become acidic and so forests and lakes will be harmed.

Air pollution in London
Until the 1950s, smoke from coal fires in homes and from factories was the main air pollution problem. Dirty fog or 'smog' was a major winter hazard. In December 1952 London was affected by a particularly severe smog (Figure 1). Transport was crippled by visibility of only a few metres. The most severe effect, however, was on people's health: 4 000 deaths resulted from lung and heart complaints.

The Clean Air Acts of 1956 and 1968 were passed to prevent such disasters and to reduce air pollution generally. Smokeless zones were created and industry was made to control emissions from factory chimneys. These have helped to cut the smoke content of London's air by over 75 per cent. However, sulphur dioxide concentrations have shown little decline, largely because of the rising of fuel oil, burnt in factories, heating boilers in buildings and power stations. Most of the other major pollutants, such as carbon and nitrogen oxides, in London now come from vehicle exhausts, not controlled by the Acts (Figure 2).

Q1
Describe how London's air pollution problem today differs from the situation in the 1950s.

Acid rain
In the early 1980s acid rain became a pollution issue of great concern. Surveys showed that over one-third of West Germany's forests were damaged and that fish were being harmed by acidic water in 20 000 lakes in Sweden and Norway. These countries pointed to Britain as a major source of acid rain pollution and further surveys showed that acid rain was also affecting much of Britain itself (Figure 3). Rain becomes acidic when it falls through air polluted by sulphur dioxide (produced by power stations and factories) and nitrogen oxides from vehicle exhausts. The building of tall chimneys to disperse waste gases has contributed to the problem as winds will blow the pollutants considerable distances. Thus the prevailing southwesterly winds carry the sulphur dioxide from Britain's power stations over Scandinavia. Areas with high annual rainfall totals are, of course, particularly vulnerable to the effects of acid rain. Many hill areas have acidic rocks such as granite; here streams are already relatively acidic and only slightly acid rain may bring acidity to a dangerous level.

Q2
Describe and explain the pattern of acid rain in Scotland (Figure 3). You will need to consider the sources of pollution (also shown on Figure 3), annual rainfall patterns (see Section 2.2, Figure 3) and geology (see Section 1.2, Figure 1).

Figure 1
A bus creeps through the London smog of 1952

Figure 2
London's air pollutants

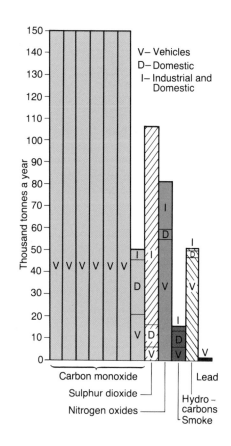

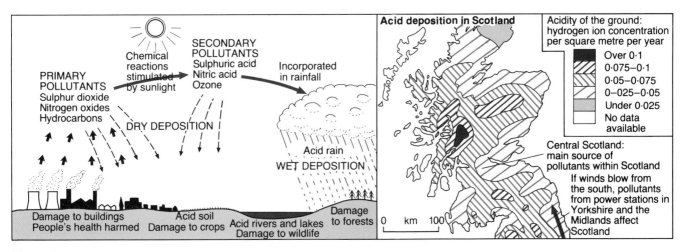

Figure 3
Acid rain

Solutions

In parts of the USA and Japan where pollution by vehicle exhausts has been extremely bad, measures have been taken to reduce exhaust emissions. They include the use of unleaded petrol and engines fitted with devices to transform exhaust gases into harmless compounds. These devices, known as catalytic converters, are expensive and cut fuel economy. In Britain, unlike some other European countries, no steps have been taken to make catalytic converters compulsory.

Equipment for removing sulphur from power station waste gases (Figure 4) is being installed in some power stations, but because of the high cost involved, progress is likely to be very slow.

Figure 4
Reducing sulphur dioxide emissions from a power station

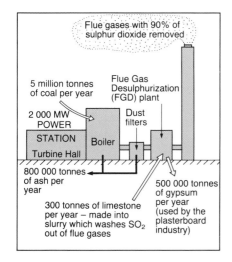

Q3
(a) Should Britain make catalytic converters and unleaded fuel compulsory, even if exhaust pollution is not as severe as in parts of the USA? What costs would be involved?
(b) Is more costly electricity a price worth paying for reduced sulphur dioxide emissions and less acid rain? Give reasons for your answer.

Land pollution

Besides being unsightly, the pollution of land damages the natural environment and can be a health hazard to people and animals. The main types of land pollution include:

● Litter, both in urban areas and the countryside.

● Poorly managed refuse tips.

● Scars on the landscape resulting from mining and quarrying.

● Waste tips remaining from past industrial activity and mining.

● Derelict land and buildings.

● Vegetation killed by toxic waste and fumes.

Q4
(a) In what types of area are problems of land pollution likely to be greatest?
(b) Refer to Section 5.3, Figure 6 and Section 11.2, Figure 5. For each of these areas describe (i) the original land pollution problem and (ii) the measures which have been taken to tackle the problem.

Waste disposal

About 50 million tonnes of domestic, commercial and industrial waste has to be disposed of in Britain each year. In addition, mines, quarries and power stations produce large amounts of waste. About 85 per cent of the waste is tipped in quarries and pits or is used to reclaim derelict land and coastal marshlands. The selection of tipping sites and the transport of waste involves a number of problems:

1 It is uneconomic for collecting vehicles to transport it a long way.
2 The cost of transferring waste from collecting vehicles to trains or barges for longer distance transport is high.
3 Most suitable tipping sites are far from the urban areas.

Some industrial wastes are a major health hazard. Toxic liquids are particularly difficult to deal with. Although the dumping of toxic waste is now closely controlled and sites have to be specially licensed, there remains the difficulty of locating and treating sites where such dangerous substances were dumped in the past. Figure 5 shows many of the hazards associated with waste dumping.

Many local authorities incinerate waste so that the volume to be dumped is reduced. In a few cases the heat from incinerators is used for district heating schemes. Waste metals, paper and glass can be recycled but high costs and few incentives for individuals or industrial firms to recycle material have meant that the amount of waste which is reclaimed stays small.

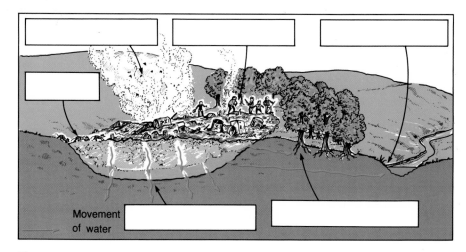

Figure 5
Hazards of a badly managed waste tip

Q5

(a) Make a copy of Figure 5 and add labels to describe the dangers shown.
(b) Look at Figure 6. Why has Essex become 'England's dustbin'?
(c) (i) Name examples of how waste materials are recycled. (ii) What incentives could be introduced so that bottles and cans might be recycled?

Figure 6
Waste disposal in Essex

Water pollution

Rivers and canals

Industrial waste, sewage and agricultural chemicals pollute considerable lengths of Britain's rivers and streams (Figure 7). Older industrial areas such as the North-West (Figure 8) are particularly affected. However, water pollution can be avoided and many rivers have been improved. Water authorities have invested in sewage treatment works where solids and sludge are separated from liquid, which is then purified before being discharged into rivers. Many regulations have forced industry to treat waste discharges more carefully than in the past. The Thames is an example of a river which has been greatly improved.

Forty years ago it was lifeless, black and bore a floating toxic scum. Huge investments in London's sewage works and the control of industrial pollution have raised oxygen levels considerably and so fish and birds have returned to the river. In 1974 a mature salmon, the first for 140 years was caught; by 1982 adult salmon had returned in quantity to the Thames.

The sea

Figure 7 also shows how the sea is polluted by untreated sewage and industrial waste. Some

Figure 7
Sources of water pollution

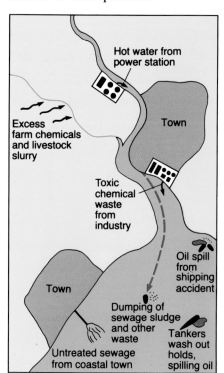

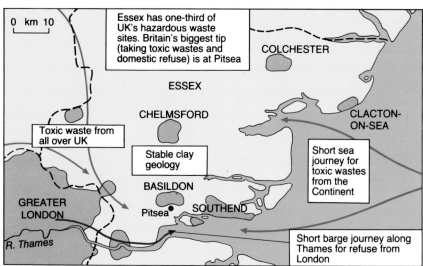

stretches of coastline are particularly badly affected (Figure 10). The beaches of many popular holiday resorts have been made smelly and unsightly by sewage. Swimmers may catch stomach, eye and ear infections. Marine life is harmed. Shellfish are particularly affected and so the livelihood of inshore fishermen is put at risk. The solution to the problem is the building of sewage treatment plants and the construction of outfall pipes which discharge further out to sea. However, limited financial resources have led to little being done.

The sea is also used for dumping sewage sludge from the treatment works of cities such as London and industrial waste, often containing toxic metals such as mercury. In Cumbria much controversy has been caused by the discharge into the sea of low-level radioactive waste from the nuclear waste reprocessing plant at Sellafield. Relatively high levels of radioactivity have been recorded in nearby marshlands and on beaches. Opposition to the dumping of nuclear waste well out in the Atlantic Ocean led to this practice being ended in 1983.

An additional threat to the sea is from oil spills (Figures 9 and 10). They can occur through accidents at ports which handle oil and in the North Sea oilfields, through shipping accidents and when oil tankers illegally wash out their tanks at sea. Despite many preventative measures, accidents have occurred: in 1978 many seabirds were killed by a spillage at the Sullom Voe terminal in the Shetland Islands. The government and the oil companies have spent much money on equipment to deal with oil spills.

Q6
(a) Refer to Figure 8. Explain why the pollution problem is greater in the Rivers Mersey, Irwell and Weaver than in the Ribble.
(b) Make a list of the measures which could be taken to reduce water pollution problems in the area shown in Figure 7.
(c) Explain the pattern of oil spills shown in Figure 10.

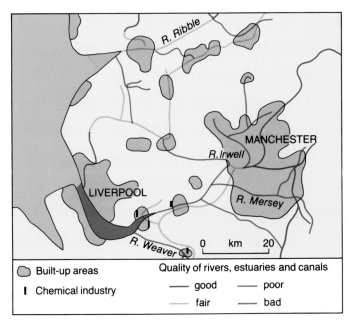

Figure 8
River and canal pollution in North-West England

Figure 10
Pollution of coastal waters

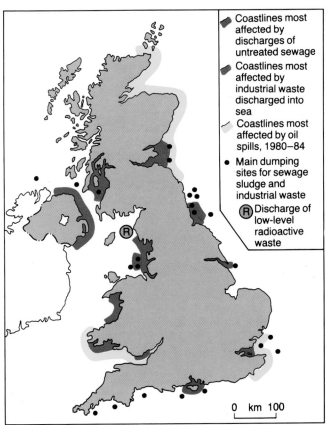

Figure 9
Seabird killed by an oil spill

12.5 Flood protection

Most floods happen when rivers overflow onto their flood plains. This usually occurs after periods of heavy rain or rapid melting of snow. In Section 3.2 we saw that it was very important to understand the factors which affect the movement of water in drainage basins, whether for planning the use of water resources or planning flood protection measures. In low-lying coastal areas the main flood threat comes from the sea at times of very high tides.

Flood protection in urban areas

When land is covered with buildings and roads, much of its surface therefore becomes impermeable. Runoff follows rainfall more quickly and peak flood levels rise greatly. Most towns in Britain are protected from floods which may occur, on average, once every hundred years. Figure 1 shows how Nottingham is protected from flooding by the River Trent.

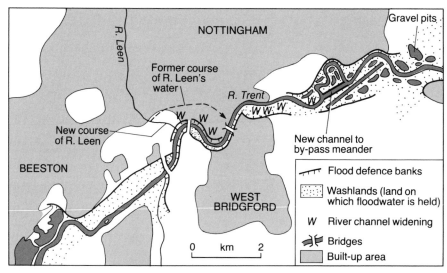

Figure 1
Flood protection measures in the Trent Valley at Nottingham

Figure 2
Flood protection in the Fens

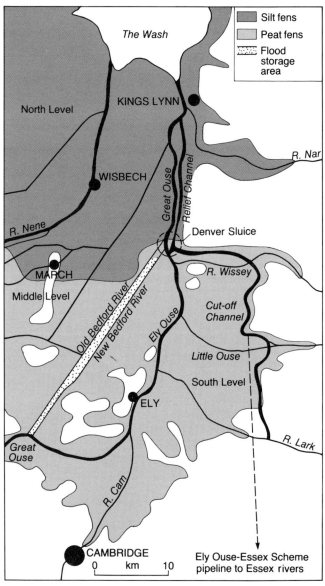

Q1

(a) Look back at the storm hydrographs in Section 3.2. Draw a sketch hydrograph of a stream in a heavily built-up area following a severe rainstorm. Label it to show how it differs from a storm hydrograph following the same rainfall in a rural area.

(b) Look at Figure 1. List the flood protection measures shown and, for each one, explain its purpose.

148

Figure 3
A sea wall protecting a low-lying coastline

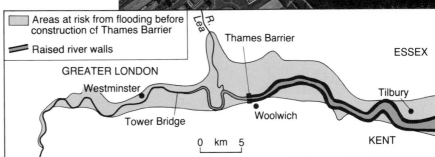

Figure 4
The Thames Barrier

Flood protection in the Fens

In the Fens of eastern England (Figure 2), major works have been needed to protect the land from flooding. From the 17th century onwards, the Fens were drained and reclaimed for farming. Large drainage channels such as the Old and New Bedford Rivers were cut. As the peat dried out it shrank, leaving much of the southern Fens below sea level. As a result, the problem of getting winter flood waters away to the sea became greater and five major floods occurred between 1936 and 1953. More complex flood protection measures including the Cut Off Channel and the Relief Channel were therefore needed to tackle this problem (see Figure 2).

Q2
(a) Why have the Fens been particularly liable to flooding?
(b) Refer to Figure 2. Explain the purposes of:
(i) the Cut Off Channel
(ii) the Relief Channel.

The Thames Barrier

Flood prevention measures are also needed in many low-lying coastal areas. The usual method of protection is the building of sea walls (Figure 3). In the Thames Estuary, sea wall construction has been accompanied by the building of the Thames Barrier (Figure 4) to provide flood protection for one million Londoners. In South-East England the land is gradually sinking. London and the Thames Estuary area are under threat from floods

Figure 5
A storm surge in the North Sea poses a flood threat to the east coast of England

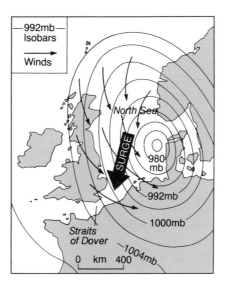

when storm surge tides occur in the North Sea. These are very high tides which involve the rapid movement (or surge) of water across the North Sea towards the Thames Estuary. They occur when a deep depression moves southeastwards through the North Sea and produces strong northerly winds (Figure 5). In January 1953, such conditions drove water southwards faster than it could escape through the Straits of Dover; the resulting high tides, two metres higher than normal made 25 000 people homeless on the Essex bank of the Thames alone. The Thames barrier aims to prevent such a disaster occurring again.

Q3
(a) Suggest what the effects of a major flood in central and riverside London would be.
(b) Refer to Figure 4.
(i) Describe the location of the Thames Barrier.
(ii) Why did new sea walls have to be built at the same time?
(iii) Describe how the barrier works.

13. Britain and the world

13.1 Britain and Europe

After the end of the Second World War in 1945, two major groups of countries emerged in Europe, one made up of western countries, most of which had democratically elected governments, the others made up of the communist states of Eastern Europe. Within these two broad groups, a variety of international organizations, economic, political and military, developed (Figure 1).

The European Economic Community

The European organization of most concern to the United Kingdom is the European Economic Community (EEC). In March 1957, France, West Germany, Italy, Belgium, the Netherlands and Luxembourg signed the Treaty of Rome to establish the EEC in 1958. The aims of the EEC were to reduce and then finally end all restrictions on trade, movement of money and movement of workers between the member countries. Common policies on agriculture, transport and external trade were to be worked out.

The United Kingdom, together with Denmark and the Irish Republic, joined the EEC on 1st January 1973. Greece joined the EEC in 1981 and Spain and Portugal in 1986. Turkey, Malta and Cyprus are associate members of the EEC, together with a large group of developing countries, mainly former colonies of France in Africa. These countries have special trade terms with the EEC members and receive aid for development. To run the EEC there is a variety of bodies ranging from the European Parliament to the Court of Justice.

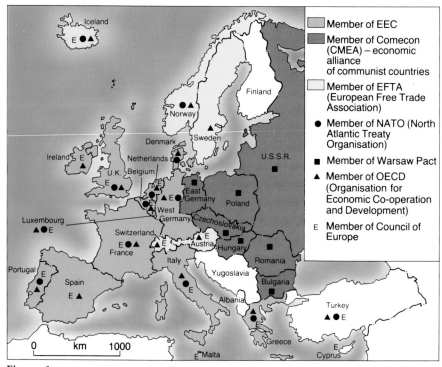

Figure 1
Membership of major European organizations

Legend:
- ▢ Member of EEC
- ■ Member of Comecon (CMEA) – economic alliance of communist countries
- ▢ Member of EFTA (European Free Trade Association)
- ● Member of NATO (North Atlantic Treaty Organisation)
- ■ Member of Warsaw Pact
- ▲ Member of OECD (Organisation for Economic Co-operation and Development)
- E Member of Council of Europe

Farming and the EEC

Farming in the EEC is regulated by the Common Agricultural Policy (CAP) (see Chapter 6). The CAP has been the source of much friction between the members of the EEC. This is partly because of its high cost. Guaranteed prices have resulted in surpluses such as the 'butter mountain'. Farming varies greatly in prosperity and efficiency between and within the member countries (Figure 3). Many people feel that too much EEC money is going to countries with many inefficient farmers. It has now been agreed that the CAP is costing the EEC far too much money and that subsidizing farmers to produce surplus food is not a sensible policy. As a result, levels of support for farming in the EEC are being lowered.

Figure 2
The EEC countries

	Population (millions)	Area (thousand km²)	GDP per head (US dollars)
UK	56.7	245	6514
France	54.9	547	8115
W Germany	61.2	249	9064
Italy	57.0	301	5549
Belgium	9.9	33	7638
Netherlands	14.4	37	7716
Luxembourg	0.4	3	9289
Denmark	5.1	43	9834
Ireland	3.5	70	4733
Greece	9.9	132	2966
Spain	38.3	505	3853
Portugal	10.2	92	2344

Gross Domestic Product (GDP) is a measure of a country's total production of goods and services

150

Q1

(a) Take each feature of farming shown by the statistics in Figure 3 in turn. For each one, draw bar graphs to compare the UK with Denmark, France and Greece.
(b) Describe the contrasts shown in the nature of farming between these four countries. Suggest why the EEC countries find it difficult to agree over farming policies and the amount of money used to subsidize farming.

	UK	DENMARK	FRANCE	GREECE
Area of farmland (1 000 hectares)	18644	2847	31337	9234
Share of agriculture in GDP (%)	2	5	4	15
Percentage of labour force in agriculture	2.6	7.1	7.6	28.9
Average size of farm (hectares)	69.9	30.2	27.9	5.3
Average size of dairy cow herd	62	28	20	3
Average annual milk yield (kg/cow)	4855	5379	3967	2946
Average wheat yield (kg/ha)	6270	5890	6060	2050

Figure 3
Farming contrasts in the EEC

Trade and the EEC

Countries control their trade with tariffs (taxes on imports) and quotas (limits on amounts of imports). The EEC aims to have no such internal trade barriers eventually. Adjustments are made gradually so that industries are able to adjust to new conditions. The EEC also aims that its members should have common trade policies towards other countries. Joining the EEC gives Britain relatively free access to the markets of the other EEC countries, but also gives those countries freer access to the British market. A major effect of being an EEC member is that British trade with Europe has greatly increased, at the expense of traditional trade links with Commonwealth countries.

Q2

(a) An example of developing a common trade policy towards other countries has been the 'rationalization' of the iron and steel industry, to make EEC made steel competitive in world markets.
(i) What is meant by 'rationalization'?
(ii) Why is working out such a policy difficult?
(b) 'Being a member of the EEC means that Britain's industries must be competitive and efficient.' Explain why a leading industrialist would have made this comment.

Movement of labour

People within the EEC are free to seek jobs in other member countries, work permits not being required. In 1981, 27 800 people emigrated from the UK to other EEC countries, while 23 000 people entered the UK from the same countries.

Q3

(a) What factors limit the movement of labour between the EEC countries?
(b) The EEC countries with the largest movement of people to the UK are Ireland and the southern countries. The movement from the UK is mainly to the northern countries and Spain. Suggest reasons for the patterns of these movements.

Regional development

Some of Britain's less prosperous regions have received aid from the EEC's European Regional Development Fund. Almost all of this EEC aid goes to Northern Ireland and the Development Areas. Most is spent on projects which improve a region's infrastructure (for example, roads and bridges). Much of the rest goes to industrial developments (Figure 4).

Figure 4
Two projects in Birmingham funded by the European Regional Development Fund: Aston Science Park and the new Moor Street railway station for suburban services

13.2 World links

Britain has a complex pattern of economic, military, social and cultural links with other countries of the world. Britain belongs to many international organizations, including the United Nations. Money, expertise and people are contributed to the various United Nations agencies, such as UNICEF (United Nations Children's Fund) and the WHO (World Health Organization).

Economic links: trade

Britain's share of world markets for manufactured goods has steadily declined. Despite this, as Figure 1 shows, Britain remains an important exporter of manufactured products. A more noticeable trend in the pattern of trade is the increased importance of manufactured imports. Now more manufactured goods are imported than are exported. Competition from other countries in both the British and world markets has been increasingly successful.

Other important trends in the changing pattern of trade have been the reduction in food imports and the increase in fuel exports. Figure 1 deals only with the 'visible' trade in 'goods'. One-quarter of Britain's export earnings and one-fifth of imports are accounted for by 'invisible' trade in services, for example, tourism, banking, insurance and shipping.

The direction of Britain's trade has also changed (Figure 2). Britain's main trading partners are now the EEC countries together with the USA and, for imports, Japan. The countries of the Commonwealth (Figure 3) are much less important trading partners than they were in the days of the British Empire, when they provided cheap raw materials and food and were a major market for British exports.

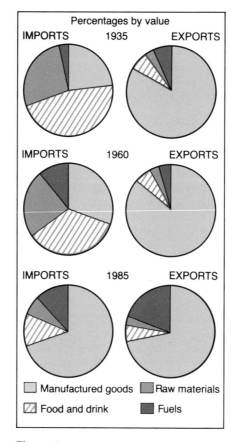

Figure 1
United Kingdom trade; changes in types of product

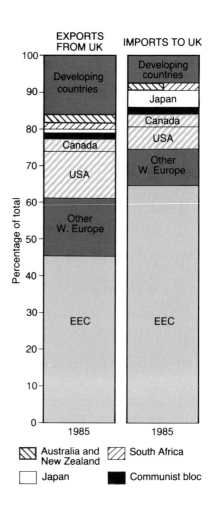

Figure 2
The directions of United Kingdom's trade, 1985

Q1
Refer to Figure 1. Describe how the pattern of (i) Britain's exports and (ii) Britain's imports has changed over the past 50 years.
(b) What effects have the increasing importance of manufactured imports had on British industry?
(c) How might the government limit the amount imported of a particular product? What are the risks of such protection measures?

Economic links: investments

Economic links between Britain and the rest of the world also involve investment by British companies in their overseas branches and subsidiary companies and the investment by foreign companies in Britain. The USA is by far the largest foreign investor in Britain, owning over £10000 million worth of British industry. Japanese investment in Britain is increasing particularly rapidly.

British companies invest abroad to an even greater extent than foreign companies in Britain. Thirty per cent of this investment abroad is in the USA. Even greater sums of money are invested abroad in what are known as 'portfolio' investments, for example, in shares in foreign companies.

Q2
What are the advantages and disadvantages of (i) foreign companies investing in Britain; (ii) British companies investing abroad?

The Commonwealth

Most of the countries which used to be part of the British Empire chose to retain links with each other within the Commonwealth

Figure 3
The Commonwealth

when they became independent countries. Every two years the Commonwealth heads of government meet together to discuss world affairs. The older Commonwealth countries of Canada, Australia and New Zealand have particularly close links with Britain because many of their people are of British descent. Most of Britain's recent immigrants are from Commonwealth countries. Almost all the Commonwealth countries use English as their official language of government.

Military links

The United Kingdom belongs to the North Atlantic Treaty Organization (NATO), a military alliance of most western European countries together with the USA and Canada. NATO was formed after the end of the Second World War in response to the threat to western Europe that was felt to come from the USSR and its allies. The stationing of British troops in West Germany is part of the country's contribution to NATO.

The USA has a large military presence in Britain with air bases, submarine bases and surveillance and communications centres. The question of whether the USA should continue to have bases with nuclear weapons in Britain is part of the fiercely-argued debate over nuclear arms.

Britain itself has military bases abroad, besides those in West Germany, for example, in Hong Kong, Cyprus and the Falkland Islands.

Q3
(a) (i) What are the advantages of the Commonwealth? Why might some people consider it to have little point?
(ii) What factors contribute to the future survival of the Commonwealth?
(b) (i) Why does the USA have military bases in Britain?
(ii) Why does Britain have military bases abroad? Why are they far fewer in number than thirty years ago?

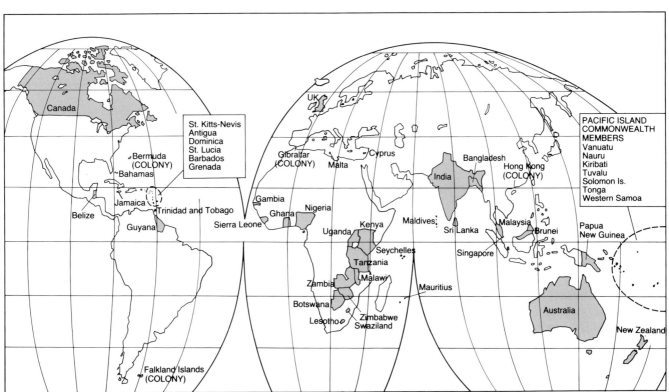

Index

Place Index